the Music NEVER Stops

A Journey into the Music of the Unknown, the Forgotten, The Rich & Famous

Dick Weissman

Design & Typography by Roy "Rick" Dains
FalconMarketingMedia@gmail.com

ISBN 978-1-57424-333-8

P. O. Box 17878 - Anaheim Hills, CA 92817
email: centerstream@aol.com • web: centerstream-usa.com

Acknowledgements

Special thanks to ***Stephen Wade*** for encouragement and his eagle eye reading of the manuscript. Stephen is a a dedicated performer and scholar of American roots music, and the author of the superb book, *The Beautiful Music All Around Us.*

While this book was in its final edits my old friend, ***Steve Young*** passed away. Steve was a superb lyricist, an under-rated guitarist, and a soulful singer. Much of my motivation in writing this book is to encourage readers to seek out neglected or under-publicized musicians. Steve ranks very high on this list. The internet gives everyone the opportunity to explore music, and I hope my readers will explore ***Steve Young's*** songs and recordings.

Without the editing, critical input and encouragement of ***Susan Planalp***, this book would not exist. Many thanks.

Additional kudos to my publisher, ***Ron Middlebrook***, for his enthusiasm for this project. If my book leads you to listening to the work of the various musicians mentioned, it will have accomplished my goal in writing it.

Table of Contents 

Prelude

This book began when numerous friends told me that I ought to write a memoir to collect all the stories that I have told them over the years about performers, the music industry, a variety of interesting people that I have known, and my life in academia and the world of the musician's union.

To prepare myself for this task, I have read over fifty memoirs that cover every style of music. This has been a real education for me. I discovered that many memoirs by famous musicians are simply travelogues of their monetary, romantic and popular successes. Others, like Linda Ronstadt's autobiography, are frank in revealing how difficult it is to maintain any sort of sensible life that puts the focus on music in today's music industry. Similarly, some of these autobiographies would have the reader believe that the writer can do nothing wrong, and any failures in their lives are the fault of other people.

I do not have a single, overwhelming point that I want to make in this book. I am not famous, although I have had dealings with some major stars. What I do have to offer is a look at what it is like to pursue a career in music that moves in multiple areas, and changes over the years. I will offer the reader a number of themes, which I will return to in various sections of the book. The music business is a difficult path, and a hard one to navigate. There is little correlation, positive or negative, between mass popularity and actual musical talent. The notion that "the cream rises to the top," is vacuous and inaccurate. Any serious artist, whether in music or other art forms, must be capable of developing sufficient objectivity to understand her own limitations and failures, in order to pursue a rewarding long-term career. Many of the most talented singers and musicians do not achieve a significant level of popularity or success. This happens for a whole host of reasons. If you want to pursue a musical career, you are going to need to choose whether you want to spend most of your time and energy on promoting yourself or on developing your musical skills. The internet and social media can help you, but they are also tools that can be counterproductive if you become obsessed with their value. The major players in the music industry still control the game, more than ever. The handful of YouTube and crowd funding successes that have occurred are the exceptions to the rule. In every town there are unsung heroes who are unabashed music fans. They will do their best to help musicians, and do not desire, solicit or expect a piece of the action. Provided you don't insist on stardom, the dream of becoming a full-time professional musician is still attainable.

In the course of my long career in music, I have been a performer, studio musician, songwriter, composer, record producer, author of numerous books, university professor and union officer. I didn't plan to do any of these things. If you wish to be a long-term musician, this book should provide some models for developing a multdimensional music career. Along the way there will be humorous and tragic stories of people that I have met.

Part 1 • Chapter 1 

My first musical memory dates back to when I was four or five years old. I was sitting at home in Brooklyn and the radio was playing. A group of convicts came on, and sang the song Red River Valley, substituting the lyric of "the warden who loved you so true," for the original lyric "the one who has loved you so true." For some reason I have an unforgettable memory of this performance, sung in country vocal harmony. I don't have other musical memories from my years in Brooklyn.

I was born in January, 1935, in the northeast section of Philadelphia. My father was a pharmacist who had a small drugstore with a soda fountain. My mother was a schoolteacher who taught in the Williamsburg section of Brooklyn. After a couple of years in Philly, she took my brother Sherwood and me back to Brooklyn, and my parents had what we call a commuter marriage today. It was the middle of the Great Depression, and teaching school was a good job, because the government kept the paychecks coming no matter how badly unemployment was ravaging most of the country.

Both of my parents came from a small town in the Ukraine called Lubar. It was part of the USSR at that time, but has gone back and forth between Russia and Poland. These days it is under Polish rule again. My mother had come to America as a very young child, but when my father came he was still a student at the local gymnasium, basically the equivalent of a junior college. My mother's family was so poor that in order to attend Hunter College, one of the tuition-free city colleges in the 1920's, she had to win a $400 scholarship. Her family had no money to buy books, lunches or even the nickel subway carfare.

My father's parents were divorced, a somewhat scandalous situation in a Jewish family in Russia during the early years of the 20th century. His mother scrambled to make a poor living, and she died in the influenza epidemic of 1919. A year later my father embarked to America, carrying a fake Polish passport, not speaking a word of English, and staying with his aunt in Philadelphia. She had her own family, and it was quite a sacrifice for her to offer him lodging.

DEFERRED DREAMS

My father applied to Temple University's pharmacy school. He really wanted to become a doctor, but felt that the extra year of school was beyond his limited resources. He began his career with a lie, telling the college that he had finished gymnasium, when in fact he attended for one year when the Russian Revolution intervened and the school was closed. He worked his way through college selling Singer Sewing Machines door to door in a rough part of Philadelphia, and managed to complete his education. He then opened a small drugstore on Wyoming Avenue, in the part of Philadelphia where I was born.

My brother is four and a half years older than I am. From an early age, my father impressed upon my brother and me that we should become doctors. In my father's view this was a secure and lucrative profession, and he always regretted that he had not had the opportunity to join it. My mother went to graduate school part-time at Columbia some years after graduating from Hunter College. She never discussed with us what had happened in graduate sæchool, but apparently the stress of working full-time and then getting married caused her not to finish her graduate degree. It is my impression that my mother wanted to write short stories, but she never discussed that. In retrospect, neither my father or my mother were able to entirely fulfill their ambitions, and this became an important part of the background music of my life. Another recurring theme was that neither of my parents had much connection to their families, once my grandmother died. Nor did they ever yearn for their homeland. Working six and a half days a week, taking only occasional vacations, and enthralled with his life in the United States my father had in effect as my brother put it, became the perfect American.

When my father died, I called his cousins and asked them about their life in Lubar. None of them were willing to talk about it. As best I can tell, the town had around ten thousand people, including four thousand Jews before World War II. Almost all of them died in the Holocaust. The current Jewish population of the town, which is now in Poland, is ten.

When I reached the age of two my mother returned to Brooklyn to resume her teaching job, bringing my brother and me with her. I only saw my father on weekends and in the summer. Until I started kindergarten, my grandmother was my constant babysitter. She was a very authoritarian, unpleasant woman, and I was not a particularly obedient child.

PHILADELPHIA AND MY INTRODUCTION TO THE PIANO

By the time I was seven years old, my father had sold his drug store and was working as a pharmacist in a private hospital in downtown Philadelphia called The Wolfe Clinic. He was able to convince my mother that he would be able to support the family on his income. My mother quit her job, and left all of her friends and family and we all moved to a house in the West Germantown neighborhood of Philadelphia. My grandmother came with us, something my father was not thrilled about, but which he accepted as part of the responsibilities of marriage. Soon my grandmother began to demonstrate signs of dementia, and this was aggravated by the fact that she only spoke Yiddish and knew no one in our mixed Catholic and Jewish neighborhood. Within a couple of years she was consigned to a nursing home in New Jersey, not far from where two of her sons lived.

My mother played the piano, and liked to sing standards and show tunes. In one of her rare extravagances, she convinced my father to buy a Steinway baby grand piano. I believe it cost $1500 (this was around 1942.) My mother then decided that my brother should take piano lessons. Since I was only seven years old, she took me along with them, and we rode the train to the piano teacher's studio in downtown Philadelphia. I sat in the waiting room as the teacher worked with my brother. After about five minutes, she determined that he was tone deaf, and appeared to have no musical aptitude whatever. She turned to my mother, pointed at me, and said "what about him?" Seven years of piano lessons followed. I learned how to read music, but nothing about chords. Improvisation was out of the question.

Since my mother could only play from sheet music, it did not occur to her that this was a problem. I became reasonably proficient on piano, but I had no special interest in it. It was simply something that I was able to do. I didn't really relate to classical music as something I wanted to study, and since that was the only style my teacher taught, I never got beyond being able to read music in the bass and treble clefs, but not really grasping the underlying musical concepts behind the music that I was playing.

I played sports every day in elementary school, except for Tuesday, which was reserved for piano lessons. I have already mentioned that our neighborhood was pretty much entirely Catholic and Jewish, and on Thursdays I was the only Jewish kid out on the ball field. Every other Jewish kid went to Hebrew School. The sum total of my religious experience was that I attended Sunday School at a reform synagogue twice, and had no interest in it. No one ever said anything about this, but it seemed odd to me that on Thursdays a third of our ballplayers were absent.

HIGH SCHOOL

I chose to go to Central High School, a city wide school that was intended for children who intended to go on to college. The trip to Central involved two trolley rides, and took more than a half hour. I have a vivid memory of the first day. Central had two thousand students. After my first class ended, I thought I would be trampled by the hundreds of kids going from one class to another. At the time I was barely five feet tall, and weighed about ninety pounds, and I felt as though a herd of buffalo were running over me. There were so many people that I couldn't see the stairs that I was climbing. After a while I got used to it.

Most Central students went on to college, and a large percentage of them became doctors, lawyers, teachers and social workers. I had one year of chorus, which was a required class, and one year of art. Most of the classes were fairly rigorous studies in English, history, math, science and languages. My high school career was a bit schizophrenic, because I invariably got high grades in English and the social sciences, average grades in French, and struggled a bit with math and science. I have no real spatial intelligence or ability, I barely passed geometry.

My brother had convinced my parents to buy a ping pong table, and when I got to high school I became a member of our championship ping pong team. Other than playing ping pong, about the only other things that I did were to be on the debating team for a year and to read every book that I could find in the Philadelphia Library about American Indians. I had a friend named Joe Stempel who helped me get a part-time job at a Ford dealer. Joe was a big influence on me. He was reading Freud and other psychology authors. I had never heard of any of these people, so I discovered the joys of Freudian theory. I've often wondered what became of Joe, who had a sort of cynical world-wise view unusual for a fifteen year old kid in the fifties.

THE BANJO AND PING PONG

There were two highlights of my high school years. When I was thirteen, my brother took me along to the 1948 Progressive Party national convention, where I saw Pete Seeger play. I was immediately fascinated by the five string banjo. I had never heard anything like it. There was something about the texture of the instrument that fascinated me, as it still does today, almost seventy years later. I started buying recordings on the Disc label, the predecessor to Folkways. These recordings included Seeger, Woody Guthrie, Cisco Houston, Brownie McGhee and Sonny Terry, and Lonnie Johnson. For reasons that I don't really understand today, blues and mountain music developed an equal significance in my life.

By the time I was thirteen, I could beat any of my brother's friends at ping pong. I joined the Central ping pong team, and also played in a local league two nights a week. The best players at that time were in New York City. I entered some tournaments there, even winning the New York State Open Junior title one year. The peak of my career was receiving a national ranking of seventh in the country for boys under eighteen.

PING PONG AND BEBOP

Most of my the kids I competed against in New York were actors who attended the Professional Children's School. Some of them had acted in Broadway shows at an early age. They all seemed to be inveterate bebop fans. I stayed over at their apartments on several occasions, and listened to their Thelonius Monk and Charley Parker records. This was a revelation to me, because I knew nothing about the contemporary jazz of the 50's. In retrospect I imagine that some of these kids were smoking pot. In those days, I wouldn't have had a clue what that meant.

THE END OF HIGH SCHOOL, AND MY ONE YEAR SABBATICAL FROM SCHOOL

I hated high school, because I found most of the teachers and students dull, and the stress on getting good grades didn't interest me. I went to summer high school at another location so that I could graduate one semester faster. I then announced to my parents that I was going to work for a year before applying to colleges. This choice was entirely confusing to them, because their projected path for me was to breeze through college and to join the working world. Night after night we would have bitter arguments, and my mother would warn me that if I didn't head right to college I would never get there. I have no idea of why she felt this way. Between my unwillingness to attend college, and my older brother's penchant for getting involved in every radical political organization that he could find, it was a tough period for my parents. My father harbored the fantasy that both of his sons would become doctors and immediately go to work in one of the two hospitals that he was now managing. It became clear that my brother had no intention of fulfilling our father's dream, and it became apparent to both of my parents that I wasn't moving in that direction either.

THE BANJO BECKONS

Shortly after I finished high school I sent off for Pete Seeger's banjo book. At that time it was mimeographed, and he sold it directly through the mail. I think it cost $2.95. In the book he suggested that the way to find a decent banjo was to haunt pawnshops. In 1951 the banjo was a minor fixture in Philadelphia musical culture. Philadelphia had an annual Mummer's Parade on New Year's day, when tenor and plectrum banjo players paraded through the streets. These were four string banjos, played with a pick held in the right hand. What sets the five string apart is that it has a short fifth string that doesn't go up the entire length of the banjo neck. The good news was that because no one wanted them, when they did appear in music stores or pawn shops they were cheap.

My brother and I went down to a pawnshop in the skid row section of Philadelphia, and there I found a fancy old Weymann Five String Banjo. It had some nice pearl inlay on the neck and the name Eddie Maples was inlaid on one of the high frets. The pawn shop clerk told me that Maples had pawned five of these banjos, and this was the last one. I was hooked, and bought it on the spot. It cost all of twenty five dollars with a case included.

I could barely contain my excitement. I raced to my room, where Seeger's book was in residence. I took the book and the banjo, and went over to the piano. Because I had never seen anyone play the banjo up close and I had never played a string instrument myself, I immediately broke two strings while trying to follow Pete's instructions about how to tune the damn thing. The banjo then went into residence in my closet.

AFTER HIGH SCHOOL, BEFORE COLLEGE

After high school I got a job operating a mimeograph machine at a downtown Philadelphia department store. For younger readers, mimeograph machines were the state of the art method of duplicating copies in 1951. A secretary at the store would type a stencil on a special blue paper, and my job was to run off multiple copies. I worked forty hours a week, and was paid $30. Most of the secretaries working with me were young women, mostly in their early twenties. It was quite a change from attending an all boys high school. I spent all of my time working, playing ping pong, and listening to records. I bought Seeger's first Folkways 10" LP, called Darling Corey. I'd listen to it every night before I went to sleep. To this day it is the only long playing record that I ever wore out. I also haunted Walgreen's Drug Store, which was selling 78RPM records by blues singers like Memphis Minnie and Big Bill Broonzy, five for a dollar.

That was pretty much my life, until my brother, who was going to graduate school in Detroit, came home for a visit half way through the year. Basically he asked me why I was wasting my time working in an office, when I could be working in a factory and getting in touch with the working class. I quit my job about two weeks later, and spent most of my time playing ping pong. I wasn't all that eager to go back to work, but I did one day at the Aristocrat Ice Cream factory, pouring fifty pound cans of cherries into vanilla ice cream to make cherry vanilla ice cream. Since I was an underweight teenager the lifting was too tough for me, so at the end of the seventh hour of work, I took an hour long shower and then quit. Next I worked in a cotton mill. All of the other employees were kids from the southern mountains, and they were just as skinny as I was. My job was to replace empty spools with new ones. That lasted two days. I worked for John B. Stetson Hats for a few more days. I had to take the finished hats to the basement, using a dumb waiter. By the end of the second day I realized that I was just piling the hat racks up, and had no idea how I was supposed to store them. I figured it was time to move on, before the boss figured out that I had no clue what I was doing.

My last employment triumph that year was to pick blueberries in New Jersey. I answered an ad in the paper, and a bunch of guys and I met downtown and rode in a truck to South Jersey. They paid us six cents a quart. Most of the guys I worked with were marginal Skid Row folks, but another group of workers were Puerto Ricans. They were getting five cents a quart. I've never spent a day where I was hotter and more tired than that one. I think I made three or four dollars. I did use the experience as part of a song that I recorded with Pat Foster about eight years later. It was called Talking Migrant.

I HEAR THE MUSIC COMING OUT OF THE RADIO

Somewhere in my middle teen years I heard a radio show with a DJ named Mert Coplin. Mert was doing free form FM radio before FM radio existed. He seemed to particularly like both folk music and jazz, and played quite a bit of music from each of these idioms. For some reason the song that has stayed in my memory bank was a duet between Louis Armstrong and Bing Crosby called Gone Fishin'. There was something about the joking rapport between these two artists that intrigued me. For some reason Mert seemed to broadcast on an irregular schedule, and I often tried to find his show, but couldn't locate it. I had never heard of Mert, who later had a career as a producer, writer and actor. Unfortunately he is best known for being an Associate Producer of the scandal-ridden TV quiz show The $64,000 Question. At the age of fifteen I discovered the radio hit parade, and I listened to Philadelphia's Top 40 radio programs which featured such people as Eddie Fisher and the early rock and rollers. I also bought Billboard Magazine at a local newsstand and followed these records up the charts for a year. By the time I was sixteen I lost interest in pop music. That interest was replaced by my discovery of the satirical radio comedians of the day, especially Bob and Ray. For years I could lapse into an imitation of Bob's character Wally Balou, reporting from the lobster pots in Maine. My parents didn't buy a television set until I was in college, so other than occasionally watching Ernie Kovacs at a friend's house, I wasn't really exposed to it.

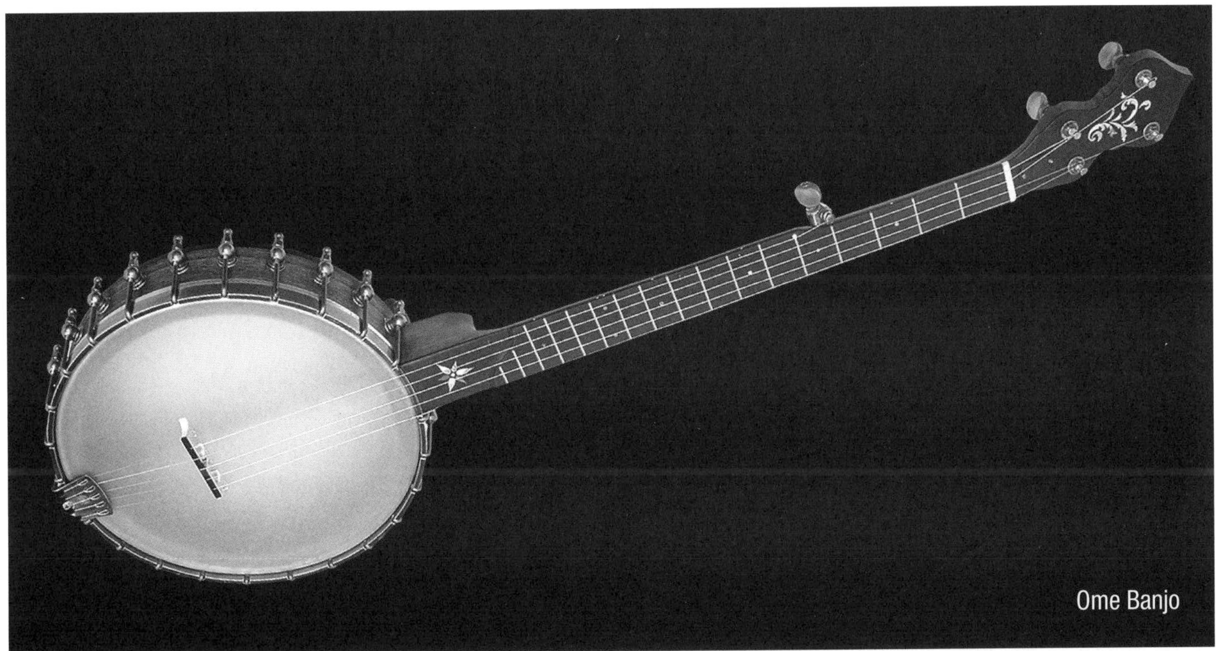
Ome Banjo

Part 1 • Chapter 2

GODDARD COLLEGE

My choice of a college entailed looking for something opposite to my highly competitive high school. There were four or five "progressive" colleges in the 1950's that offered liberal arts majors, but didn't give grades. Bard College was up the Hudson River from New York, Bennington College was a girls' college in Bennington, Vermont, Black Mountain College was located near Asheville, North Carolina, and Goddard was in North Central Vermont. Black Mountain was in serious financial trouble, although it hung on until 1957. Bard was a little too artsy for me, so Goddard was my choice. In the summer of 1951 my parents and I visited Black Mountain while on of a vacation trip to the Smoky Mountains. The dorm was saturated with beer cans and trash, and my parents were appalled. After that experience I'm surprised that they consented to my attending Goddard.

I took a train to New York City, plus an all night bus ride from there to Montpelier, the capital of Vermont, about fifteen miles from Goddard. No one met me at the bus, and I ended up calling the college. They sent a student named Ward Stewart to pick me up. He was a perfect introduction to life at Goddard. On the half hour ride he dropped every curse word that I had ever heard, and added some new ones. Welcome to the bohemian world of the progressive college.

That night there was a party to welcome new students. At the time Goddard had all of seventy students. There were two rooms of entertainment. In one of them a former student named Jane (Jerry) Mink was picking away on her banjo. In the other a jazz trumpet player named Burrill Crohn held forth, playing Louis Armstrong records and such. You would think I would have spent my time in the banjo room, but in fact I opted for jazz.

My room-mate was Piers Jacob, who later became a successful science fiction writer under the name Piers Anthony. I became good friends with another student, Richard (Richie) Reinitz, a New Yorker, and Greenwich Village habitué. Like my high school friend Joe Stempel, Richie was heavily into Freud, with a touch of Marxist ideology as well. We spent many hours talking about various things. Richie was very literate, and much more knowledgeable about literature and life than I was. He quickly became involved with a young coed named Lil (Lillemor) Blos. Besides being the daughter of one of Freud's last living associates, Lil played the banjo. Since I was hanging out fairly regularly with Richie and Lil, I got to hear her play the banjo, and I told her that I really liked her playing. She asked me if I'd like to learn how to play. I explained that I had a banjo in my closet at home. She told me that if I brought it back, she'd teach me how to play it.

That Thanksgiving I went home and carted the banjo back. Sure enough she taught me how to play what is called basic clawhammer today. She wasn't fancy, but she was accurate and musical. Lil also taught me how to change strings, and how to tune the banjo without breaking strings. Our lessons weren't like anything that takes place today. We used no music, and no tablature. She showed me what to do with the right hand, and drew a few chord diagrams. That was how I first learned to play the five string banjo.

PING PONG FINALE

Meanwhile Goddard had a ping pong table, and of course I challenged all the local players. One was a student from Baltimore named Guy Parr. I played him left handed for money, and he accumulated a sizeable debt. We both realized that this couldn't go on, because he really didn't have any money. He invited me over to his room, to figure out how he could pay off his gambling debt. He had a Harmony Monterey F Hole Guitar, which he didn't know how to play. I accepted that in place of the $50 or so that he owed me. It was a pretty wretched guitar with high action, but at least I now had a guitar, and I didn't have to buy one.

As the climax of my table tennis career, I entered the Vermont State Table Tennis Championship. Since I was unknown there, I was not seeded. I almost lost in the first round to a quirky player from New Jersey who was a University of Vermont student. From there on in, it was smooth sailing. I beat the best player in Vermont, Ed (Pinhead) Le Stage 21-10, 21-12, or something like that. This placed me in the finals against a Middlebury College student, whose name I have conveniently forgotten. That competitor had broken his leg, and had made it to the finals with his leg in a cast. I couldn't believe it. How do you play someone who has a broken leg? I devised a strategy where I hit very sharp angles, so that he wouldn't be tempted to chase the ball. It was all working well until near the end of the match. I miscalculated one shot, and hit it pretty close to him. He went after the ball, and fell down in a heap. I turned around. I couldn't look at him.

When I got back to Goddard my friend Burrill Crohn made an announcement at dinner that I had won the tournament. He paused for a moment, and added "he beat a kid with a broken leg."

THE PIANO

Burrill knew that I played the piano, and he asked if I wanted to jam with him. I didn't really know what he was talking about. We sat down together, he played the trumpet, and I tried to follow him. I had no idea what to do, and the little I could do didn't sound very good to me. I bought a couple of jazz piano instruction books, including one by Mary Lou Williams. Williams was a Kansas City jazz player and arranger and her book gave me enough to go on so that I could play behind Burrill without being entirely ridiculous. We started playing together pretty regularly, and it was a great musical outlet for me.

GODDARD

Goddard was kind of an anomaly in North Central Vermont in those years. Today when people think of Vermont politics, they conjure up Bernie Sanders, the independent socialist senator. In the 1950's Vermont was conservative, but in kind of a quirky way. The two senators were Republicans George Aiken and Ralph Flanders. They were fiscal conservatives, but social progressives. Later Aiken was a lonely vote against the war in Viet Nam.

The locals sometimes referred to Goddard as "little Moscow, the whorehouse on the hill." This was their tribute to the politics and morals of our humble campus. Most Goddard students came from New York, or other East Coast cities, and we also had a Nigerian student and a Moroccan student, who received some unpleasant attention from the locals. The campus was lovely but kind of bedraggled and the buildings were always in need of some repair. Across the road there was a footpath that led into the woods. If you followed it for about a couple of hundred yards, you came to the end of the path, and you were overlooking the Winooski River below. A few times a day a train would go by, but otherwise you could be alone with your thoughts, looking out at a pastoral vista a few hundred feet below you. I spent many hours sitting there, playing the banjo or reading.

The professors at Goddard were a varied if small bunch. My advisor was Gabriel Jackson. He was a brilliant scholar, and later wrote several significant books about the Spanish Civil War. He had taught at a private school, but apparently was fired because he refused to sign a loyalty oath of some kind. Thomas Yakhub was an East Indian sociologist, and his wife Una was a member of the famous Ritchie family of Kentucky mountain singers. John Pierce was the only science teacher, and he was an intrepid hiker-camper and square dancer, who also played the fiddle. Tim (Royce) Pitkin was the president of the school, and taught some education courses. He was a pioneer in the world of progressive education, and wrote and lectured on that subject. Part of the concept that he developed at Goddard was that students also worked menial jobs on campus. We bussed tables, did dishes, cleaned, gardened and planted. We were supposed to work about an hour a day, although some of us managed to do a fraction of that. The concept was that we would get to know one another in an informal environment outside the classroom.

Another Goddard innovation was the winter work term. January and February are cold months in Vermont, and during this two month period students left the campus and went to work at temporary jobs. This was way before the advent of internships, so it was basically up to students to find employment, wherever they wanted to go. My list of jobs during the work terms included working at factories in Philadelphia, doing filing at the New York Public Library, and distributing free toothpaste samples in New York City. The college expected us to tell the employer that we were temporary employers, but the reality of the situation was that many of us lied or we would never have gotten jobs in the first place.

POLITICS, GIRLS AND MUSIC

By the end of my first year, I realized that I was not going to follow my brother's path, and dedicate my life to social change. My political views shifted from Marxism to anarchism, with a dose of cynicism. Like many students in the 50's I became impressed with existentialism, and the works of Jean Paul Sartre. My distrust for the American position in the Cold War remained, but I became almost equally skeptical of what Russia was up to.

My initial discoveries of the mysteries of the opposite sex initially brought me into the position of being the trusted confidant of women whose interest in me didn't extend to any further encounters. At the same time I finally began to grow taller and felt all of the consequent awkwardness that rapid growth carries in adolescence. I went from a height of five feet four inches when I entered college at the age of 17, to just over six feet by the time I graduated at the age of twenty one. Like a lot of teenagers I spent far too much time feeling sorry for myself. In my case, this meant many late night hours listening to records by Ma Rainey and Bessie Smith. I think that the attraction of blues for many middle class white kids is that the elements of anger and self-pity in many blues songs tie in very nicely to insecure late adolescence. That isn't the context in which they were written, but they can be interpreted that way.

I continued to play piano with Burrill and although Lil had transferred from Goddard after my first year, I spent hours playing the banjo. I played in front of the community center, in the woods, at parties, and anywhere else I went. One of my classmates, Dick Mulliken, was a decent guitar player, and we spent hours playing together. A fellow student named Jim Roos nicknamed my banjo, the "tin can" and I'm certain that he and many other students were hoping I'd either drop the thing or start to play better.

In my second winter work term, I was working in the bindery at the New York Public Library. I was living on sardines and bad food and buying lots of records. I contracted a virus in my left eye, and had to go home to Philadelphia. I was diagnosed with herpes virus in my left eye, and had to take a drug called atropine. This stuff was so strong that the slightest amount of light made feel as though a searchlight were being shined directly in my eye. During the six week course of the disease, all I could do was to play the banjo or listen to the radio or records. I returned to Goddard in mid-March, a week after the start of the semester

In my sophomore year at college, I developed the brainstorm of booking Pete Seeger to sing at Goddard. The school had no real money for student activities. We were able to convince Pete to come up for the princely sum of $35. Part of the deal was that we gave him a ride to Montreal, where he had a real gig the next day. I had a friend named Anne Stokes who had a car and she and another student and I drove Pete to Montreal after a wonderful concert at Goddard. Mostly I just listened to Pete talk. He seemed to have an insatiable curiosity about almost everything, and he gave me my first lessons about Canadian politics.

During my sophomore year I realized that Goddard was too small for me to spend four years there. Transferring to another school was a doubtful procedure, because Goddard was not accredited by the regional accreditation authorities. I decided that the easiest path to take was to take my junior year away from Goddard and to return for my senior year. I applied to the New School For Social Research in New York, and the Metropolitan Music School in New York. I wanted to continue academic classes at the New School, while studying banjo and guitar at the Metropolitan School with a well-known teacher named Jerry Silverman. For the spring semester of my junior year, I applied to the University of New Mexico.

Studying banjo and guitar certainly made sense for me but I'm not sure exactly how I justified going to Albuquerque in the spring. The plan that I devised included studying southwestern anthropology and government. In any case Goddard accepted my plan, and the other schools admitted me as a provisional transfer student. Goddard dutifully placed on my transcript a sort of warning that the six credits I would receive for studying banjo and guitar would quite likely not be accepted by another college and might make me ineligible for graduate school.

PETE SEEGER AND CAMP WOODLAND

I spent the summer of my sophomore year as a camp counselor, mostly playing banjo and guitar at a progressive summer camp called Camp Woodland. I was a terrible counselor. I didn't know anything about teenage kids, hell I was still growing myself. I didn't swim or camp and I wasn't much interested in doing those things. Beyond singing with the kids, there wasn't much I was qualified to do, and I wasn't all that good at even that.

While I was working at Camp Woodland, one night Pete Seeger, who was a friend of the camp's director, came by to sing and play for the campers and counselors. This was a great opportunity to do a little bit of playing with Pete, although for the most part I listened. That same night we had another guest, a banjo player named Dave Sear. He was renowned in New York folk circles as having learned almost every Pete Seeger strum and lick. As we sat around the campfire, the two often played identical banjo parts. Dave even affected Pete's mannerism of raising his head and neck as he sang. It was kind of embarrassing. Pete showed no outward signs of being annoyed, but when he and Dave were playing a song called Round The Bay of Mexico, at the end of the second verse they came out of the verse and started to play identical instrumental breaks. Suddenly Pete broke into tremolo, a technique where several fingers of the right hand play the same repeated notes. It is an effect often used on the mandolin. Dave apparently either didn't know this technique, or decided not to try to imitate it. No one ever said anything, and all of this transpired in a matter of seconds. In jazz this mechanism is called "cutting" a competitor, as in cutting him down. I didn't know what to make of this, but it was kind of a tense moment. It seemed to me that there was more to playing music with other people than I had thought.

NEW YORK

I had been dating a Goddard student named Emeline Schick for about four months. At the end of the summer, we met up in New York, and I broke up with her. We had gotten along well, and I really liked her, but I had some subconscious realization that my world was entering a period of extensive changes, and I didn't feel able to continue any sort of romantic commitment. She didn't really understand what I was trying to say, probably because I had a great deal of trouble trying to explain it.

I found a place to live on the west side of town, not too far from the Metropolitan Music School, and Richie Reinitz's family often invited me to dinner at their house. Richie and my friend Burrill had both left Goddard, so I had some friends in the city.

At the New School I took classes in short story writing, physical anthropology and a wonderful class called Music of the World's People. This class was taught by Henry Cowell, a famous experimental composer who was one of the first "serious" musicians with a deep interest in the music of the entire world. This class had a tremendous impact on me, because Henry lectured and played recordings of music from

Asia, Africa and the Americas. He was in the process of compiling a set of recordings that would later be released on Folkways Records.

The New School was founded by a group of social scientists who were refugees from Nazi Germany, and in its early days it functioned primarily as a school where students who had two years of college completed their education. In those days the school had only one building on West 12th Street between 5th and 6th Avenues, just North of Greenwich Village. Metropolitan Music School was further uptown, and I started taking guitar and banjo lessons as quickly as I could get enrolled. My instructor Jerry Silverman was involved with the People's Song Hootenanny movement. In other words he was deeply involved in political folk music. He had just completed his master's degree in music at NYU, where he transcribed and analyzed the music of blues singer Josh White.

Studying with Jerry helped me to gain an understanding of the banjo and guitar fingerboards. He was a versatile guitarist, and a decent enough mostly Seeger-style banjo player. After ten or twelve weeks I stopped taking banjo lessons, and we doubled up on the time spent on guitar. My Harmony Guitar was not up to the challenge of playing anything that required moving up to the higher positions of the fingerboard. I was able to overcome my parent's severe resistance, and to purchase a reasonably decent Favilla Guitar through Jerry for $50. My parents were extremely unhappy about spending this money. They had seen my interests go from ping pong to music. They viewed both of these endeavors as frivolous and useless. I'm sure they had many difficult discussions between them about what sort of future their younger son was going to carve out for himself.

TINY LEDBETTER AND GARY DAVIS

Bob Harris was the son of the man who had started Asch-Stinson Records, with his then partner Moe Asch. Various disputes led the partners to split up, and Stinson became a stand-alone label. It had a retail store in its office on Union Square. I wandered into it, looking for some Woody Guthrie albums. Bob told me that on Tuesday nights Leadbelly's niece Tiny hosted an informal music gathering where a musician named Gary Davis would come over to play music. I was vaguely aware that Gary was a gospel singer who played a blues-influenced guitar, and decided to check it out. I will never forget the first time I heard Gary Davis play live.

Tiny lived in an apartment on East 10th Street between Avenues A and B, an area that later became known as the East Village. As I walked east, the neighborhood seemed to deteriorate a bit. I found the address, 414 E. 10th and as I walked into the building, I could hear the guitar music floating down from the apartment, one story above street level.

Tiny (Robinson) Ledbetter was Leadbelly's niece, and his widow Martha Ledbetter lived in a separate apartment in the same building. I knocked on the door and entered a world that was vastly different from anything that I had ever experienced.

Tiny was very friendly, and introduced me to Gary, who was playing, along with his (then) prize pupil John Gibbon. John became the first of a whole series of aspiring young white blues guitarists Gary continues to influence today, years after his death. For the next couple of months, this would be my real music school, one where credit was sparingly awarded by (Professor) Reverend Gary. Gary Davis was a blind man who had come to New York from the Durham, North Carolina area, where he had played and recorded with Blind Boy Fuller. Fuller was one of the legends of the Carolina blues guitar style. His music was very ragtime-influenced, and danceable. This wasn't the intense bottleneck blues style of the Mississippi Delta blues men, but a lighter, more technically difficult, more party-oriented music. Davis had taken the style to a much more technically complex place than anything Fuller had attempted. He could reproduce John Paul Sousa orchestral marches on the guitar, played ferociously up and down the neck, and he sang religious songs in a growly, emotional voice.

For the remaining several months of my New York semester I would spend every Tuesday evening at Tiny's house. At various times twelve string guitarist Fred Gerlach and young guitarist Barry Kornfeld played along, and one time I met Woody Guthrie and his third wife Anneke there. Everyone was under Gary's spell, and the experience served as a kind of combination storefront church and a music school.

Following Gary's music was like taking a really tough class in music school. Most musicians in the folk revival learned how to play with other musicians by watching their left hands. The idea was that you knew what chords they were playing by watching their left hand fingers. This technique didn't really work with Gary. As a child he had broken his left arm, and his arm had not been properly reset by the doctor. Because Gary's left wrist was always bent, you could only follow him by listening, not by watching his hands. It was like an ear training class in music school.

Many times I came away in a state of musical bewilderment. After a while I relaxed a little and tried to follow where the music was taking me, rather than trying to think about it or mimic his playing. Since I always played banjo during these evenings, there was no question of trying to follow his playing note for note. One night towards the end of my stay in New York, Gary was playing a tune called Oh Lord, Search-a My Heart. This was a particularly intense song, whose theme was that the singer asks God to search through his life, and to lead him on the right path. Something happened to me that night. I had no idea what I was playing, but somehow the banjo seemed to play the part of a second voice, answering Gary's pleading with its own voice. Gary himself offered me a rare compliment. At the end of the evening I left Tiny's house with a full heart, and the beginnings of a feeling that I could indeed develop my own musical voice and follow it wherever it would take me.

Gary Davis' music was ringing in my heart and ears, and thanks to Henry Cowell I was now seriously interested in music from distant parts of the world. It was time to complete the academic year in Albuquerque.

THE UNIVERSITY OF NEW MEXICO

I flew from Philadelphia to Albuquerque. It was an all-night redeye flight that left Philadelphia in the early evening, and arrived in Albuquerque about five in the morning. It was also the first time I had ever been on an airplane. The plane was a DC 3, and it made three or four stops along the way. I had no idea what was in store for me, and I was so excited that I couldn't sleep. I got off the plane in Albuquerque with my banjo and guitar and a suitcase. A taxi took me to the dorm by around 6AM, but of course nothing was open. It was fairly warm, by my standards, for January, and I sat outside the dorm, looking at the biggest sky that I had ever seen. The sun was coming up, and I had never seen anything so bright and welcoming. I didn't know a single person in Albuquerque, but I was too wired to be tired. At 9 o'clock the dorm office opened, and the next phase of my life began.

Goddard had dormitories, but nothing had prepared me for UNM. There were thousands of students, and the Mesa Vista Dormitory was huge. I signed up for classes, which included Cultural Anthropology, Social Psychology, Government of New Mexico, and a Modern Poetry class. I also signed up for a sight singing class. Sight singing is the ability to reproduce the notes on a written page of music without the use of an instrument. It turned out that these students had been sight singing since high school or earlier. I felt as though I had entered a foreign country. I had no idea what was going on, and dropped the class almost immediately.

My room-mate was a student from Missouri, who had aspirations to enter the diplomatic service. Most of the students at the dorm came from various parts of New Mexico. There were quite a few students who were basically partying for a year before going to work on their family's ranch.

THE GUITAR

In 1955 not that many college students were playing guitar. When you saw someone with a guitar case, it was a natural thing to talk to the person carrying it. I quickly met Helmuth (Muty) Naumer, son of a fairly well-known visual artist from Santa Fe. We started hanging out together, and playing guitar. Muty, his brother Carlos and their friend Tom Dickerson became friends of mine, and gradually I began to meet other people around the university who were interested in American folk music. Tom was fluent in Spanish, and was recording songs for a music professor named J. Donald Robb, who was compiling a huge collection of such songs. Periodically Tom would insert a current Mexican-American pop song into the mix, confident that Robb never listened to contemporary Mexican-American radio stations. A somewhat sullen twelve string guitarist and blues aficionado named Max Drake appeared somewhere in this circle. He told me that there was a really fine banjo player named Stuart Jamieson, who lived up in the nearby Sandia Mountains. I remembered that I had heard about Stuart from Margo Mink, a friend of my New York friend Richie Reinitz. Her older sister Jane (Jerry) Mink was the first one that I heard play the banjo at Goddard. Jane had spent a year at UNM, and had met Stuart there. This vague remembrance encouraged me to pester Max to make the contact. Max called Stu, and a few weeks later, I found myself driving with him to Stuart's house. Along for the ride was Max's girl friend, and a fellow student named Jim Edgar. Jim was a street-wise hard-drinking Korean War vet from New York. I met him at the dorm, and his interest in guitar cemented our friendship.

PHASES OF STUART JAMIESON

Stuart lived outside Albuquerque in a house high up in the Sandia Mountains. His house was guarded by a very large and mean blue goose who Stuart had to call off so that we could access the house without being attacked by this militant bird.

Stuart sat in his living room and played the banjo, and occasionally Max or I would join in. I felt that I was on a similar voyage of discovery to the one that Gary Davis had guided me on. Stuart's playing was crystal clear. This was the old time mountain style, not Pete Seeger's simulation of it.

The highlights of the evening for me were Stuart singing a song called The Blue Goose and his final song of the evening. I had heard Pete Seeger do this song Cumberland Mountain Bear Chase, but Stuart did the original version by Uncle Dave Macon, which he called Cumberland Mountain Deer Chase. I had never seen anyone play the banjo with such power and conviction, and the song seemed to exhaust Stuart and all of us as well.

I only saw Stuart play one other time, this time on another trip to his cabin without Max. Stuart was much more interested in some of my Piedmont style guitar work than in my banjo playing. I wasn't offended because in my own view I had gone beyond the beginner phase, but I wasn't someone who had developed an original or interesting style on the banjo. Later I found out that Stuart was one of the pioneers in collecting music by black banjo players for the Library of Congress, and that he had studied banjo with the legendary and somewhat obscure Kentucky banjo player Rufus Crisp.

After the two evenings with Stuart, I had little interest in playing with other Albuquerque musicians. I realized that I had a whole lot of work ahead to figure out where the five string banjo could take me.

YELLOWSTONE

Through my UNM friends Muty and Carlos, I got a summer job selling fishing trips on Yellowstone Lake in Yellowstone National Park. I worked six days a week, and spent the rest of my waking hours trying to figure out how I wanted to play the banjo. Yellowstone workers got one day off, and on those days, or even on weekday nights, we would find someone who had a car and go to the neighboring towns. The problem was that all of these towns-West Yellowstone, Gardiner, or Cody, were at least sixty miles away.

Yellowstone Park is very large, and the scenery varies from waterfalls, to canyons, geysers, mountain passes and verdant hills where buffalo graze. On one of my days off I borrowed a bicycle and rode from the lake to the Grand Canyon of the Yellowstone. About five miles into the journey I encountered a large brown bear. I quickly realized that with a swipe of his paw he could bring my journey to a permanent end. I rang the feeble bell mounted on the bicycle, and fortunately for me he ran the other way.

At the end of the summer of 1955, I caught a ride most of the way back to Goddard, and prepared to enter my senior year of college. During my year away, I had taken banjo and guitar lessons, had met Gary Davis and Stuart Jamison, and lived in New York, Albuquerque, and Yellowstone. It would take me years to comprehend how significant that year had been for both my musical and personal development.

Photo: Herbert Grossman

Reverend Gary Davis, being recorded by Stefan Grossman. Stefan's first wife, Matesa, watches the proceedings.

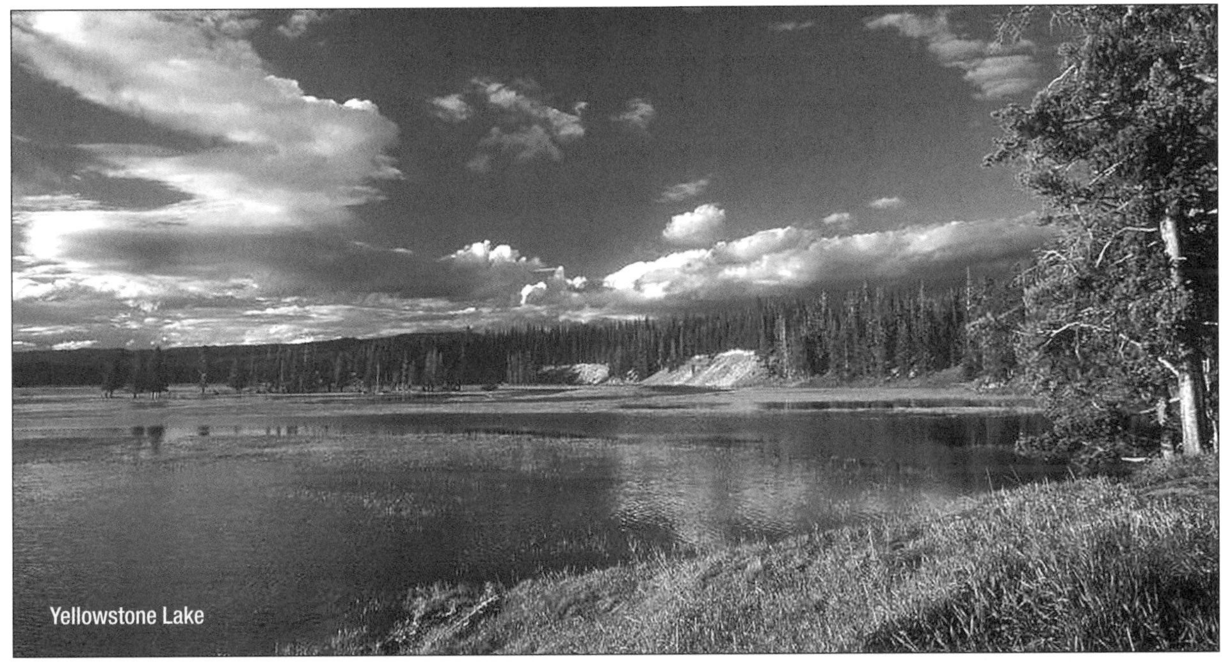

Yellowstone Lake

GODDARD AGAIN

The Goddard that I returned to was quite a bit different from the college I had left.

Goddard always operated on the borderline of financial stability. During my junior year the population had fallen to about sixty, and the board of directors made a concerted effort to recruit a new population. Somewhere they obtained some scholarship money, and suddenly there were some ten African-American students who were recruited from Philadelphia and Baltimore. Although Goddard prided itself on its "liberalism," most of the black students ate together in the cafeteria. Whatever their shared experiences had been, they were different from the ones of their white fellow students. Jim Spruill was an exception to the rule, and we quickly became friends and later we roomed together in New York.

BOB COLTMAN

A friend of my fellow student, Dick Mulliken, visited him and brought along a Dartmouth student named Bob Coltman. Bob had collected folksongs in the south on some trips with his father, and he was an excellent banjo and guitar player, and a good singer. He had developed an original three finger picking style that was in a bluegrass vein, but not exactly like the way Earl Scruggs played. I was aware of bluegrass, because late at night you could get WWVA and WWRV on the radio in Vermont. Broadcasting out of Wheeling and Richmond respectively, these stations were high wattage stations. When the less powerful stations went off the air at sundown, the signal for these stations could be heard hundreds of miles away. Bob was at a more advanced stage as a player than I was, and he was a positive musical influence on me.

MORALS AND POLITICS

One of the creative projects that had emerged at Goddard during my first two years as a student, was that several students, with some help from some others, built a cabin in the woods. It was generally known as Roos' cabin, after Jim Roos, one of the architects. The cabin was far enough off campus that students could use it for romantic purposes without attracting unwanted attention from students, faculty, or neighbors. Because they began to be concerned about students' dating habits, the summer before I returned to Goddard, the faculty instructed the maintenance staff to tear down the cabin.

Just after this one particular young woman who decided that she was going to systematically sleep with the thirty male members in her class. For whatever reasons, she also elected to inform her counselor about this.

Remember that we're talking about the 1950's, and those college kids were not part of the peace, love, sex and drugs era that emerged ten years later, some of the students were indeed romantically involved. When the counselor heard about what her student was doing and reported it to the faculty, they decided that they would have to crack down. Students tended to congregate in the lounge of the women's dormitory. The faculty instituted a curfew for that lounge. They informed us that after 10PM, no one was allowed in a lounge of the opposite sex.

Meanwhile, my guitar playing friend Dick Mulliken, who like me was in his senior year, was pursuing a serious relationship with another student. Somehow they were able to keep the details of where they stayed together quiet. One night one of the maintenance men noticed that there were fresh footsteps in the snow leading to the college library. He followed the footsteps to the library, but couldn't figure out where Dick and his girl friend were. Finally he started shining his lantern and telling them with shouting that he wasn't going to leave the library until they came out of their hiding place. After an hour, the couple concluded that the maintenance man wasn't going to leave, and they came down from their makeshift apartment. It turned out that they had constructed a little loft, complete with lamps, a mattress and bookshelves in the upper portion of the library. The faculty immediately suspended Dick for a week, although they did nothing to his partner. (I'm certain that today's feminists at Goddard would have their own opinions about that decision, but remember, this was 1955.)

Meanwhile Piers Jacob, my ex-roommate who was also a senior, committed an act of civil disobedience by breaking the dorm curfew with his girl friend, joined by another student. The same maintenance man that had discovered Dick Mulliken's library love nest issued a formal warning to them. When they refused to leave the two men were suspended for a week.

COMMUNITY MEETING AND THE MOMENT OF TRUTH

Goddard was ostensibly governed by a town meeting system similar to the one that many towns in Vermont still use today. The next day President Tim Pitkin called a meeting of the entire college, and basically told the assembled students and faculty members about the suspension, and that the school intended to enforce its rules. I was the only leader left who hadn't been suspended, and I posed the question about what the school was to do if students confiscated the offenders car keys so that they couldn't leave campus. With very little hesitation, Tim said that if this happened, that by authority vested in him by the Board of Trustees, he would close the school.

I looked around the room at the sixty odd students and dozen faculty members. I was a senior and if the school closed no seniors would graduate. I was also concerned that everyone would have trouble transferring their college credits, since Goddard was still not an accredited college. I also thought to myself that we were in the middle of the McCarthy period, and very likely most of us would have trouble even getting into another college, since we would clearly be labeled as troublemakers.

I blinked. We didn't take the car keys, the students were suspended, and the school continued as though nothing had happened. All of the eight seniors took the position that there was only another six months left, so let's move on. To this day there is a part of me that regrets that I didn't call the president's bluff. Would he really have closed the school? I have no way of knowing.

SENIOR THESIS

When I entered Goddard College I had no idea what I wanted to do with my life. At various times I harbored the fantasy that I could be a novelist and short story writer. Taking a creative writing class at the New School convinced me that my talents in this area were not significant. I decided to try to combine my interest in social sciences and folk music by writing a thesis about the Life and Music of Leadbelly. Gabriel Jackson, my original mentor, had left the college so I utilized a new professor who had a background in history and scholarship. He knew absolutely nothing about Leadbelly, so I realized he could help with the research design, but I'd have to do most of the planning on my own.

I prepared a brief questionnaire about Leadbelly's life, and sent it out to Pete Seeger, and to two music critics, Frederic Ramsey Jr. and Charles Edward Smith. Both of them were quite familiar with Leadbelly's music, and Ramsey had even recorded the Leadbelly's Last Sessions albums for Folkways. I also contacted the authorities at the Angola Prison, one of the two institutions where Leadbelly had been imprisoned. Everyone was very cooperative, and I then spent hours transcribing the lyrics to Leadbelly's songs. Because he had a thick accent, and many of the recordings were poorly recorded, I had to listen to many of the songs over and over. One day my black friend Jim Spruill laughingly referred to what I was doing as "translations from the original Negro."

MY FIRST PAID PLAYING JOB

John Pierce, the science teacher at Goddard, also played some fiddle, and could call square dances. He hired me to play banjo at a square dance in nearby East Calais, Vermont. I didn't really know any of the tunes, but enthusiasm carried me through the night.

The next day John informed me that I had no left hand technique on the banjo. It hurt my feelings, but he was right. He could have added that I didn't know many chords either. I'd gotten through my first paying job playing music.

GRADUATION AND A DAY IN THE KENTUCKY MOUNTAINS

Dick Mulliken and I decided to do a concert of American folk music at graduation. Still under the spell of Stu Jamieson, I decided to write a five part suite called A Day In The Kentucky Mountains. Prior to coming up with that idea, I had written a few songs, and I thought that writing instrumental music would provide me with some interesting challenges.

I wrote most of the piece outdoors. It was divided into an opening section, a second part called Waterfall, a song with lyrics called Chase The Rising Sun, a blues at sundown, and a reprise of the entire piece. The idea was that the piece depicted reprise of a day in the Kentucky Mountains. At the time I had never been to Kentucky, but I definitely was inspired by the music of Stu Jamieson, Uncle Dave Macon, and other banjo players. Each section had specific musical themes, and then I would improvise on the themes as the section continued. I don't know why I came up with the idea of placing a song in the middle of an instrumental piece, but it seemed logical to me. Because the Waterfall and Blues sections were relatively quiet and lyrical, I tried to play the banjo quietly, and to be expressive rather than frantic. Because I had little contact with other players at that time, I challenged myself to come up with techniques that would make that possible. To this day there are relatively few banjo players who seem interested in exploring the instrument as an expressive tool, rather than a vehicle for technical virtuosity.

It took me several months to get all of the music together, and I did play it at graduation as part of a folk concert. I thought that it was an effective way to acknowledge that the banjo had been a major part of my college life. Within two years I would record the piece, and it would become the jumping off point for all the music that I would play on the banjo during my entire musical career.

GOODBYE GODDARD

As the end of my senior year approached, I started to think about what I would do after college. I took the state exam that would qualify me for a job as a social worker for the state of Vermont. A passing grade was 80, and I scored slightly above that. The job would have required me to get a car. I did not know how to drive at the time, didn't really want to invest in a car, and the prospect of visiting rural homes in Vermont in the winter didn't appeal to me.

I was involved in a difficult relationship with a student named Carol Cohen who was a couple of years younger than I was. I urged her to take some psychological tests, and after resisting the idea, she agreed to take the Rorschach and Wechsler-Bellevue tests if I would take one as well. A woman named Marjorie Townsend who was a psychiatric social worker, lived next door to Goddard, and I went to her office. The Rorschach test is a sort of psychological diagnostic test. The tester shows the subject a series of ink blots, and asks them to describe each one.

A week later I went back to get the results. Marjorie asked me several questions about what I was doing, and how I felt about various things. She the informed me that I had a very high score in the Wechsler-Bellevue test for verbal ability, but an extremely low score for spatial understanding. That didn't particularly surprise me, because it reflected my inability to do shop projects, to know how to take things apart or to understand geometry. She also told me that I didn't have a single common response to the ink blots. She looked at me carefully, and said that normally someone with my combination of characteristics was a schizophrenic, but that I seemed to be doing well at school, and to have fairly normal personal relationships, so I probably shouldn't be too worried about that.

YELLOWSTONE AGAIN

I decided to go back to Yellowstone Park to work

for a second summer. I was also able to help Carol get a job as a maid working at one of the lodges at Yellowstone Lake. The Yellowstone Park Company had a policy of paying employees $25 to help them get to Yellowstone. That money paid for a bus ticket from Vermont to Nebraska, and then we planned to hitchhike. By the time we got off the bus, Carol began to have an attack of tonsillitis. We got her a cheap hotel room, and I slept out in a field with my sleeping bag. I had forgotten how enormous the western sky is. There was heat lightning all around, and I was terrified and couldn't get to sleep. I ended up dragging myself into a prefabricated dog house. Since the dog house was most likely an excellent conductor of electricity, this was probably the dumbest thing I could have done. The next morning the sound of railroad workers going to work woke me up at around 5:30. I went to the hotel to collect Carol, and we decided to take a bus to Cheyenne. I left her at the hospital there, and started to hitch rides to Yellowstone. I had told my boss that I would get to work at a certain date, and I correctly figured that Carol could make it on her own a few days later.

The going was very slow, but I finally got to a town called Dubois, south of Yellowstone. A fellow dressed like a cowboy drove by in a pick-up truck, saw my banjo case, and turned around and asked me whether I wanted to work that night. It was close to twilight, so I happily accepted his offer. He told me that the pay would be $15. He turned out to be the town hero. He had played bass with the country star T. Texas Tyler (Courting In The Rain) and had been on the Grand Ole Opry and toured with Tyler. My employer, who I'll call Cal, because I don't remember his name, outfitted me in a western shirt and boots, and we went over to the bar.

The band included a tenor banjo player and a drummer. When Cal played guitar I played five string banjo, and when he played bass I played guitar. The club had the longest bar that I had ever seen. We mostly played Hank Williams songs and other current country hits.

Around midnight a half dozen Cree Indian kids, probably underage, came to the bar. One raced up to the bandstand, and started singing Cree songs. I was the only one interested, and he was booted off the bandstand.

At the end of the long night Cal invited me to stay on the floor of his cabin, but he only paid me $5. He said the boss said that he wasn't expecting to pay another musician. That was my second job in the music business, and already I was being partially stiffed. When I got to Yellowstone, one day I was practicing the banjo, and a tourist asked me if I could play Under The Double Eagle. I only knew the first half of the tune, but I played that for him. He tossed me a silver dollar, and told me that I was the greatest banjo player in the world. That was the first tip I ever got for playing music.

When Carol arrived a few days later, we broke up almost immediately.

KEITH HILLIARD

One of my dorm mates at Yellowstone, Keith Hilliard was an art student at Eastern New Mexico University. He was a very quiet, self-deprecatory guy. Like me was interested in exploring as many parts of Yellowstone as possible. We managed to get some of the same days off, and we kayaked around the lake. This wasn't the smartest move for me, since I didn't know how to swim. On the other hand, the lake was at an elevation of 7500 feet, and supposedly the water was so cold that anyone falling in the lake would be in a state of hypothermia within ten minutes. Everyone liked Keith, especially the women who worked at the lodge. He was one of those unassuming people who seemed totally unaware of his own charms.

Part 1 • Chapter 4

GRADUATE SCHOOL AND NEW YORK CITY

When I graduated from Goddard I was twenty one years old. I had no idea what I wanted to do, but I knew that if I didn't continue going to school, I would be drafted. Despite the warnings that Goddard had placed on my transcript, I decided to apply to graduate school in sociology. I applied to CCNY (City College of New York) to the social work school at New York University and to Columbia University. The program at NYU was an innovative program that involved combining studies in the social sciences with social work. It seemed to be the most interesting of the three programs, but I was not admitted. I was accepted by the other two programs, and chose to go to Columbia.

By this time I had started to teach banjo and guitar, and to play my first professional gigs. My parents agreed to pay my tuition, if I paid my living expenses. With the help of my friend Richie Reinitz, I got myself an apartment on the lower east side of New York. It was a five story walk up apartment, with no heat, and a bathtub in the kitchen. There was a wood stove in the kitchen that could be used to heat the apartment. The rent was $22 a month, but in order to sublet the rent controlled apartment, I had to agree to purchase the furniture for about $200. What that actually meant was that you bribed the previous tenant in order to get into the building. This practice was illegal, but common.

COLUMBIA

I had chosen to attend Columbia because of two well-known politically radical professors named C. Wright Mills and Robert S. Lynd. Both of them had written some interesting sociological works. Mills' books contained a politically radical analysis of American capitalism, and Lynd had written the pioneering community studies Middletown and Middletown In Transition.

I soon discovered that Mills was at war with most of the other professors at Columbia, and they had basically agreed that he could teach undergraduate programs, while the other senior faculty controlled the graduate school. The research emphasis in the department was on the then new field of market research, and a number of professors there were involved with questions about why people bought specific products. During my year and a half at Columbia, Lynd had a visiting professorship in England. The only contact that I ever had with him was to attend one guest lecture.

Other than one class in social psychology, my classes involved sociological methods and statistical research. I had virtually no interest in any of this, and I struggled through the classes, barely maintaining the required B average.

The most peculiar part of my graduate work was that I could more or less follow what my professors said, but whenever my fellow students would say something in class, I had no idea what they were talking about. Except for working on my statistics homework with a fellow student named Burt Prelutsky, I had no social contact with any of my fellow students. Without Burt's help, I probably would never have even made the minimal C grades that I was able to obtain.

One day I was walking across campus to a class. The quad at Columbia basically cut off city streets. A young Puerto Rican grocery delivery man was pushing a grocery cart. He seemed very puzzled. He asked me if non-students could walk across the quad. I told him that of course he could walk there. I looked up at the hundreds of students scurrying to classes, and thought to myself, I'm like the delivery guy, I don't really belong here.

GREENWICH VILLAGE DAYS

By hanging out in Greenwich Village, I met an aspiring bookseller named Israel (Izzy) Young. He was selling books about folk music and dance out of a warehouse office and by 1957 had opened a retail store at 110 MacDougal Street, in the heart of Greenwich Village. Oddly enough, my mother had hung out in Greenwich Village before she was married, going to parties with various literary types.

The Folklore Center became the headquarters for anyone interested in American Folk Music. It was a long and narrow store, and was the site of numerous jam sessions and impassioned discussions about the future of American folk music. The habitués included a bunch of young semi-professionals like me, as well as Logan English, Gina Glazer, Roger Abrahams, and Paul Clayton. I began to spend more and more of my time at the Folklore Center, and on Sundays, I would periodically join the musicians who gathered to play music around the fountain in Washington Square.

HAPPY TRAUM

I started performing with Happy Traum, a guitar player and singer who I met in the Village. We did occasional concerts in New York and Philadelphia, and played the Swarthmore Folk Festival at Swarthmore College. It was at this concert that I did one of the first live performances of A Day In The Kentucky Mountains. Happy and I continued to play occasional concerts over the next couple of years.

FIRST RECORDING

Bob Harris still had his record store and Stinson Record label, and I wrote a set of liner notes for a Bob Gibson album and did my first professional recording session for Stinson, playing guitar for an actor-singer named Dick Silvera. Dick was a trained art singer, who had a rich and strong voice that would have probably been better suited to piano accompaniment. We recorded in Bob's basement, and drove up to Harlem, where Bob or his wife Nadine took the album photo of Dick singing on the steps of an apartment building with me playing guitar and dozens of local black kids staring at the camera.

DAVE VON RONK

One Sunday afternoon I was playing in Washington Square and a rather bear-like individual approached me. He told me that his name was Dave Van Ronk. He was a member of the Merchant Marine, and had just come off a ship. He told me that he played guitar, and asked whether you could actually make a living playing this kind of music. I told him that if you combined teaching, recording, and some performing that it was possible.

Decades later he died, and I was unable to attend the memorial service. I did share that memory with his wife Andrea, saying that it seemed to me that making a living as a musician still involved the same challenges forty years later. She read it to the many attendees at the memorial, and told me that many of his peers nodded when she read my reminiscence about those days.

LORENZ GRAHAM AND BAMBOO

The summer before my last stand at Columbia, I got a call from a singer named Lorenz Graham. He was an actor-singer cast in the Harry Belafonte mold. Lorenz didn't play any instruments and he was looking for an accompanist. He had a two week gig at a club in Boston, in the so-called Combat Zone of Boston. This was kind of a rough area of town that featured burlesque shows, tough bars, and a few clubs. I told him that I could do the first week, but that the second week was my first week of graduate school, and I didn't think that I could get away with missing my first classes. I arranged that Fred Gerlach, an excellent twelve string guitarist could sub for me during the second week. The pay was $125 a week.

I went up to Boston, and got a cheap hotel room. The club that we were playing in had a room called the Limbo Room, and the general theme of the club was all calypso all the time. We did our first set, consisting of four songs. Three of them were calypso songs, and we did one ballad, Every Night When The Sun Goes In. The last song in each set concluded with the performers and some of the audience doing the limbo. This involved squeezing under a net. It was quite funny watching some of the older and heavier audience members trying to squeeze under the net. When we finished the first set, the manager said to us, "that was pretty good, but you need to do more calypso." I guess three out of four songs wasn't enough. Lorenz had advanced me $75 for the gig, but when the gig ended he told me he'd pay me the rest later. The English translation of later is never.

Lorenz claimed that he had written a Jamaican song called River Come Down. I happened upon two versions of it in a book of Jamaican folk songs in the New York Public Library. In 1961 John Phillips, Scott McKenzie, and I started a pop-folk trio called The Journeymen. Our first album consisted of songs from my repertoire, and a few songs that John had written. I had worked out a very complicated banjo arrangement of River Come Down, using all five fingers of the right hand. This was one of the songs on our first Capitol album. John and I copyrighted all of the traditional songs that we did, using the phrase "arranged and adapted by John Phillips and Dick Weissman." In this case that was literally true.

A year later I was walking in Greenwich Village and ran into Dave Van Ronk. Dave had heard me do the song before I was ever in The Journeymen, and he told me he had re-arranged the song further, and changed the title to Bamboo. Dave said that he wanted to copyright the song in his name and mine, and asked if that was acceptable to me. I told John Phillips what was going on, and since neither he nor I had actually written the song he agreed that this worked for him.

THE BIG BUCKS AND THE COMPLICATIONS

Shortly thereafter, the song was recorded by a new group called Peter, Paul & Mary. It was on their first album, which went multi-platinum. On the initial pressing of the album my name appears as co-composer with Dave's. Royalties from radio and television airplay are distributed by three performing rights societies. At the time, I was a member of BMI, while Dave was a member of ASCAP. The problem was that in those days, you were not permitted to write with a member of the other society. Neither Dave nor I knew this nor did we care about performing rights in those days. Dave and I were summoned to the offices of the music publisher, Warner Music. The head of the company was a corpulent cigar-smoking music business fixture named Herman Starr. Mr. Starr proceeded to read me the riot act, telling me what a terrible organization BMI was, and what a miserable person I was for joining that group. After about ten minutes of this, I had had enough. I pointed out that much of the income his company was enjoying came from the re-arrangements of traditional folksongs, and all of us knew that this was a bit of a farce because we had no idea who the actual authors were. Mr. Starr screamed at me, and turned entirely red in the face. He then kicked me out of the office. I was escorted out by his assistant Artie Mogull, a well-known music business character and bon vivant. Artie said to me, "No one talks to Mr. Starr like that." I looked at him and said, "I guess I did."

My name was taken off the re-pressings of the album. To Dave's eternal credit, he continued to send me half of the royalties from the sales of the record. Ultimately that came to fifteen or twenty thousand dollars for each of us.

Bamboo became the gift that kept on giving. Years later I got a phone call from Dave, telling me that he had used the song in a German shoe commercial and that I would be getting a bunch more money. So in the early 1990's I received another seven or eight thousand dollars for my part of the song.

In 2013 the Coen Brothers made their movie Llewyn Davis. It was very loosely based on Dave Van Ronk's autobiography. Smithsonian Records then produced a boxed set of Dave's music. One of the songs on the albums was of course, Bamboo. It continues to pay modest but regular royalties, more than 46 years after I heard the song for the first time. As for Lorenz Graham, I have no idea what became of him. I found a single reference on the internet to a performance that he did in 1969 in North Carolina.

I blacklisted Lorenz with the musician's union for

not paying me my full salary in Boston. A couple of years after the Boston gig Lorenz joined the musician's union, and in order to be accepted he had to pay me the balance of the money that he owed.

DROPPING OUT OF GRADUATE SCHOOL

After a year on the Lower East Side, I moved to a slightly better apartment at 110th Street and Amsterdam Avenue. I had to "sell the furniture," when I sublet the apartment on East 3rd Street. I placed an ad in the Village Voice and someone called and threatened to report me to the city, because selling the furniture was considered an illegal scam. I took the ad out of The Voice for a few weeks, put it back in again, and someone rented the apartment, and bought the furniture.

The new apartment was a ground level one bedroom apartment, that actually had heat and hot water, and was within walking distance of Columbia. I completed my course work in sociology and started to prepare to write my thesis. I wanted to continue combining my musical and sociological interests, so I dreamed up a thesis project that involved studying a group of blind black blues singers. My hypothesis was that a black blind musician growing up with little or no education would act as a kind of living museum of the culture that he experienced in his childhood. I wanted to include Gary Davis, Blind Lemon Jefferson, and several other blues and gospel musicians in my research. I went to see my adviser, Professor Morris Zelditch Jr. I assumed that he was doing market research, like most of my professors. Unbeknownst to me, he was actually an authority on social status. I described the research that I wanted to do, and he made a rather odd comment, something to the effect that his wife was an artist, and so he understood creative people. I concluded that he had no idea what I was talking about. As I left his office, I realized that I was not going to write this thesis, and that I was going to drop out of graduate school without completing my degree.

PSYCHOTHERAPY AND THE DRAFT

Although I didn't enjoy my time at Columbia, it had provided me with specific tasks that I needed to undertake. I went to classes, for the most part, took exams, and was able to preserve the illusion that I knew what I was doing. The truth is that I was close to being a lost soul. I continued to see Carol, who lived on the extreme north side of town, which meant endless late night subway rides to and from her house. Neither of us had the courage to end our relationship, or to invest any real energy in expanding it. Under the influence of my friend Richie, I undertook two years of psychotherapy. It helped me to understand my behavior, and I began to spend more time on exploring other people's ideas and emotional issues.

In the midst of my therapy, just after I left Columbia, I was called up for my physical for the draft. The army psychologist was a suit with a cigar, and he seemed to want me to get angry at him. When he succeeded in doing so, he decided I was not suitable material for the Army. I think my primary concern at the time was that I imagined myself spending hours and hours in vain attempts to take apart a rifle, in the same way that I had tried to plane a piece of wood in my high school shop class. The year was 1958, after Korea and before Viet Nam, and my guess is that at the time the army wasn't desperately in need of new recruits.

Part 1 • Chapter 5

WORKING AS A MUSICIAN IN NEW YORK: BANJOS, BANJOS AND MORE BANJOS

Two of the most interesting musicians that I had met in the Village were a guitar player named Frank Hamilton, and banjo player Billy Faier. Frank was a wonderful guitar player, who was playing music from various parts of the world long before anyone else that I knew in the folk world was even aware that such music existed. Billy was a very interesting banjo player, who played variations on everything from fiddle tunes to lute music. Although he could play traditional banjo as well, most of his music was derived from classical music and/or ragtime. Billy was much more worldly, with an awareness of the process of making a living by playing music.

In the late 1950's Riverside Records, known for its jazz recordings, hired folklorist Kenny Goldstein to produce a series of folk music records for the label. Billy persuaded Kenny to do two albums. One was basically a solo album for him, accompanied by Frank on guitar. For his other album he came up with the concept of doing an album with three different banjo players, all playing in different styles. I was quite surprised when Billy asked me if I wanted to be one of his two cohorts. I was happy to join the party.

To record for Riverside, I had to join the American Federation of Musicians. To become a member in those days, you had to pass an audition. Because of my piano lessons, I could read music, but Billy told me that when I played, I should just tell the union official that I just sang and accompanied myself. I followed those instructions, and started to sing and play an old murder ballad called Pretty Polly. I got through one verse, and the union guy told me he had heard enough. I was quite insulted but I didn't realize that this was all a game.

In later years a topical singer named Charley King told me that he had auditioned in Massachusetts, and he sang a song he had composed about the Italian anarchists Sacco and Vanzetti, who were sentenced to death for their alleged anarchist acts in Massachusetts. Charley was singing with his eyes closed, and he was really involved in performing the song. He looked up, and the union official auditioning him was snoring!

The third banjoist on our album was a very young bluegrass picker named Eric Weissberg.

The name of the trio album was Banjos, Banjos, and More Banjos. I asked Billy if I could record my banjo suite, A Day In The Kentucky Mountains. He ran that idea by Kenny, who told him that he only wanted to record traditional music. I was crushed. When we got to the studio Billy told me to record it anyway. It turned out that Kenny really liked the piece, and when he had to remove one of Billy's pieces because of a technical flaw, he had me come over to his house and I recorded another short original piece called Cape Cod Blues. In addition to our solo pieces we also did some duets. My duet was played with Eric, and it was the traditional tune Going Down The Road Feeling Bad. I played in clawhammer style, and Eric played bluegrass.

The Banjos album was favorably reviewed in the New York Times, and the Times music critic Robert Shelton, specifically cited my banjo suite. When the album came out, it didn't especially do anything for my career, but it was a big boost to my self-confidence.

PAT FOSTER

Around the same time that I was doing the Banjos album, a singer named Pat Foster wandered into the Folklore Center. Pat was a balding, 35-ish intense fellow who at his best had a wonderful golden voice. I was soon to learn that among his other qualities he sought out girl friends who could pay his bills, and he was a very mean drunk who would periodically get into fist fights during his barroom flings. Pat confided in me that his real name was David Feinberg, which may or may not have been true. My friend Frank Hamilton recently told me that he had heard Pat preach an evangelical hellfire and damnation sermon in Los Angeles. No one in my circle of acquaintances knew who Pat really was. He decided that he and I should develop a performing duo, with him doing most of the singing, and me taking instrumental solos. Through my connection with Kenny Goldstein in short order we became part of the Riverside Records folk roster. Kenny wanted to do a series of albums of songs of different periods of American history. Possibly because Pat claimed to be from Idaho, and had spent some time in California, Kenny decided that we should do an album of Gold Rush songs. I spent some time in the New York Public Library researching songs of the period, and we came up with enough material for an album. After we recorded the album, Kenny asked us to do another album of Songs of California and the Pacific Northwest. That album was recorded, and we were paid to do it, but it never was released.

In the midst of all this activity, Bill Fox wandered into the Folklore Center. He had a record company called Esoteric, which utilized the same concept that Nonesuch Records was to implement a decade later. Fox leased European recordings of baroque and pre-baroque music, and also issued some of the first albums of world music, as well as some unusual jazz recordings of early bebop recorded live at Minton's in Harlem. For some reason, Bill had gotten it into his head that he wanted to do an entire album of Talking Blues. Talking Blues are a sort of odd fusion of country and blues forms that are spoken but not sung. The first person to record a talking blues was a country artist named Chris Bouchillion, but the famous songwriter Woody Guthrie found the form perfect for many of his monologues. He wrote Talking Columbia about the Columbia River, Talking Sailor, and with Pete Seeger and some of the other Almanac Singers, Talking Union. Bill Fox encountered Pat Foster at the Folklore Center, and Pat immediately convinced him that with my help he could put together a terrific album of talking blues songs. Bill agreed almost immediately.

This left Pat and me with the problem of how to do a dozen songs without any real singing, and make them interesting to anyone other than Bill and a handful of folklorists. The first thing we did was to come up with an original song of our own called Talking Migrant. We interpolated little sections of the folksong Worried Blues into Talking Migrant, and Pat "sold it" to Bill by claiming that he had collected the song in California. The song includes a spoken reference to my teenaged gig picking blueberries in New Jersey for a penny a quart more than the Puerto Rican workers in an adjoining folk were making. Ironically, our "folksong" was cited ten years later in a serious study of hobo life by English scholar and journalist Kenneth Allsop. Bill Fox wasn't the only one we had fooled. Much to my surprise the album was re-issued as a CD in 2009.

The Talking Blues project was the beginning of the end of my association with Pat Foster. Pat spent too many nights drinking and being thrown out of Bob Dylan's favorite bar, the Kettle of Fish. The few performances that we did were nerve wracking, because when Pat drank he would become hostile to the audience and anyone else around. One hitchhiking trip to Massachusetts got us a pick-up job for a bunch of business executives in Harriman, New York. That was the extent of our touring. For a while Pat was living in a loft in the Village that had formerly been rented by actress Veronica Lake. The loft had huge ceilings and a swing that could make you float through most of the apartment. The bills were being paid by a woman named Florence Goldberg, a very sweet if plain looking woman that Pat had picked up somewhere in his New York travels. When she eventually tried to kick him out, he developed a rapid case of amnesia, and pretended not to remember who he was. By that time I decided that I'd had enough.

In the late spring of 1961 I was playing at the hungry i in San Francisco with The Journeymen. One night Pat magically appeared as we were about to enter the club. I didn't ask him whether he wanted to see the show. I figured that he'd probably get into a fight with one of the waiters, or insult someone in the audience. That was the last time I ever saw him. I don't think he ever recorded again.

106TH STREET

When I quit Columbia I decided to move out of my one room apartment on 110th Street. My friend Burrill had just vacated a five room railroad flat on 106th Street between Amsterdam and Columbus Avenue. The rent was $105 a month, and there were three bedrooms, a kitchen, and a bathroom. I invited two friends to move in with me. One was my Goddard friend Jim Spruill, the other was a guy that I met in New York, David Wolkenberg.

All of us were having various levels of relationship problems. I had been seeing my friend Carol who I had met at Goddard. Our relationship was on and off for about three years. Somehow it seemed better to settle for something predictable rather than to look for someone new.

My first summer at 106th Street I got a job teaching guitar at two summer camps in Massachusetts, near Stockbridge. It was a great time for me. I rode up there on a bicycle from New York. I'd teach guitar at one camp in the morning, and then in the afternoon I'd bike three miles to the other camp. Whenever I wasn't in one place, the camp directors assumed that I'd be in the other one. The weather was cool, a lot of the students were talented musicians, and towards the end of the summer I started dating Sara Jo Samuels. When I got back to New York, we continued to see one another.

PHILADELPHIA

Someone in Philadelphia who had been teaching guitar contacted me, and asked me if I'd like to take over her students, because she was leaving town. Two days a week I'd go to Philadelphia and teach guitar and banjo. I'd take the train from New York on Sunday, and stay with my parents. Most Sunday afternoons I'd go over to a coffeehouse called The Gilded Cage. In the back room there was a musical round robin, where everyone there would perform a song. It was there that I met Harry Tuft and a young medical student named Morrie Schambelan. Harry became a lifelong friend, and he later moved to Denver partly under my influence, and I moved to Denver under his influence about ten years later. Almost all of the Philadelphia folksingers would show up for the Sunday afternoon sings, so I got to know quite a few of the Philadelphia folksingers. A number of them later became professional musicians, performing or teaching, but most of them stayed in Philadelphia.

On Sunday or Monday evenings I would often drift over to a downtown folk club called The Second Fret. It was there that I met Jerry Ricks, a young black aspiring musician who worked first in the kitchen, and then managed the club. Jerry became a superb guitarist, and a close friend.

I put an ad in The Village Voice, advertising that I was teaching guitar and banjo, and got some students in New York through that ad. Meanwhile I played on several other albums. Kenny Goldstein hired me to accompany Ruth Rubin, who was a scholar and performer of Yiddish Folk Songs. I did an album with her, and I also periodically would perform as a solo act in the Village, usually at a coffeehouse known as a basket house. The name of the club was The Commons. Basket houses were coffeehouses where we instructed the audience that we were not paid, but we passed around baskets at the end of each set. In fact we were paid. Something like $3-$5 a night. On a good night you might go home with all of ten dollars, with tips. The performers included a flamenco guitarist. Dominic Chianese, who later played Junior in the Sopranos TV show, sang Italian opera flavored songs, and occasionally the so-called beat poets like John Brent would perform.

MY FIRST REAL STUDIO GIG

At this point, all of my studio gigs were accompanying folksingers, or playing banjo. One of the places musicians hung out in New York was a music store on West 49th Street, called Eddie Bell's. I became friendly with Eddie and his wife Paula, and they recommended me to play banjo on a commercial. The music was written and conducted by Raymond Scott, a New York composer who wrote all sorts of experimental music. The two guitarists were Al Caiola and Barry Galbraith. Both were incredibly busy studio musicians, and Barry also had a reputation for being a superb jazz player. The music involved playing some chords that were unfamiliar to me. I worked them out, with Raymond suggesting I continue to practice during a five minute break for the other musicians. It all worked out fine, and was my introduction into the world of New York studio players. Barry had a Stromberg Guitar, a rare jazz make, and I asked him if I could try it. I played a couple of Piedmont-style riffs on it, kind of in the vein of Blind Boy Fuller. Barry and Al looked at each other. I don't think they had ever seen anyone play fingerstyle ragtime blues guitar before.

FOLK CITY AND THE BLUES PARTIES

Just east of Greenwich Village was an old restaurant-bar called Gerde's. Izzy Young and his business partner Tom Prendergast talked Mike Porco, the owner, into starting a live music folk club at Gerde's. Izzy was very supportive of my music and shortly after the opening, he asked me if I wanted to be the opening act for Brownie McGhee and Sonny Terry, the well-known blues team. Of course I was thrilled.

The original engagement was for a week, but we were held over for a couple of weeks. Virtually no one came to see me, but Brownie and Sonny were a well-established act and drew lots of patrons. I did a short opening set and then they would tear the place apart. One night Brownie was late, and I actually did a set with Sonny. I was almost entirely naïve about singing in those days. About two songs into the set I realized what a lame singer I was compared to either Sonny or Brownie. Even so, it was the highlight of my three weeks at Folk City.

One weekend night Brownie asked me if I wanted to host a party at my house. Since our apartment could hold quite a few people, I enthusiastically agreed. A few minutes later, Brownie announced the party on the microphone, and gave out my address. By the time I got home the doorbell started ringing. Eventually about a hundred people showed up.

A few weeks later we hosted a similar party. My roommate Jim Spruill and I looked around and determined that we knew maybe ten of the hundred people in the house. Sonny Terry suddenly realized that he had invited both his wife and his girl friend to the party. Brownie and Sonny had something of a contentious relationship and every time the doorbell would ring, Brownie would tell Sonny that either his wife or his girl friend was there. Among the other people at the party were guitarists Bruce Langhorne, Erik Darling and John Lee Hooker.

Most of the playing took place in our dining room-kitchen, which was at the end of the hall that ran adjacent to our three bedrooms. Soon Brownie and John Lee started to play together. Brownie was a sophisticated, experienced guitarist. Besides playing with Sonny Terry he had done quite a few solo records, and also played with his brother Sticks McGhee. John Lee had a very distinctive, but basically simple guitar style, utilizing identifiable techniques that were original but not especially complex. Brownie, who could be competitive when he wanted to, began to basically obliterate John Lee, guitaristically speaking. John Lee, who had a severe stutter when he wasn't singing, told me that he wanted to go out to his car to get his amplifier. I had to explain to him that he couldn't do that, because our house had DC current. In order to use any normal electrical device like a record player or a guitar amplifier, it was necessary to plug it into a converter. Otherwise the amplifier or record player would literally blow up. John Lee didn't understand what I was talking about and when I explained it to him several more times, I still had the sense that he didn't believe me. In any case, I was able to convince him not to bring the amplifier in. It occurred to me that here I was, a graduate student at Columbia whose technological expertise wasn't adequate to meet the demands of this "primitive" blues singer. During the course of the evening, John Lee became intrigued with my blues banjo playing. He told me that he wanted to learn how to play the banjo.

We then had another surrealistic discussion where I explained to John Lee that the banjo might not fulfill the image that his fans had of him. Meanwhile, I watched John Lee demonstrate his pick-up routine on various women. He would simply go up to them, and say "do you want to sleep with me tonight?" I have no idea whether this technique worked for him, but it certainly got my attention.

BRUCE LANGHORNE

Bruce Langhorne was one of the few young black musicians in the early years of the folk revival. Bruce was born with a couple of deformed fingers in his right hand. Not one to feel sorry for himself, he bought a sweet old Martin Guitar and developed a beautiful tone on the instrument. He went on to play for Odetta, Peter Paul & Mary, and on some of Bob Dylan's early albums. He is supposedly the protagonist of Dylan's song Mr. Tambourine Man. Bruce had an interesting way of expressing himself. His goodbye greeting was "be good, but don't take any shit." Later he moved to Hawaii, wrote some commercials and did New Age workshops on music.

THE NEW YORK MUSIC SCENE

The music scene in New York was incredibly varied, and easy to access. On Sunday afternoons folksingers gathered in Washington Square and sang and played all afternoon. In the evenings many of us walked over to the American Youth Hostel on West 8th Street and did some more singing. Sometimes the sessions spilled over to various apartments. There were a bunch of jazz clubs in and around the Village and downtown. I would take the subway down to the Half Note club near the Holland Tunnel. At various times I saw Wes Montgomery and John Coltrane, nursing a beer through their shows. I wanted to see Thelonius Monk at the Five Spot Café, near my old apartment on East 3rd Street, but every time I'd go there he was always late, so I never did get to see him. There were plenty of other clubs that featured jazz, but they were uptown and too expensive for me. There were also a large number of classical concerts at Town Hall and Carnegie Hall, and at schools and other performance spaces. I saw Julian Bream play twice, as well as Andre Segovia, and I attended several concerts with the French flute virtuoso Jean Pierre Rampal, accompanied by harpsichord master Robert Veyron Le Croix. Later I saw the Janacek Quartet from Prague play music of Leos Janacek from memory at a wonderful performance at an elementary school. I really liked Town Hall, which held about 1200 people, because you could see and hear perfectly from any seat. As I recall, these concerts typically cost around $5. In all the time I attended classical music concerts I never ever ran into any of my friends from the folksong world.

MUSIC WASN'T EVERYTHING

My friend Jim Spruill was one of the first actors in the black theater renaissance in New York. He performed in a number of off-Broadway plays, and I met some of his cohorts, including Lou Gossett Jr. Jim was fascinated by my prison song records, and he used to go around singing a couple of the songs. Years later I was watching a movie starring Lou and I heard him singing one of these songs without accompaniment. I feel certain that he learned it from Jim.

One night I was having dinner with Tanis Fletcher, a friend of mine from Goddard. Tanis brought along two friends. The boy friend of her friend Carol Kolmetz was a young architect. He told us that he had just designed the world's first shopping mall. This meant nothing to the rest of us, until he detailed exactly what it would look like, and correctly described how malls were going to change the nature of American cities. He told us that he was going to Europe, because he didn't want to live in a country that was going to be populated by shopping malls. I don't know where the mall was or if it ever got built, but his predictions turned out to be disturbingly accurate.

ERIC WEISSBERG, HOAGY CARMICHAEL AND THE FOLK YEARS

One day in 1960, I got a call to appear on an NBC TV special called Those Ragtime Years.

The show was designed as a history of ragtime. The narrator for much of it was songwriter Hoagy Carmichael, composer of Stardust and Georgia On My Mind. The featured guest was ragtime pianist Eubie Blake and there was a large orchestra consisting of NBC-TV musicians who were on staff at the network. My role was to play banjo for Robin Roberts, a folksinger best known for singing Irish and English ballads. They asked me if I knew a fiddle player, and I suggested that they use Eric Weissberg.

The show involved extensive rehearsal time, even though we were only going to be on camera for a grand total of about twenty seconds. We sat through the laborious two days of rehearsals, and during one of the many segments that we weren't involved with, Eric leaned over to me and said, "do you think that in twenty years they'll do a show about us called The Folk Years." I absolutely cracked up with laughter. Unfortunately right at that time Hoagy was blowing one of the lines that he was reading off the teleprompter. He looked over at me angrily, and asked me what was so damn funny? I tried to explain to him that I was laughing about something that had nothing to do with him, but he obviously didn't believe me. He proceeded to embarrass me in front of the entire cast.

Over the years I had completely forgotten this incident. Around 2004 Eric and I were both hired for an educational television show that was intended as a fundraiser for the network. Many people from the folk revival were on the show, including the Clancy Brothers and Judy Collins. I looked over at Eric and said, "they did exactly what you predicted." He smiled broadly. He knew exactly what I was referring to.

THE PARTY AT MARTHA LEDBETTER'S HOUSE

Leadbelly's widow Martha lived one flight above Tiny Ledbetter's apartment on E. 10th Street. During the time that I had jammed with Gary at Tiny's apartment, I had never met Martha. One night Tiny invited me to a party at Martha's apartment. Lots of blues royalty were gathered in an apartment that basically was maintained as a shrine to Leadbelly. Gary was there along with several of his protégés when John Lee Hooker walked in. John Lee walked up to Gary, and said "Mr. Lead, I been hearing your name everywhere I go." The entire room became totally silent. Someone had to explain to John Lee that Leadbelly had died in 1949, and the person that he was talking to was Gary Davis. The silence ended, and the party resumed.

HEDY WEST, WIN STRACKE, HARRY TUFT AND CHICAGO

In the fall of 1959 I got a call from a Chicago folksinger named Win Stracke. He was coming to New York to record an album of Civil War songs, and someone told him that he should hire me to play banjo and guitar. Win invited a friend of his to the sessions. Her name was Hedy West, and she was a singer, banjoist and flute player, who was studying for a master's degree in theater at Columbia. The sessions went well, and one day he invited me to come to Chicago. With Frank Hamilton and a woman named Dawn Greening, Win had founded a school called The Old Town School of Folk Music. He told me that they were looking for an assistant music director for the school, and that it paid $75 a week. This doesn't seem like much money in 2016, but in 1959 dollars I guess it was the equivalent of six or seven hundred dollars today.

It turned out that my Philadelphia friend Harry Tuft had an older sister in Chicago, and he was up for visiting her. Harry also had a car, so that solved the transportation problem. We set out for Chicago, where his sister and her husband invited us to stay at their house.

I went down to Old Town to meet with Win. It turned out that the situation was a bit more complicated than he had led me to believe. Frank had recently married a woman who was more ambitious than he was. For whatever reasons, the other people at the school thought that she was going to pressure him to leave Chicago. I concluded that hiring me was a sort of an insurance policy for the school. This was a difficult situation for me, because Frank was one of my heroes, and it was clear to me that no one had exactly explained to him why they wanted to hire me.

Meanwhile I learned about the operation of the school. Frank had instituted a learning program initiated by Bess Lomax Hawes, Alan Lomax's sister. She had taught large group classes at UCLA's Extension Department. For the first hour guitar players would get together and work with an instructor, or even two instructors, while banjo players were in another room. They would work on the same repertoire, and after a short break, they would all get together and sing and play the songs together.

Old Town attracted many students, and still exists today, but in three buildings with many more classes. I thought that this was really an interesting way to teach large numbers of student simultaneously.

One of the nights that I was there, Frank invited me down to The Gate of Horn nightclub, where he was the house guitar player, accompanying anyone who performed there. Odetta was supposed to be performing that night. Frank and I and Victor Sproles, the house bass player, were jamming away in the dressing room when Al Grossman, the club's owner, came in and told us that Odetta was sick. He asked if the two of us could do a guest set. Frank and I had never really played together, but we quickly agreed. As we took our places on stage, the club MC mentioned that Odetta was sick, that we were doing a guest set, and that anyone who wanted a refund of the cover charge could get one. Two middle aged women in full length mink coats immediately got up before we had played a note and left. I guess that one look at Frank and me told them this wasn't what they wanted to pay to hear.

I don't remember anything else about the set, except that it went smoothly considering that we barely knew one another, let alone having never performed or rehearsed together. I knew Al Grossman from New York, and he graciously thanked us for doing the set. Al being Al, he never offered to pay us for our services. Truthfully I hadn't even thought about that aspect of things.

I elected not to accept the job at Old Town. My thinking was that it was a very politically fraught situation, and I certainly didn't want to make an enemy of Frank Hamilton. I also had no particular reaction to Chicago. It seemed me quite a bit like New York, only a bit smaller. I was already thinking about the possibility of leaving New York, but I decided that I wanted a more extreme change of scene when I did decide to leave.

HEDY WEST

When I got back from Chicago, Hedy West and I began a romance that over time turned into a long-term friendship. Hedy had an impeccable folk pedigree. Her father was Don West, a radical poet, preacher, and organizer. Hedy knew dozens of folk songs that she had learned from her family. Her grandmother in particular, taught her songs like Cotton Mill Girls, and One Sunday Evening. She also taught me 500 Miles, a song that was to become the ultimate folk standard. Hedy didn't think much of the folksingers that were hanging out in New York. She had studied voice and flute, and could read music fluently. She made fun of the authenticity fad that so many of the New York-based folksingers advocated. She also had no compunctions about using syncopation in her traditionally based banjo picking. Although my banjo playing was more complex than Hedy's was, she knew a lot of things about music that were new to me. We did a few gigs together, playing at my friend Burrill's short lived coffee shop The Lorenzaccio, and later at the Café Lena in Saratoga Springs, New York.

THE CITIZENS

By the time I was twenty five, in 1960, I started to take stock in my music. I had turned down the job in Chicago. Outside of the occasional recording date, I was teaching, performing here and there, and trying to figure out how I was going to make a living in music. I realized that my singing and somewhat introverted stage presence would never bring me any sort of secure income. Although my own taste in music leaned strongly towards traditional music, I was deeply involved in writing instrumental music and some songs. This tended to disqualify me from the traditional music camp. I couldn't seem to resolve this puzzle.

I answered an ad in the Village Voice, asking for someone to play banjo and guitar in a new pop-folk group called The Citizens. This group was the brain child of two Tin Pan Alley songwriters, Sid Jacobson and Lou Stallman. Many pop music fans are familiar with the songwriting mills that centered in the Brill Building in midtown Manhattan and 1650 Broadway, a few blocks north. The concept that songwriters like Carole King and Gerry Goffin utilized was to write an endless stream of songs, hoping to get some of them recorded, and hoping that a percentage of those songs would become hits. Many of these writers wrote three songs a day. Of the approximately twenty songs a week that they came up with, they hoped that four or five would get recorded, and one or two of those became hits. Anyone that could write, say twenty hits a year, could make a fine living in the music business. Lou Stallman and Sid Jacobson were lesser known versions of the above phenomenon.

Together or with other writers, they had enjoyed successful recordings of their songs by Johnny Mathis, Steve Lawrence, Dion & The Belmonts and Perry Como. Sid had another day job, but Lou spent all his time writing songs and hustling his creations. The two of them had come up with a series of songs about life in New York City.

I auditioned for the group, and was quickly accepted. The other members included Lennie Levene, who later became a comedy writer for television, and his friend Al Wenger. I brought in Hedy West, and soon we were rehearsing. I thought that the songs varied from acceptable to mediocre to horrible. In no case did I think that they were either artistically or commercially excellent. I also felt unsure that I was equipped to judge the quality of this sort of music. Al had some problems learning to sing parts, and Lou replaced him with himself.

Jacobson and Stallman had an independent production deal with Laurie Records. This meant that the contract was between them and Laurie. They gave each of us a contract to sign, which obligated us to them, not to the record company. Considering my naivete at the time, it is surprising to me that I actually read the contract. I noticed that it stated that they would get 20% for any of my musical earnings. Since a fair percentage of my income was coming from playing on recordings, and Sid and Lou had nothing to do with these calls, I told them that they needed to take that part of the contract back and re-write it. I returned the contract unsigned. Fortunately for me, they never re-wrote it.

KAREN DALTON

Ever since my summers in Yellowstone I was interested in returning to the Rocky Mountain region. I took one trip with Happy and Jane Traum to Colorado. The only notable occurrence on that trip was that I wrote half of a banjo piece called Trail Ridge Road while we were driving on that road, in Rocky Mountain National Park. A year later I had caught a ride with Bob Harris of Stinson Records to western Ohio, and planned to hitchhike from there to California. This was because Dave Van Ronk had told me that there was a club in Hermosa Beach, California that I could work at. This turned out to be an endless trip. I couldn't seem to catch anything but local rides. One was from a hot rodding teenager who was disgusted with me because he wanted me to drive while he caught a nap. Unfortunately at the time I didn't know how to drive. When I got to Colorado, the state police escorted me to Denver, and told me that hitchhiking wasn't allowed in Colorado. I took the bus east to western Kansas and hitched back to Philly. I got one ride from a working stiff who offered me raw hot dogs, and who said things like, "sometimes I feel like a jackrabbit kicked out from under the barn."

This wasn't exactly the kind of talk I was used to from Greenwich Village folksingers. Another time I got a short ride, and noticed that the people just behind the car had stopped as well. They followed my ride until he dropped me off. They were a young married couple, and he was from Bowling Green, Kentucky. He had seen my banjo case, and I played him the song I Wish I Was In Bowling Green.

By the summer of 1960 I had accumulated a little money. I had a guitar and banjo student in Philadelphia named Art Benjamin, and he and I decided to head to Denver. In my previous travels I had run into a folksinger named Walt Conley. He had been very friendly, and basically told me that if I came back, he'd try to get me some work. I bought a 4CV Renault, a tiny car, and Art and I set out for Denver. The Renault was a stick shift car, and I could barely handle it. We were riding on old US 40, a two lane highway around Effingham, Illinois, when a truck came over into my lane. I had two choices. I could either hit the truck head on, which didn't seem like a great idea, or I could go off the road, and try to stop the car on the grass. Art told me later that he had opened his eyes and saw that we were drifting off the road, but then he closed them again, figuring that I knew what I was doing. He was wrong. Instead of hitting the brakes I pressed down on the clutch. Fortunately for us, the car came to a halt in a mass of branches, in front of a big tree. Everyone who saw the accident was convinced that we would be killed. Amazingly, neither one of us were even injured. The front part of the car, however, was caved in.

The truck driver told us that he had tried to pass a car, but that he had no brakes, which is why he came into our lane. Because he acknowledged this, there was no question that his insurance company would have to pay for the damage. My car was towed to St. Louis, where we stayed over at a cousin of Art's, and waited a couple of days for the repair. Then it was on to Denver.

We made it to Walt's house, not far from downtown Denver. It seemed that every musician in Denver knew Walt. They either had worked with him or had been to parties at his house. Sure enough there was a party going on when we arrived. Art and I met two sisters, Karen Dalton and Joy Carriker. Karen was tall and willowy, and Joy was a sort of Brigitte Bardot lookalike. During the week or so we were in Denver each of us asked the sisters whether they wanted to come back East with us.

Art's situation was a bit different from mine. It seems that Joy had been married for about ten days to another musician, Dave Hamill. Furthermore, she was all of seventeen years old. Karen was 22, and seemingly a calmer individual. She was divorced, and as far as I could tell, she was coming to the end of a relationship with my friend Walt. In any case, both of them agreed to go with us. The four of us in my tiny Renault struggled across the Midwest. Dave was the cousin of the former Lieutenant Governor of Colorado, and supposedly he called in a few favors. Since Joy was 17, we were technically violating the Mann Act. The Mann Act is the federal law that prohibits transporting anyone under the age of 18 across a state line for "immoral purposes." Supposedly state troopers were looking for us, but if that was true, we got to Kansas before they did.

I dropped Art and Joy off in Philadelphia and proceeded to New York. Karen moved into the 106th Street apartment, and we tried to make a go of things. Karen and I went to Klein's Department Store and I bought her some clothes. I still remember the yellow turtleneck sweater that became a regular part of her wardrobe.

Karen and I never worked together, but we did sing and play at the house. My friend Harry Tuft came up to visit, and Karen revealed another side of her character. Harry was struggling in architecture school, and Karen attacked him head on. She told him that he was wasting his life, that he ought to move to Colorado and ski and sing, and so forth. I was saying some of the same things, but in a more gentle way. Karen hit him like a steamroller. I began to see that Karen had varying agendas of her own, and she wasn't someone you could argue or reason with.

A more unpleasant side of Ms. Dalton emerged when she drank. She became hostile, nasty and out of control. She reminded me of my ex-singing partner Pat Foster. After a few months of being together, Karen told me that she was going to go back to Carbondale, Illinois where her ex-husband Don Dalton lived, and kidnap her daughter. I didn't think that this was a great idea, but I realized that when Karen decided to do something arguing with her was futile. Karen told me that her plan was to pretend to reconcile with Don, gain his confidence by being entirely available to him, and then to come back to New York. I had no idea about whether she really intended to come back to New York, but I reluctantly drove her to the Greyhound Bus Station. About ten days later, she was back with her daughter Abra, an active four year old.

JOHN PHILLIPS

Sometime after I came back to New York from Colorado, I got a call from musician John Phillips. He had been at the Folklore Center, looking to find someone who played banjo and guitar. John was the leader of a vocal group called The Smoothies. They were four young singers from the Alexandria, Virginia area who had made some unsuccessful pop recordings for Decca. Their songs were mostly written by John, and were in the vein of The Four Preps or The Four Freshmen. Influenced by the burgeoning popularity of the Kingston Trio, John had decided that the group should try its hand at pop-folk music. The problem was that no one in the group knew much about that music, and John was the only one who played a musical instrument. He played basic rhythm guitar, but didn't know any of the folk picking styles. We got together, and I played a bunch of things for him. He asked me if I could recruit some other musicians for the session, because he didn't know any folk instrumentalists who played in these styles. I called Eric Weissberg and we both played on the session.

This was a typical New York studio session, with a musical contractor who called the other musicians. The contractor was Sandy Bloch, a bass player who I would later see on quite a few other recording sessions. Sandy told me that he thought this was the first real "pop-folk" session in New York. Eric and I represented the folk aspect of things and Sandy, electric guitarist Don Arnone and several other musicians came out of the New York pop-rock world.

The only thing that I remember about the session was that I played a hand-made twelve string guitar with a very high action. (The action is the way the height of the string is set.) The tempo was ridiculously fast, and listening back to John's song, Ride, Ride Ride, on a CD re-issue, I can't believe that I was able to play that fast on that particular instrument.

The unique and talented Karen Dalton, a folk and blues singer later marketed as a Billie Holiday-esque stylist. She was my girlfriend just before The Journeymen began.

Part 1 • Chapter 6

THE JOURNEYMEN

John and I started to hang out together. He went to the last of the Citizens' recording sessions with his band-mate Scott McKenzie, where I was playing a finger picking solo. Shortly after this, John told me that he didn't think The Smoothies were going anywhere, and he wondered if I would be interested in forming a folk-pop trio with him and Scott.

Since I was interested in leaving New York, and I really didn't have any other offers at the time, I decided that this might be an interesting idea. There was one impediment, though. That was Karen Dalton. I fantasized that she could become part of the group. John and Scott came up to 106th Street and we actually had two rehearsals with the four of us. It was a complete disaster. John's idea of rehearsing was that he would give out vocal parts, and that I would come up with the instrumental solos. Most of the rehearsals were spent with Karen arguing about the parts that John wanted her to sing.

John was remarkably patient with this process. In retrospect I realized that his thinking was that he would play along with the quartet idea, but he was correctly anticipating that my relationship with Karen wasn't going to last very long. In short order Karen was out of the musical loop, and we were rehearsing as a trio.

The Smoothies had one more gig, in January, 1961, playing at the Elmwood Casino in Buffalo, New York. The Elmwood was an old-time barn of a night club, complete with cigarette girls, comedians, and a burlesque show. Something for everyone. Meanwhile I picked up a three week gig, accompanying Martha Schlamme. Martha was an international singer, who sang songs in a variety of languages, and she was playing at a folk club in LA called The Ash Grove, followed by a college concert in Long Beach, California. Meanwhile Karen and I seemed to be fighting all of the time. She was basically bored. I was busy with recording sessions, and rehearsals with John and Scott, and she spent all of her time taking care of Abby. We were invited to a party at Harry Tuft's house in Philadelphia, and we broke up during the party. While we were arguing back and forth, I wrote a song called I Met The Blues In Kansas, which I recorded many years later. I told Karen that she was welcome to stay on 106th Street while I was in California, but I expected her to be gone by the time that I came back in late January.

THE ASH GROVE

Karen Dalton had indeed "talked a hole in Harry Tuft's head," as my roommate Jim Spruill liked to say. Harry decided that he was going to quit school, and go skiing in Colorado. Since I was headed towards Los Angeles, we schemed to get a driveaway car from Philadelphia to Denver. Driveaways are cars that need to be delivered from one place to another when the owner of the car is unable or unwilling to drive there. The driver generally is only responsible for getting the car to wherever the owner wants it to go, and may or may not have to buy gas. Our plan was that Harry would stay in or around Denver, and I would take the train from Denver to Los Angeles.

The beginning of the trip was a bit ominous. Harry had a long-term girl friend who was not happy to see him leave the area. She decided to put sugar in the gas tank of our Volkswagen driveaway. Fortunately she told our mutual friend Morrie Schambelan about this. Otherwise the car would have been disabled, and I suppose we would have been responsible for any repairs. Harry spent the first morning of the trip having the gas tank totally drained, and we proceeded onward.

I left Harry Tuft in Denver, and took the train from Denver. In those days was a pleasant trip. When I got to Los Angeles I went to the club. It was the closing night for the acts playing there. There was a young fiery seventeen year old flamenco guitarist named Rene Heredia, a bluegrass band called the Kentucky Colonels featuring guitarist Clarence White, and the closing act was The Tarriers, with Eric Weissberg.

I found myself a cheap hotel, and the next night our show began. Martha Schlamme was the headliner, there was a theater group called Jewels by Feiffer, who did vignettes based on the clever cartoons of Jules Feiffer, and I opened the show. Initially I felt entirely lost as a performer. I could certainly play, and I could more or less sing, but I didn't have a clue about how to talk to the audience. One of the actors in the Jewels show was named Frank Mahoney, and he took pity on me. He spent a fair amount of time explaining to me what a performer had to do to get the attention of the audience. He also explained matters like pacing, not doing three similar songs consecutively, and so forth. It was kind of a Performing For Dummies approach, but I was indeed close to that level of performing intelligence. By the time the engagement was over, I had became an acceptable performer, if not a brilliant one. Martha's music was challenging, and it included a Burt Brecht-Kurt Weill song. Hedy West had helped me work out the banjo chords for that one. There was also a Greek song in a 7/8 rhythm, which was truly Greek to me when I started learning it.

I enjoyed working with Martha, and mid-way into the gig a fellow named Shelly Tolin invited me to stay at his house in one of the canyons. I was astounded to be able to pick lemons off the tree right in front of his house. I also met some other people that I have stayed in touch with over the years, especially a young woman, Lisa Citron. She was very young and idealistic, a great change for me after the drama-filled time with Karen Dalton.

During the gig I met Barbara Dane, a blues and jazz singer. She asked me if I wanted to do a tour of the Pacific Northwest with her after the gig with Martha ended. This was a very attractive idea to me, but I also felt that I needed to check out the degree of John Phillips' commitment to our new group. I called him up at the Elmwood Casino, and explained the situation. I asked him how serious he was about our new group. He started to laugh. After a few minutes he explained that an old friend of his had asked him whether he wanted to hang out on the beach in Ibiza, but John had told him that he was putting together a new group. That was enough for me. I told John I'd see him soon in New York.

I flew back to New York, and returned to my apartment. I wasn't shocked to see that Karen Dalton hadn't moved out. John Phillips offered to drive her down to the Village, where she was moving in with John Stauber, an excellent guitar player. John Phillips moved into what had been Abra's room, and we began rehearsing the group that became known as The Journeymen.

BILL GRIER AND THE FBI: "SOMETHING HAS COME UP IN THE GRIER MATTER"

After David Wolkenberg moved away from 106th Street, a friend of mine recommended our next tenant, Bill Grier. Bill was an easy going, pleasant fellow who fit into our household without any trouble. For the most part, Bill wasn't hard to get along with. Every once in a while, he would go on an occasional drinking binge, and would do odd things, like walking on neighbor's rooftops. After about a year, Bill moved to Washington, D.C. Not long after that, I got a phone call. The caller explained that Bill had applied for a job with the State Department, and he was doing a security check on him for the FBI. He asked if he could talk to me, and I invited him over to the apartment.

This was during the time when JFK was running for president against Richard Nixon. We had placed two photos on our dining room wall. One was the famous photo of Nixon wagging his finger in Nikita Krushchev's nose. The other was a photo of JFK when he was taking shots for his back problems, and he looked like a living corpse. We had the two photos side by side, with no commentary on our part.

The FBI man came to visit and asked me the usual questions. Did I think Bill was loyal, was he normal, that is interested in women but not too much so, did he drink to excess, etc. I gave Bill a ringing endorsement as a good American. The agent also arranged to meet with Jim Spruill at the office where he was doing market research work. I don't know what the agent thought about a black and white guy living together in the same apartment in 1954, but it didn't come up.

Around the time that Karen moved out, the Journeymen started rehearsing six days a week. One day the phone rang, and the same FBI agent asked if he could come and talk to me again. The next day he came over to the apartment. The scene was totally chaotic. I had told our landlord that we would be vacating the apartment, because we were negotiating with a managerial group in San Francisco. He immediately arranged for a Puerto Rican housepainter to come by and re-furbish our ancient paint job. John had just moved in, and his dirty clothes were everywhere. Into this little bohemian scene came my friend from the FBI. He hemmed and hawed, and I started to lose patience. I asked him what this was about. He said "something has come up in the Grier matter." I asked him what that meant. He mumbled something about a question of loyalty.

At first I couldn't figure out what he was talking about. Suddenly it hit me. He must have checked up on us with our neighbors. The people downstairs were an older Italian couple who fought every single morning at dawn, before the old lady took her three little dogs out for a walk. One weekend when my friends from Philly had come up on a motor scooter it started to rain very hard. The rain was severe enough that they decided not to drive back in the rain. Since this was New York, and our neighborhood was a bit rough, I suggested that we carry the scooter up the flight of stairs to our apartment. We got a large wooden board, and started pushing it. The lady downstairs heard us, and she followed us up the stairs as we escorted the scooter into our dining room. She muttered, "you can't do that, YOU can't dothat, you can't do THAT, " over and over. As we put the kickstand down, I looked at her and said, "I guess we did that." She was entirely convinced that the scooter would leak oil and burn the building down.

Anyway, I suddenly realized that she had followed us into the dining room and had seen the pictures of Nixon with Krushchev and Kennedy, and she must have told the FBI agent that we were communist agents, or something on that order. I marched the FBI agent into the dining room, showed him the two pictures, and explained that this was our idea of a joke. He had a totally blank look on his face, and it was obvious to me that he didn't think this was the least bit funny. He quickly left. I don't know exactly how things developed, but I do know that Bill didn't get the job.

CHARLEY RYAN, CANADA DRY AND THE BIRTH OF THE JOURNEYMEN

After John moved into the apartment on 106th Street, Scott McKenzie would come up six days a week. We rehearsed intensively, about eight hours a day. We'd break for dinner at the neighborhood Greek restaurant, where we could eat dinner for about $3. I had never worked with an agent or a manager, but John and Scott had been managed by an old-line manager named Charley Ryan. He had a string of one liners, usually tending towards the bawdy. Walking down the street with him was an experience, because he would kept intruding on your space, until you found yourself walking in the street. None of us wanted Charley to represent our new group, because he was steeped in the old style night club business. We wanted to perform at colleges, and our goal was to create a musically superior version of The Kingston Trio.

John had a wife and two kids who lived in Alexandria, Virginia. He was in debt to Charley from advances that he had talked Charley into. Because The Smoothies didn't work all that much, and didn't make much money when they did work, John hadn't been able to pay these advances back. Charley was an inventive fellow, and one day he called and invited us to audition to do some Canada Dry radio commercials. The agency told John what they wanted, and he quickly wrote four different jingles. Scott sang them while John played guitar and I played banjo. The key line for all the jingles was their slogan, "America's first family of beverages." We rehearsed the four jingles, and took a cab to the agency office. Inevitably the office was on Madison Avenue.

We were ushered into an office with a large conference room mahogany table. There were seven or eight agency executives sitting around the table listening to us. They quickly eliminated two of the four jingles. Most of the people seemed to like jingle#1 the best. Suddenly an older, more distinguished looking gentleman with a more expensive wardrobe joined us. He was introduced as the president of the agency. We sang the two remaining jingles again. Mr. Big looked up and said, "I like the second one. Of course I'm tone deaf." Everyone laughed nervously. One of the agency's creative directors put in a few words favoring the first jingle. John looked up and averred that he also preferred the second jingle, saying that it seemed to have a special quality. The creative director who had favored the first jingle looked up at John, and said with a touch of bitterness, "kid, you'll go far in this business." He got that right.

We shook hands all around, and recorded the jingle a few days later. I was paid union scale for playing on the session. I don't know what or how John and Scott were paid for writing and singing the jingle. I know that they never got a nickel of that money. My guess is that Charley recovered the advances with a nice profit for himself. After all, he was an old smoothie.

THE RECORD DEAL

We realized that there were three things that we had to do to get our group off the ground.

We needed a record deal, a booking agent, and a manager. John and Scott were still under contract to Decca as members of The Smoothies. We didn't want the new group to be on Decca, but we went down to their offices on 57th Street and performed for Milt Gabler, their head of artist and repertoire. John had told me that Milt hated banjos, and that I should play as loud as possible. Later I found out that this was one of John's fairy tales. In fact Milt had been the producer for The Weavers, with Pete Seeger. Anyway we didn't put much effort into the Decca audition, and Milt decided that John and Scott could be released from their Decca obligations.

Even in 1961 the basic path to a record deal came from cutting some sort of a demonstration tape. We didn't want to do that, because John and Scott were just about dead broke, and I was not much better off. We leafed through the pages of Billboard, the weekly music trade paper, selecting six record companies to call. It was obvious that John was the logical person to make the calls. Neither Scott nor I were smooth enough to pull of this sort of sales job. Five of the companies told us that they would be happy to listen to a tape but that they did not do live auditions. The sixth company was MGM, and they agreed to listen to us at their office.

We sang for two of their producers, Danny Davis and Jim Vienneau. They both liked us, and said they wanted to sign us. However, they didn't feel that any of the songs that we sang for them had the potential to be hit singles. In 1961 record companies looked for one or two hit singles, and would then promote and sell an album that contained these hits. They told us that they would hook us up with various songwriters who might have some hits for us.

Our next step was to find a booking agency. While reading Billboard we noticed that an agency called ITA, International Talent Associates, seemed to be booking the Kingston Trio, the Brothers Four and other folk groups. We made an appointment to audition for them, and went downtown to their offices a few days later. Our audition was like a Hollywood fantasy. Initially we were singing for three or four people. Other agents could hear us and they drifted out of their offices to check us out.

At the time, we thought that we were good and also commercially viable, but we didn't understand exactly what a booking agent would see in us. First they heard ScottMcKenzie's angelic tenor voice. Then they were impressed by my instrumental skills. John clearly was the best front man for the group, the one who was going to do most of the talking on stage. They were also impressed by his songwriting skills.

I don't intend to deny that there were some talented people in the other folk groups. The Kingston Trio projected lots of energy and a perpetual party, and Bob Shane was a decent singer. Glenn Yarbrough of the Limeliters was, like Scott, an excellent tenor singer and Lou Gottleib was a hilarious front man for that group. None of the groups that ITA represented had the combination of ingredients that we represented. ITA was enthusiastic, and wanted to sign us immediately. We told them about the pending deal with MGM Records, which certainly was a positive sign.

RENE CARDENAS AND FRANK WERBER AND THE $50 MARTIN GUITAR

The ITA people asked us if we had a personal manager. We told that that we didn't, and they quickly introduced us to Rene Cardenas. Rene had been taken on as sort of a junior partner by Frank Werber, who managed the Kingston Trio. We quickly signed with ITA as our booking agency. Shelly Brodsky, one of their agents, gave us our name by thumbing through a dictionary until he came to the word journeyman. We all agreed that that was an appropriate name, so our group became The Journeymen

We were unaware of what was going on with the Kingston Trio. Dave Guard had announced that he was leaving the group. Werber and Cardenas were interested in us as an insurance policy, in case the trio was unable to find a replacement. Cardenas dangled a possible engagement at the legendary hungry i in San Francisco as something that they could make possible. He also suggested that we might want to leave New York, and move out to the Bay area to work more closely with them. The three of us were tired of the New York rat race, and it all sounded good to us. In rapid order we had accumulated an agency, a personal manager, and seemed on the verge of signing a record deal.

I flew out to LA, to visit my friend Lisa. A day later I took an all night bus up to San Francisco, to check out Frank Werber. I arrived around 8:30AM. I got off the bus and noticed a pawn shop across the street. I really liked old Martin Guitars, and hanging in the window was a small-bodied guitar that looked for all the world like an old Martin. It was too early to head up to Frank's office, so I hung out for a little while, and went into the shop just after 9. I asked if I could see the guitar in the window. The proprietor said, "that's funny, you're the third guy that wanted to see that thing since yesterday afternoon." The guitar was a New York Martin guitar made in New York City before 1905, when the factory had moved to Nazareth, Pennsylvania. The asking price was $50, including the original wooden so-called coffin case. It was called that, because it resembled a child's coffin.

I had about $20 in my pocket, plus my ticket back to New York. I knew that we were coming to San Francisco a few weeks later, so I put $5 down on the guitar, and told the proprietor that I'd be back in a few weeks with the rest of the money. That guitar, by the way, would sell for about $4000 or so today. It was the beginning of what became an active hobby. Wherever we traveled, if I had some spare time, I'd haunt pawn shops and music stores looking for old instruments. In many instances I found them.

RENE CARDENAS, MGM AND CAPITOL RECORDS

We had a number of meetings with Rene Cardenas. Our dealings with MGM Records had come to an impasse. In an effort to find us a hit song, they paraded a number of songwriters in front of us, and gave us demos of other songs. We felt that none of these songs were in the ballpark of pop-folk music, and we rejected all of them. Rene arranged a meeting at MGM with Davis, Vienneau, the three of us and himself. He came in with two demands: a minimum two album a year commitment, and a $5000 promotional guarantee for each album. These days most artists are hard pressed to complete an album a year, but in those days the recording process was not as complicated as it is now. The promotional guarantee was not really much of a commitment either. The two MGM executives seemed flabbergasted, and they totally rejected these demands. Vienneau even told us that we would never, ever get a deal like this in the record business.

Rene had a surprise for us. He had made an appointment at the New York office of Capitol Records with A&R man Andy Wiswell. After a ten minute walk, we were at Capitol auditioning live for Andy. He was very enthusiastic, and asked what our demands were. Rene explained what we wanted, and Andy placed a call in our presence to the senior A&R man at Capitol's Hollywood headquarters. The deal was sealed in about two minutes.

I date my interest in the music business to these two encounters. I felt that any business where you can hear two absolutely contradictory views from people involved in the same process must be more complex than I had understood.

THE JOURNEYMEN AND AVERTING SOME LEGAL PROBLEMS

About the same time that we were getting together, there was a vocal group called The Mystic Journeymen, who made a few 45 RPM records. They read about our signing with Capitol in Billboard, and tracked down my phone number. They called and threatened legal action. It is possible to protect the name of a group, by either registering it with one of the talent unions, the secretary of state in the state where you are working or you can apply for a trademark. If you do that, and you can point to having used the name regularly in performances, road tours, and recordings, you can prevent someone else from using that name. Once you establish the name of a group, you tend to build up a following, and changing the name confuses your fans. There are instances where groups have done so. For example, Pearl Jam's original name was Mookie Blaylock. They named themselves after a basketball player, who refused to allow them to use the name. I know of other instances where a band accepted a financial buyout from the band that was infringing on their name. In any case, the Mystic Journeymen never followed through with their threats. It may be that lawyers told them that the names were not similar enough to undertake a successful legal action.

Right around the same time, Sid Jacobson and Lou Stallman, who created the group The Citizens and owned its name, also read the Billboard story. Sid called me and told me how happy they were to hear about my new group. He also assured me that they would be taking 20% of any money that I earned in The Journeymen, due to their contract with me.

I let Sid speak his piece. I then reminded him that I had never signed the original contract, and that they had never re-written it. There was a pause at the end of the line. End of story.

WHO IS REGISTERED HERE?

ITA started getting us some gigs. We played at Gerde's Folk City in New York, and the Second Fret in Philadelphia. These gigs were a bit strange for me, because they were folk clubs where I had played alone, and where I was regarded as one of the folk revivalists who was a bit of a purist. They also got us a gig on CBC TV on a show called Norman Sedawie's World of Music. We flew to Toronto, and took a cab to a fairly new motel on a Bloor Street. The cab driver laughed at us. Apparently Bloor Street had been in the heart of a red light district a bit before then. The show went well, and after the show John encountered a woman that he had met when The Smoothies had played in Windsor. Because we were a new act, the show had only paid for two rooms, so John and I were ostensibly roommates, and Scott had the other room. John asked me if I would move in with Scott for the night. I did so, and shortly after that there was a knock on both of our doors. The registration clerk, who had a thick German accent, said, "Meeseter Philleeps, Mr. Veisman, who is rehgistered here?" After a few minutes of this comedy act, he informed us that women were not allowed in the room, and John's companion was hastily kicked out of the motel. I guess the cabdriver knew what he was talking about. For the rest of Scott's life, we would frequently greet each other with the question, "who is registered here?"

The recording at Capitol went smoothly. We finished the album in about a week. We used bebop bass player Arnold Fishkin, and on River Come Down we added a bongo player. I played both banjo and guitar on a bunch of tracks, which was the first time I had ever over-dubbed parts. I thoroughly enjoyed doing that, which I still do today. About the time we finished the album, Rene arranged a gig for us at the hungry i, and we all prepared to move out to San Francisco. John drove his wife and two children there, and Scott and I flew. I shook hands with Jim Spruill, and we vacated the 106th Street apartment.

John Phillips and Scott McKenzie performing with The Smoothies, the group which was the precursor for The Journeymen.

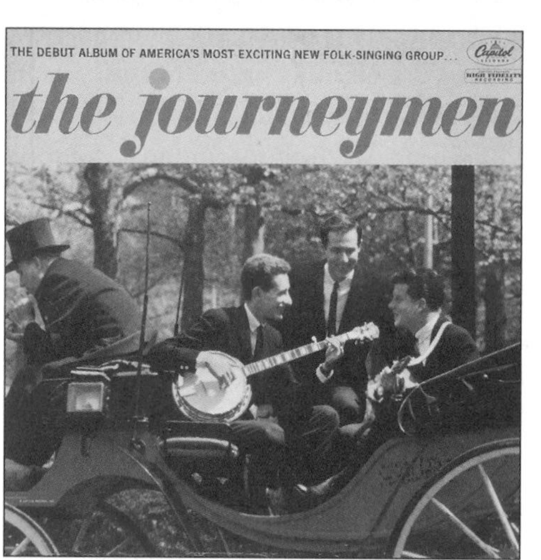

Above: The debut album from The Journeymen on Capitol Records.

Right: Promotional photo of The Journeymen, represented by International Talent Associates, Inc.

Part 1 • Chapter 7 

THE JOURNEYMEN HIT THE ROAD: SAN FRANCISCO

We played the hungry i for a month. We were the opening act. The middle act was a guitarist and singer named Frank D'Rone, and the closing act was comedian Mort Sahl. On opening night Frank Werber came to see his new act, and seemed pleased. We seldom saw him after that. We found that Rene Cardenas was really the one acting as our manager.

The Smothers Brothers were playing across the street at a club called The Purple Onion. We became friendly with them, and they invited us to go for a ride on their boat in Sausalito. As John and I drove down the main street, John saw a familiar face driving a cab. He asked me if that wasn't Harry Tuft driving the cab? We followed the cab, and sure enough it was Harry. I hadn't seen him since I had played the gig with Martha Schlamme six months earlier. Harry's girl friend had become his wife, but they were already in the process of splitting up. He was living in a $50 a month cabin in Mill Valley, and asked me if I wanted to split the rent with him. That sounded a lot better and a lot cheaper than living in a motel, so I moved in with him for a month or so.

We did two sets at the i, and only played for a grand total of 45 minutes so at the end of the night I felt like I was just getting warmed up. There was a coffeehouse near the i called the Fox and the Hounds, and Harry and I would often go over there after the shows at the i.

The owner was a visual artist wannabe named Lee, who always wore a beret and was very friendly. A young singer named Hoyt Axton was playing there every night, and I'd do guest sets in between his gigs. I didn't care about getting paid, because I was making decent money at the i.

One morning I woke up in Mill Valley, picked up a guitar and immediately started playing a new piece on the spot. It was called Mill Valley Serenade. It wasn't like anything I'd ever done before, and had a long series of chord changes. It was inspired by my short time living in this idyllic setting, a sort of guest house on a larger property in a really beautiful area. These days Mill Valley is an expensive and highly gentrified town.

TROUBLE IN PARADISE

It turned out that the Kingston Trio was indeed breaking up. Meanwhile we discovered that Werber and Cardenas were engaged in a bitter feud with ITA, our booking agency. It mostly had to do with bookings involving the Kingston Trio. Rene reassured us by saying that he was going to get us out of our contract with ITA and get us a deal with another agency. He was able to do this, because the musician's union had a provision in their booking agreements that if an agency didn't get an act work for a certain number of weeks, the act could get out of its contract with the agency.

To complicate the situation, John had met a young woman named Michelle Gilliam at the hungry i. Despite the fact that he, his wife Susie and his two children were living in another section of Mill Valley, John found himself seriously involved with Michelle. Desperate for some source of income, John started writing songs with John Stewart, Guard's replacement. Scott was living with a woman he had met at the i who was a friend of Michelle's, and I was ensconced in a luxurious $9 a week hotel in Chinatown. We were all broke and depressed, and the very existence of The Journeymen was in question.

Through some of my folkie friends, I found out about a club in San Jose that booked pop-folk music. We auditioned there, and were hired. We started with a one week contract, but did very well, and ended up playing there for about six weeks.

BEN AND ME

John and I started to write some songs together. Usually my part was more like editing than writing. John seemed to have a million ideas and he would exhale them, one after the other. One Monday we had stayed over in Berkeley, and were sitting around the house, and John got the idea to write a song about a young hobo and his older brother freezing to death while riding in a freight car. He called the song Ben And Me. As the song took shape, John and I disposed of the contents of a bottle of vodka. We finished the vodka and the song at about the same time.

Scott came over, and we prepared to drive down to San Jose. I have never been terribly interested in alcohol, but in this instance I was pretty much drunk out of my mind. On the drive down to San Jose I remember listening to Scott and John plotting about how we were going to get through this show, when I was pretty much incoherent. We tuned up, changed clothes, and went on stage. Our opening number was the old square dance tune Old Joe Clark. I would play an instrumental chorus, while we sang oohs in harmony. I got through the instrumental, and John opened his mouth and started to laugh. He continued to laugh for thirty seconds. Scott and I suggested that he go off stage. I sobered up instantly as though someone poured a gallon of coffee in me. We did the rest of the show as a duo.

Another night in San Jose a woman leaped on the stage with her trumpet. She announced her name, and said something like "Joyce Watkins, Local 47." (Local 47 is the Los Angeles local of the musician's union.) She never asked us whether she could play with us, and none of us had ever seen her before. She proceeded to play swing trumpet with our pop-folk songs. The three of us were laughing hysterically. John and Scott left the stage laughing, leaving me to play St. James Infirmary with her. Another night in paradise.

SPOKANE

By the time we left San Jose, Rene had arranged for us to be booked by ABC. Rene or ABC, I don't know which, contacted an agent in Spokane named John Powell. John hired us to play at a club called The Plantation Inn. When we had been in San Francisco, I had left a nice but inexpensive Mexican guitar in the trunk of John's car. The trunk had gotten stuck, and we had to force it open at the airport so that I could get the guitar out. When we arrived at our hotel in Spokane, I opened the soft leather gig bag that the guitar was stored in. It was the rainy season in San Francisco, and the guitar emerged from the case in pieces.

When we got to the club, we noticed that there was a light jazz trio that played between our shows, and we were the main event. John endeared himself to the trio by writing them a short intermission jingle. It went like this: Pardon us for leaving the stand, but we'll be back, we're the only band, but with your permission, we'll take an intermission, Thank you.

They loved it, the audience liked it, and I still remember the words and music a mere 50 years later.

One night, a local disc jockey invited us to attend a party that he was throwing that weekend. The next night another fellow walked in and invited us to a party on the same night. John politely explained to him that we had already accepted an invitation to another party. He smiled and looked at John. Pointing to the well-stocked bar at the club, he said, "You see that bar. The bar at my house is twice that size." John asked if we could fold the first party into this party, and the genial host agreed.

The next night after we got through playing at the club, we drove over to a huge mansion. It turned out that the host's wife was an heir to the Gallo Wine fortune. We settled in for a pleasant evening. The next event was one we hadn't anticipated. The host's wife came on to each one of us. John and I demurred, but at the time Scott liked to become involved with people who had other commitments. He and the hostess proceeded to have a long talk. Before John or I could figure out what was going on, we saw Scott leave the house with the woman and her enormous German shepherd dog.

Meanwhile, I proceeded to drink way too much, and I played touch football in the huge living room. I wasn't drunk enough, though, to have forgotten Scott's disappearance. John and I looked up to see the host putting on his overcoat and carrying a rifle with him. Just as he was about to open the door, Scott and his wife came in with the dog. It was snowing hard, and they were both almost covered with snow from head to foot. The whole situation took on ridiculous proportions. It seemed clear that nothing wildly erotic could have possibly happened between them.

John hustled Scott and me out of there as quickly as possible. He then proceeded to take us to our hotel and to read both of us the riot act. I still remember him saying, "Dick, I would have expected something better from you." I couldn't have agreed more.

THE JAIL IN PHOENIX TOWN

We finished out the engagement, and headed for a gig that ABC had booked for us at a steak house in Phoenix. The club had featured jazz for some time, and on the bill with us was the legendary boogie woogie and blues piano player Meade Lux Lewis. He was nearing the end of a long and legendary career, and was overweight and seemed not to be feeling too well. Very few people came to the show, and those that did mostly occupied themselves eating steak and drinking. We weren't really a lounge act, and became very frustrated.

At that point Scott and I both did some really foolish things. The last night of the first week of our two week engagement I played a quiet blues piano solo during our set. Meade was very offended, and I was annoyed with myself. At the very least I should have asked his permission. After all, we weren't being booked as a blues piano act. Scott was in a similarly destructive mood. One of the song that we did was an Irish song called Gilgarra Mountain. It has a verse that includes a lyric that the singer will bid a fond farewell to the jail in Sligo Town. Scott substituted the words Phoenix town. The manager of the club happened to be there at the time, and he was greatly offended. He demanded a meeting with John, and he immediately fired us, and told John that he was going to blacklist us with every club in the United States. John was able to calm him down to an extent, and we all figured that it was just an excuse to save money on our salaries, since we clearly weren't drawing any people.

ABC AND ITA

This was not an auspicious beginning to our relationship with ABC Booking. Meanwhile our album had come out, and so had the first single. The B side was River Come Down, and it became something of a turntable hit. That expression is used to describe a song that isn't necessarily a big seller, but gets a bunch of radio play. It turned out that Burt Bloch, who was one of the owners of ITA kept hearing the song as he was driving to work.

By this time we had become thoroughly skeptical about what Rene Cardenas and Frank Werber were going to be able to do for us. They had dragged us out of the one booking agency that seemed to have a lock on pop-folk gigs and college concerts, and put us in an old line booking agency that was best known for booking Louis Armstrong. We regretted leaving ITA, and we also realized that Werber and Cardenas had lost interest in us when the Kingston Trio re-formed.

John called Burt Block, who seemed happy to talk to him. Block told us that if we would come back to New York, they would be delighted to book us, and that they would set us up with some lawyers who would help us get out of our management contract with Werber and Cardenas. John left his wife and kids in Mill Valley for the time being, and the three of us drove almost non-stop to New York, except for one night in Las Vegas. In Vegas we visited with another Werber-Cardenas act, the Four Amigos, who had a wonderful lead guitar player. We gambled all night, and took off for New York. I told John and Scott that since I wasn't driving, I'd stay up and help the driver keep awake. I promptly closed my eyes and spent ¾ of the trip sleeping.

NEW YORK AGAIN, AND THE EXPENSES OF SHOW BUSINESS

When we got back to New York, we met with ITA almost immediately. They assured us that they would move heaven and earth to get us work, and this turned out to be one of the few truthful things anyone in the music business ever said to us! They

then suggested that we consult with a law firm called Pryor & Braun. We met with David Braun, and he explained to us that we could indeed get out of our contract with Werber and Cardenas, but it wasn't going to be a free ride, and there would be some negotiation involved. Rene flew to New York, and we all met at Braun's office. John owed about a couple of thousand dollars in advances that he had been given, money that mostly was given to help pay the rent for his wife and kids in Mill Valley. The big question was what else would they demand?

We sat in a room while Braun and Cardenas came up with earnings projections of what we would make in the next three years. The numbers that they came up with were $100,000 for the first year, $150,000 for the second and $200,000 for the third year. These were grosses, of course, and didn't involved the expenses that we would have to pay to make this possible. Those would include agency commissions, airline tickets, car rentals, and lodging.

The three of us felt like animals in a zoo, whose keepers are discussing our future diet. Essentially we were all broke, and our future income was being discussed as though we were some commodity on the stock market.

After a few hours of back and forth, we agreed to pay $6000 to get out of our contract, $4000 of which represented new money on top of what we owed from John's advances. We left the meeting in a daze. We had no idea whether these earning projections were realistic or blue sky fantasies. We did know that we were now out of our management agreement.

1960s New York

Part 1 • Chapter 8 

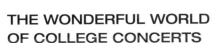

THE WONDERFUL WORLD OF COLLEGE CONCERTS

Once ITA started booking us regularly, we would do 2-4 college concerts a week, and play clubs in the summertime or in the Christmas season. Initially the way that they booked us was that a college would call and want to book one of ITA's major groups, but have a limited budget. At that point ITA would sell our services. Initially, we were getting $1000 for a concert. In those days air fares and motel stays were cheaper than they are today.

Within a year our price had gone up to $1500. We also developed pockets of popularity where we became known. The biggest one for us was Virginia. We played virtually every college in the state, and in a number of instances came back the following year and played the same school for more money. We played the University of Richmond, VMI, Hollins, Hampden-Sydney College, and lots of other schools in the state. We also did two very successful engagements at a club in Washington D.C, called The Shadows. John and Scott were both from the Alexandria area, and it seemed like every person that attended high school with them came to the club.

We also developed a following in the Minneapolis Area. Our second album was a live recording at a club called The Padded Cell. We had played there once before, and knew that we would have an enthusiastic following there. Capitol taped our shows for two nights, and we did a bit of overdubbing afterwards as well. When the album came out, we were shocked at the tepid audience response on the album. For whatever reasons, Capitol minimized the applause, and it was an embarrassment to us.

BACK TO SAN FRANCISCO

We played the hungry i again, this time with comedian Dick Gregory closing the show. I re-connected with my friends in Berkeley, and shared a large one room apartment with a graduate student named Jerry Levine. I'd stay in Berkeley all day, and take the bus home. Soon, Jerry went home to England to get married. I made the commitment to keep the apartment, even though we were no longer working out of San Francisco. The apartment was one story up, and had a large living room-bedroom, and a kitchen large enough to put a couch in for visitors. There was kind of a rooftop garden right outside the living room, and because the Bay area has a fairly mild climate. I found that I could use that space as another room most of the year. If I didn't want to use a key to unlock the door, I could push against it with my shoulder, and it would open. I never thought about how easy it would be for a thief to do the same.

WASHINGTON DC, THE SHADOWS, JOHN AND MICHELLE GET MARRIED

In December of 1962 we played at a club in Washington D.C. called The Shadows. After John's divorce from his first wife Susie, John and Michelle got married by a justice of the peace in Maryland. Scott and I were the only attendees at the wedding. We bought a lovely ladies model vintage Martin Guitar as a wedding present for the happy couple. After the gig was over, we piled into John's car and drove away. John accidentally left the guitar in the motel parking lot. When he realized what he had done, we raced back to the motel, but the guitar was gone.

BERKELEY AND LUNDBERG'S GUITAR SHOP

During our month at the i it rained almost every day. I didn't mind. It was an idyllic time for me. I spent some time with a friend named Rita Rabow, and we'd wander the streets talking about our lives, and what each of us wanted to do. I often walked over to Jon Lundberg's guitar shop, and hung out with other musicians and the people who worked there. Many of them were musicians too. Marc Silber was a fine guitarist who went back and forth from New York to Ann Arbor to Berkeley. Later he opened a music store next door to the Folklore Center in New York.

Jon and his wife Deidre would occasionally play music in their store. Deidre had a beautiful Bacon Banjo. Various people from the Bay Area or people who were playing there would wander in and play music.

Most of the histories of the folk revival have neglected to mention how music stores in many cities were a real social and cultural center for musicians and music fans. They were places to meet other musicians, to find gigs, start bands, and to make social contacts.

A young black singer named Al Young often sang at a neighborhood coffeehouse called The Blind Lemon. Al had a huge repertoire, everything from Ewan McColl to country blues. Later on he became a much published poet and novelist, and taught at the University of Michigan. It was hard for me to leave Berkeley, because I really felt at home there. Lundberg's was a good social center. The Berkeley musicians and my friends weren't like the people I encountered on Journeymen gigs.

We left San Francisco to go back to New York, and we went back on the college concert circuit. It was the easiest way for a musician to make a living that I have ever encountered. For the most part we played secondary schools, not the biggest ones. So we might not play, say, the University of Michigan in Ann Arbor, but we might play other state schools in more remote parts of the state. In many cases we were the only entertainment in the town that night, so we had a ready and willing audience. We'd come out, and after the first song, we'd hear a powerful round of applause. One exception to the rule occurred when we played Virginia Military Institute. We played the entire first half to tepid applause. During the intermission, the commandment came to our dressing room. He told us that the reason for the lack of applause was that cadets wore gloves. He ordered the students to take their gloves off in the second half of the show, and when we did the opening number in the second half, we were greeted by thunderous applause.

STAN GREESON

From time to time ITA would ask us if we had found another personal manager. After our experiences with Werber and Cardenas, we weren't eager to make another such commitment.

ITA introduced us to a manager named Stan Greeson. He was friendly, personable and very professional. He had a half dozen clients, none of whom were competitive to us. One was Peter Nero, the piano player, and others included Broadway actress-singer Dorothy Collins, comedian Soupy Sales, and some television and film production people. We liked Stan but our previous experience had left us really skeptical about managers. Stan offered us a deal that we could hardly refuse. He told us that he would work for us for two months without taking any commission. If we liked what he did, then we could sign with him, but if we weren't satisfied we could walk away.

Stan quickly went to work on our behalf. He booked us on a mid-western tour with Peter Nero. He lobbied Capitol Records incessantly, and we started to see Capitol's regional promotion people at our gigs. They took us to radio stations, and we did quite a number of radio interviews and occasional live radio performances. Stan was a constant presence at ITA, and the good job they had been doing got even better. We auditioned to do a series of Schlitz radio commercials, and signed a three year contract for them. The first year we were guaranteed $20,000, $25,000 for the second year, and $30,000 for the third year. Schlitz flew us out to Chicago for the first ones, and we recorded at a famous studio there called Universal. The agency for Schlitz put us up at a very expensive hotel, and John and Scott proceeded to order super expensive lobster dinners via room service. Scott then telephoned everyone that he knew all over the United States, running up a nice bill for the agency. When the hotel bills came in, the agency decreed that from then on when we didn't record in New York they would put us on a per diem expense account.

THE ROAD OF EXCESS LEADS TO MEDICAL PROBLEMS

We picked up a one week engagement at Freddie's

in Minneapolis. Our old haunt The Padded Cell had gone out of business, but we still had a good following in Minneapolis and St. Paul. Freddie's, along with a handful of other old-line clubs, had an odd policy which required performers to play a Saturday matinee show. Since Friday and Saturday night shows tend to be long and exhausting, most performers weren't fond of this requirement. We did our usual show at Freddie's on Friday night. Scott dreaded the prospect of doing the matinee, so he stayed up all night partying. We got to the club not long after noon, and got ready for the show. We went on stage, and I played the instrumental lead in to our opening number. Scott opened his mouth, and nothing, literally nothing, came out. Scott went off stage, and John and I did the rest of the show without him.

Within two days Scott flew out to San Francisco where our vocal coach Judy Davis arranged for him to be operated on almost immediately. Scott was diagnosed as having nodes in his throat. The first operation revealed pre-cancerous tissue, so the doctor did a second operation just to be safe. Scott was then put on six week vocal rest, which meant that he could not talk for six weeks. Meanwhile, John and I were out of work for six weeks, right at the beginning of the spring college concert season.

I GUESS HE'D RATHER BE IN COLORADO

With the future of The Journeymen in doubt, I decided to visit my friend Harry Tuft in Denver. I had met a young woman named Diane Deschanel on my last Denver trip, and with six weeks of unexpected free time we started to see each other regularly. Meanwhile Harry found us a gig in a western slope ski town called Crested Butte. I went from sharing $1500 a night to splitting a couple of hundred dollars a week with Harry. It was not lucrative, but I really enjoyed the casual atmosphere of the performances. I wrote some new songs, and we generally had a good time. When I got back to Denver, I got to know Diane better. She was a student at Antioch College at the time, and she was on her work term rotation. I began to think that this could develop into a serious relationship. Soon after that, she decided to study in France for a year!

Six weeks later John called to say that Scott was cleared by the doctor to work again, and the three of us met to do a show at the University of Western Ontario, in London, Ontario. When Scott sang his first notes, John and I looked at each other in amazement. He sounded five years younger than he did before the operations. It was as if the doctor had gone inside Scott's vocal chords and scraped away all the smoke and alcohol remnants that had been living there. The Journeymen were back in business.

THE NEW DIRECTIONS ALBUM

During our first two years, The Journeymen did two albums and a handful of singles that were not on our albums. The singles included some re-fashioned traditional, pop songs like What'll I Do, an Everly Brothers style song called Don't Turn Round, the folk standard Kumbaya, an attempt at ragtime, and one drawn from the first album. Although we had developed a good audience for our live shows, none of our recordings had sold well enough to make the Billboard charts. All of our recordings featured the three of us singing or playing, with added bass players, and occasional other musicians.

John had become friendly with guitarist and arranger Walter Raim, and for our third album he suggested that we bring Walter in to play guitar, and assist with some of our arrangements. We started intensive rehearsals for the third album. When John went into rehearsal mode, he became a different human being. Whatever alcoholic or drug scene he was involved with at the time generally became subservient to working out vocal and instrumental parts. John and Michelle were living on East 70th Street. Neither Scott nor I had an apartment in New York so we almost always rehearsed at John and Michelle's place.

THE NEW DIRECTIONS ALBUM

Walter Raim played some nice guitar on our records, although I never thought of him as having an especially original style. He certainly was capable of playing some things that I wasn't, so I didn't object. I did feel as though my role in the group was starting to diminish. At the same time, some tension had arisen because John was experiencing writer's block, and he did not have any new songs. In all of my experience with John, this was a rare event, but it was clearly bothering him. At the same time, my songwriting output was increasing. I had two songs ready for the new album, and was eager to record them.

We decided that it was time to record at Capitol's LA studios, instead of their smaller New York facility. We also wanted to try using a new producer. Andy Wiswell, our original producer at Capitol, had done the first two albums. We thought that for the most part he had done a reasonable job, although we were still angry about the muffled applause on our live album. The third album was produced by Curly Walters. Curly was an interesting, down to earth fellow, who had a farm, and drove his feed truck to the Capitol Towers building in Hollywood. It definitely stood out next to the Cadillacs and expensive foreign cars driven by the other Capitol executives. We hired studio bass player Morty Corb for the album. Morty had an absolutely beautiful 18th century German bass, probably the best sounding bass I have ever heard. One day when we were recording half way into the song Curly asked us to start over and do another take. Morty promptly got out a small notebook, and wrote something in it. I asked him what he was doing. He said that whenever he made a mistake on a session he'd write it down in this book. I asked him how often this occurred. He told me that "about every six months." I looked at him quizzically, wondering if I'd ever even played an entire show without making a mistake.

We then proceeded to record the rest of our album, including my two songs, Someone To Talk My Troubles To, and I May Be Right. Troubles ended up being a very popular song, and established some credibility for me as a songwriter. I May Be Right was a sort of modern bluegrass tune, and ended up not appearing on the album. It was never clear to me why it didn't make the cut, and in later years it was recorded by several other artists, including Cass Elliot and The Big Three and Every Mother's Son. It also eventually appeared on several of the CD re-issues of our music. Rightly or wrongly I felt that my song was excluded from the record because John was irritated that I was on a writing spree at a time when he was having trouble writing songs.

THE PROMOTION TOUR

The album had the pretentious title New Directions In Folk Music, which I have to admit was my idea. To promote the album, our manager Stan Greeson convinced Capitol to send us on a promotion tour to half a dozen cities. The New York appearance was important for us, because we hadn't played at a club in New York since our earliest days, and we got to play for writers and editors of the major New York trade papers.

We did a poorly attended show in Cleveland, and the next day we flew to St. Louis. It was a dark, rain-filled day, and the plane was an hour late. The Capitol promotion man met us at the airport, and hurried us into his car. He then proceeded to drive sixty miles an hour on the shoulder of the highway. He said that we were already late for the show, but John was able to persuade him that our lives meant more to us than the ten minutes he might save with his crazy driving.

Our performance was in the ballroom of the hotel where Capitol was putting us up. We raced to our rooms, changed clothes, and came downstairs with our instruments. Just as we were about to go into the ballroom, Scott looked at the promotion man and asked if he could tell us who our audience was. The promotion man said that we were playing for the editors of a number of high school newspapers. He added that there were originally thirty of them, but only about eight of them were still there. Scott looked at him, and said "we are not a high school act." He then turned around and went back to his room. Without missing a beat, John told the poor guy "You have to understand that Scott is a deeply sensitive boy." I tried to restrain myself from laughing, and then John and I left the promotion person to explain to the remaining high school editors why they weren't going to see a show.

That night John suggested that we go to the night club section of St. Louis, called Gaslight Square. His idea was that we would not wear our performing clothes, but would go around and sit in at clubs. Since we were all depressed, and had nothing else to do, it seemed like a good idea. We got our instruments and played at three different clubs. The audiences loved us. We were offered jobs, including one probably mythical one in the West Indies, and people were really curious about who we were. We told them that we were three college boys who played together for fun. We had everyone convinced, we were just fun-loving kids, until a singer who we had met in Cleveland wandered into the last club we were at, and blew our cover.

Of all the performances that The Journeymen ever did, this one was probably the most fun for me. There was no pressure, and were entirely loose and relaxed. We didn't do our normal scripted stage patter, and we improvised more than we ever did in our performances. John's whim turned a depressing evening into an enjoyable experience.

THE SOUTH

The 60's was a critical time in the history of the Civil Rights movement. The Journeymen were not a politically-oriented musical group, but John and I both had an extensive background and a great love for black music. My taste tended towards folk blues, while John loved Ray Charles. This made us somewhat unusual among the folk-pop groups. Erik Darling, was virtually the only one in the folk-pop world who had any serious involvement in black music (Erik was a founding member of The Tarriers, and later started The Rooftop Singers.)

We read newspapers and watched television, and were certainly aware of such matters as sit-ins, voter registration movements, and efforts at de-segregation. Our main base of popularity was in the southern states. Besides our extensive shows in Virginia, we played in the Carolinas, Florida, Georgia, and Alabama. A number of incidents forced us to pay more attention to Civil Rights issues.

We did a college concert in Virginia with Odetta. We knew her from hanging out in Greenwich Village. When we got to the show, she was clearly uncomfortable. She told us that the hotel that the student organization sponsoring the concert had reserved for her refused to allow her or Bill Lee, her bass player, to stay there. She called the fraternity that was sponsoring the show, and one of their officers came down to the hotel, and fabricated some story that she was an African princess. Finally the hotel agreed to let her stay there, but she had to use the freight elevator rather than the passenger lift. She was very upset, but we all had contracts, and walking out would have meant a possible lawsuit, and of course losing the income from the gig. The three of us were disgusted by this strange encounter with racism, but other than to commiserate with Odetta, there wasn't really anything we could do about it. I always wondered what the hotel did about Bill Lee film maker Spike Lee's father. While Odetta was sufficiently exotic enough to pull off the African princess story, Bill was simply a fine jazz bass player from Brooklyn.

At around the same time we did an outdoor stadium concert at the University of Alabama.

Outdoor concerts are often a mixed blessing, because performers have to deal with everything from barking dogs to wind noises and drunken patrons. John introduced a solo blues that was part of our show at the time, explaining that he had learned the song from Josh White. Some yahoo yelled out from the audience "that nigger?" John immediately responded by saying, "you're very crude, sir." We practically got a standing ovation, because a good section of the crowd was embarrassed by this ugly comment. When the show ended, we left the stage, and the heckler was waiting for us. We anticipated that he would apologize. Actually what he said was, "Well that's what we call them down here." John didn't feel any need to respond to this fool.

Another incident that made a big impression on me occurred after one of our many Virginia college concerts. After the show we were invited to a fraternity party. I generally avoided these affairs, because watching a bunch of over-privileged young people drinking and flirting or making out wasn't an appealing way for me to spend an evening. In this instance I was bored enough to accept the invitation. There were several hundred people gathering around lubricating their throats, hoping to pick up members of the opposite sex, and so forth. A half dozen people were gathered around the piano. A young black musician was playing and singing Smoky Robinson's song You've Really Got A Hold On Me. I thought the singer was good, and I sat down to listen to him. I soon noticed that there was a young co-ed in a low cut dress who seemed to be really into the music. She was leaning over the piano, exposing a panoramic view of her breasts. I looked up and saw a couple of white college students who were not happy to see a pretty young white woman that was interested in a black musician. The singer had his eyes half closed, and didn't appear to be paying any attention to the woman. I began to get an uneasy feeling. The co-ed was violating the ultimate black-white sexual taboo, but I was well aware of the fact that she wasn't going to be the one to be punished for it. The song went on for five minutes or so, and the tension in the room kept building, and so did my own fear of how this was going to resolve. I was really frightened for the piano player. Chances are that nothing came of this incident, but it was another reminder, if I needed one, of what life was like for a black musician in the south in 1963.

KUMBAYA AND THE SACRILIGIOUS

During the time The Journeymen were together, a number of groups had major hit singles.

We accepted the success of The Kingston Trio, because we knew that they were really the first of the college boy folk-pop groups. Although we weren't especially fond of their music, we appreciated their energy, and their ability to connect with audiences. The Brothers Four were a tougher sell for us. In our minds they were four guys out of any college glee club. Peter, Paul & Mary obviously struck a chord with their audiences, and they were the first ones to bring the songs of Bob Dylan to a mass audience. We reached our lowest point of acceptance when The Highwaymen's Michael Row The Boat Ashore became a major hit. John Phillips was particularly outraged by this record, feeling that we were doing work that was musically far superior to it. He gathered us together, and we worked out an arrangement of the old chestnut Kumbaya. The concept and the feel were imitative of the Highwaymen's work. We recorded the song as a single, and it began to hit the charts in Minneapolis, Vancouver, and it even got into the top ten records in Boston. The history of Kumbaya is that is a song from the South Carolina islands that was also sung by African missionaries.

Much to our surprise and dismay, a minister in Boston decided to attack our version of the song as being anti-religious. He counted the number of times that we sang Oh Lordy, and began a campaign to get it off the radio. Unfortunately for us, he succeeded. Our attempt to capitalize on Michael sank into oblivion.

POSTCRIPT

More than forty years later another version of the song became a hit in Belgium. The only reason that I know this, is that I received several hundred dollars worth of royalties through ASCAP for radio play. (When an American song is played on radio or TV abroad, the local equivalent of ASCAP and BMI collects the royalties, and after deducting an administrative fees pays the American organization, which then pays the writer.) The closest I can get to uncovering the mystery is that a Belgian tenor named Helmut Lotti recorded the song, and he must have credited us as the authors. Of course this is ridiculous, but that didn't stop me from cashing the checks. My friend Allen Jones in Portland, says that I am the only person in the world that could get royalties from "writing" Kumbaya. Of course he's wrong. Scott's and John's estates got an equal share.

THE ATLANTA AIRPORT

There was one week in the fall of 1963 where we played a series of concerts around the Atlanta area. There was a restaurant at the airport called the Dobbs House. In previous trips to Atlanta we would usually eat breakfast there. During this particular week, we noticed that the employees were on strike. It appeared that all of the employees were black, and they had a picket line set up around the restaurant. Scott and I looked at each other, and agreed that we were not going to cross the picket line. John ignored our comments, and went into the restaurant. We turned around and saw Peter, Paul and Mary wander towards us, looking for a place to get their morning coffee

By this time PP&M were the most popular of the folk-pop groups, and had a reputation of being involved in the Civil Rights movement. Scott looked at me, and said, "watch this." Paul was the first of the three to approach the restaurant. Scott mentioned the picket line, and Paul said to him, "You know, I've got to have my eggs." About fifty feet behind Paul came Peter. Scott gave him the same rap, and Peter proceeded to deliver an entirely incoherent verbal tirade, which continued as they approached the restaurant, and then Peter walked in. Finally Mary came up to us. Scott spoke to her, and she asked whether there was somewhere else we could go. I told her that there was a gourmet food store around the corner, and we were planning to get something to take out there and eat it in the airport lounge. She looked at us, and said, "You know, I hate the fucking South, I'm going with you." Scott and I didn't discuss what had happened, but we were definitely on the same page. Our rep in the folk community was that we were a good, but slick folk-pop group, while Peter, Paul & Mary were given a pass in folkdom because they performed Bob Dylan's music, and they were associated with the Civil Rights movement. We should have joined the picket line and launched into a chorus of the protest song, Which Side Are You On?

MENTAL SURVIVAL

Touring musicians develop various strategies to ensure mental survival on the road. When you do a series of one night shows, there is a certain disorientation that seems to accompany the gigs. There are occasions when you literally can't seem to remember what city you are in. There is also a kind of cumulative exhaustion that comes from doing shows at night and being too wired to get to sleep in a timely fashion. This is often followed by early morning flights or wake-up calls to do things like radio station visits.

The two strategies that seemed to work for me were searching for instruments, and sitting in at clubs or coffeehouses after finishing a gig. Recently I tabulated the current value of various instruments that have passed through my hands over the years, but no longer own. I figured out that had I kept all of these guitars, banjos and mandolins, I'd have well over $300,000 worth of instruments. My actual investment in them was something under $10,000! To give you an example of this scavenging, I bought a OO42 Martin guitar in Berkeley for $300 which now is worth about $50,000. I also found a OO40 model for $195 at a music store in Raleigh, North Carolina. I recently saw a similar guitar for sale for $35,000. Even before the days of The Journeymen, I bought a pre-World War II D28 Martin guitar in a hard case for $75 for my friend Artie Traum.

Looking for instruments brought me to skid row areas of towns where pawnshops were generally found and to various parts of cities where music stores were located. It was interesting to see something in a city other than the venue where we were performing. There was also something of a game in finding the stores, bartering with the storeowners, and watching the people who frequented these places. To this day I do a bit of this, although my level of enthusiasm for it has diminished as rare instruments become more and more expensive and more difficult to locate.

SITTING IN

When we would finish a show, I would sometimes feel the need to go somewhere and play my own music in a more spontaneous way than Journeymen shows permitted. My favorite memory of this kind was going to a club in Houston, and seeing a duo perform. The man was playing twelve string, and his female partner was an excellent and passionate singer. I didn't know who these people were.

During the 1980's I was playing at the Winnipeg Folk Festival, and the wonderful songwriter Guy Clark recalled that he had met me that night. I asked him if he knew who the singers were that I had heard that night. It turns out that they were a visual artist named Frank Harris and a woman named K.T. Oslin, who in later years had a successful career as a country music singer-songwriter. Guy later sent me a really raw but nice tape that they had made during those years.

HOOTENNANY, '64, KENNEDY'S ASSASSINATION, JACKSON, MISSISSIPPI AND CARNEGIE HALL & GUITAR DESTRUCTION

In November of 1963 we became part of a thirty-day bus tour called Hootenanny'63. The other people on the tour were Chicago folksinger Jo Mapes, country comedy act the Geezinslaw brothers, Canadian folk-pop group The Halifax Three, and Glenn Yarbrough, who had been the lead singer of The Limeliters. The tour took us through the midwest and south, culminating in a final show at Carnegie Hall. Most of the shows were not well attended, because the folk boom was already tailing off to meet its final resting place shortly thereafter when The Beatles toured the United States.

On the 22nd of the month, John F. Kennedy was assassinated. I have a vivid memory of our bus stopping in a small town restaurant in Illinois and dozens of people sorrowfully gathering around a television set. This tragedy certainly didn't contribute to the appeal of our tour and resulted in one date getting cancelled. The country was in a state of acute confusion and despair. Entertainment wasn't a priority for most people. A few days after Kennedy's death, we received a call from SNCC, the Student Non-Violent Coordinating Committee. SNCC was an organization that was registering black voters, and agitating against segregation. Unlike some of the older civil rights groups, it was almost entirely both young and black. SNCC found out that we were scheduled to play at the Jackson, Mississippi auditorium. The auditorium enforced segregated seating. Because the authorities in Jackson knew that this policy would be thrown out by the courts, they simply arrested any black person that came within a hundred yards of the auditorium. They would then charge the person with loitering. SNCC asked us to cancel the show, unless this policy was changed.

The tour's participants as a group decided that we would take a vote of the performers, and do whatever the majority decided upon. Jo Mapes, Glenn Yarbrough and The Journeymen voted not to play the show, while the Geezinslaw Brothers, who were Texans cast in the redneck mold, voted to play. The Halifax Three also voted to play. Their attitude was that this was an American problem, and since they were Canadians, why should they get involved. The guitar player of the Halifax group was Zal Yanovsky, and he voted to cancel, but the group didn't accept his vote, since he was only their guitar player. (Later he was one of the founders of The Lovin Spoonful.)

We called SNCC back and informed them of our decision. They responded by saying that since we weren't going to be working that night, would we consider doing a benefit performance at Tougaloo College? Tougaloo was about ten miles north of Jackson, and it was ostensibly a black college, but its students included not only black students but radicalized white students who had come down south to support the Civil Rights movement. We talked it over, and all of the people who voted to cancel the show agreed to do the benefit.

John and Scott had rented a car so that they could drive to the next gig, rather than be subjected to the tour bus. We started to leave Jackson, and drove by the Greyhound Bus Station. John handed me a paper bag, and asked me if I could check it in a bus station locker. I went into the bus station, where I realized he had given me a bag half full of marijuana.

John was basically an addictive personality. When I first met him, he was taking benzedrine and dexedrine, as well as imbibing excessive amounts of alcohol. After our sojourn in California he had turned to marijuana and occasionally hashish. As I checked his bag in the bus station it occurred to me that I should have told him to check it himself. I had visions of being busted with his grass.

We had been warned to drive very slowly to Tougaloo, and to be sure to come to a full stop at all railroad crossings. Our SNCC contact assured us that we were going to be followed to and from the college. In a short while we got to the college, and performed for and with the students. Looking around the room, we noticed that some of them were sporting bandages or other evidence of having been attacked as a consequence of their activism in the cause of civil rights.

The performance closed with the traditional obligatory performance of We Shall Overcome, with all of us locking arms. We drove back to Jackson without any problems. The next day, I got on the bus and we drove to the next show in Louisiana. The first people off the bus were the Geezinslaw Brothers. Ironically, they were met by baseball bats and threats, and people shouting that if playing Jackson wasn't good enough for us, we weren't welcome there. The brothers got back on the bus and we drove away. Apparently the story of our cancelling the show got on the AP wire service, and was carried all over the south.

BEGINNINGS OF THE BAND BREAK UP

Scott and I were both preparing to quit the Journeymen, although we didn't talk openly about it. Part of the reason for our reticence was that our third album had just come out, and we were scheduled to play The Troubadour in Los Angeles in conjunction with Capitol's efforts to promote the album. Somehow two members of the Halifax Three found out that we might dissolve the group, and at every single opportunity they would sit with John, sing harmony with him, and report how great they sounded together. The leader of the group, Richard Byrne, was kind of a dictator and the other two performers, Pat La Croix and Denny Doherty, were totally intimidated by him. It didn't surprise Scott or me how eager they were to get out from under his reign. Later Denny became a charter member of John's next group, The Mamas and the Papas.

For the last date of the tour, we played a half-full Carnegie Hall in New York. Scott and I went to Eddie Bell's guitar shop, and bought a $15 Stella acoustic guitar. We hatched a plan to destroy the guitar during our performance, thereby anticipating the act that The Who popularized a few years later. While John was doing a short comic monologue, Scott and I came on stage with the guitar, and to everyone's puzzlement we systematically destroyed the instrument. It was one of the few times that I ever saw John Phillips become absolutely speechless. It was a perfect expression of what Hootenanny '63 meant to us.

JOHN AND SCOTT

John and Scott had spent some years together before I had ever met them. Even before The Smoothies existed, they sang together informally, and in an earlier group called The Abstracts. They knew each other's comedy routines, habits and inclinations, and when they were getting along, that worked well for them, even though it made me feel like a perpetual outsider. During the entire last year of The Journeymen's existence, they did not talk to one another. They would literally converse through me, as though I were some sort of medium. Scott might say, "Dick, would you tell John that his shoes are untied?" or John might say, "Dick, tell Scott that the plane leaves at 8AM tomorrow."

In addition to being awkward for all of us, this foolishness added to our financial overhead. We would often rent two cars and I would alternate riding between the two of them. In some ways I enjoyed this because, if I wanted some stimulation and discussion, I'd ride with John, while if I wanted a quieter less raucous ride, I'd go with Scott. Neither of them ever asked me how or why I made these choices.

Anyone reading this book may well be asking themselves, how can a group perform together when two of the three people are not talking to one another? The best way that I can explain it is to think about some of the major groups and how their relationships have worked. Keith Richards and Mick Jagger of the Stones have a very similar love-hate situation, where each of them regards themselves as the indispensable person in the band, although neither of them have had any significant success when they tried to do solo albums. A similar situation exists with Steven Tyler and Joe Perry of Aerosmith. If you read any of the bios or memoirs of these people, you will see how this sort of thing can happen. Imagine yourself in a band, travelling night after night with the same people, performing on stage with them, checking into hotels with them, doing radio promotion together, going to parties together, etc. There are also sources of conflict in songwriting credits, and the question of who gets how much of the spotlight in performances. If you consider all these factors, it becomes easier to understand this sort of competitive childishness. The same situation recurred with Scott and John a few years after the demise of the Journeymen. That's a discussion I'll return to later in this book.

THE TROUBADOUR AND THE FINAL BREAK-UP

The Troubadour gig was our last major club gig. I arrived a day early and went over to the club. I found that we were sharing the gig with my old North Beach friend Hoyt Axton. Someone, maybe his manager, asked if we cared who closed the show. I have a vague recollection of saying that we didn't care. While it was true that I personally didn't care, this went against everything that show business stands for and our manager Stan Greeson quickly corrected my comments. I can only imagine how stupid he must have thought that I was.

I don't remember much about the Troubadour gig. I know that some of the Capitol people came. I vaguely remember meeting David Crosby and T Bone Burnett, and I recall getting a warning from the cops for walking in Beverly Hills between sets. I guess this wasn't acceptable behavior in that town, and it probably still isn't. The only other thing that I remember is the contrast between Hoyt Axton on stage and in the dressing room. In the dressing room he loved to do quiet fingerpicking guitar. On stage he would bash the guitar into submission. He almost never did a set without breaking a string, and sometimes he broke two strings. One night he had a huge argument with his girl friend and he came off stage and threw his Martin D28 guitar against a wall.

Outside of my early fascination with lemon and orange trees on lawns, I never cared for Los Angeles. I couldn't wait to leave, and four weeks later we were out of there. We didn't seem to arouse much interest in the Hollywood set. The folk boom was dying, waiting only for the soon to be arriving Beatles and Bob Dylan going electric to administer its final rites. In only three and a half years, we had become dinosaurs.

HOW I BECAME BOB DYLAN FOR TEN MINUTES

While we were playing The Troubadour, Capitol began to search their roster for a Bob Dylan competitor. For reasons I've never really understood, I became their choice. I don't know whether it was because I was their folkiest folk-pop artist, because I seemed a bit off-center for someone in the music business, or because John Phillips convinced our producer Curly Walters that I was just as weird as Dylan and could be merchandised in a similar way. In any case, Capitol asked if I wanted to do a solo album of topical songs.

From the first, I thought this was a crazy idea. First of all, I never thought that I was much of a singer.

I was indeed writing songs, but most of them were what my friends and I somewhat cynically would call sensitive singer-songwriter opuses. I did write a song about the murder of Medgar Evers while we were playing at the Troubadour, and I had one song about coal miners. I began to figure out how I could give Capitol some facsimile of what they wanted.

I knew that Frank Hamilton was living in Los Angeles, and I had met a young guitarist named Steve Young in Los Angeles. Steve was a wonderful and under-rated guitarist, who was playing with a pop-folk duo named Richard and Jim. They also were in Los Angeles at the time. For vocal back-up and moral support I had Capitol fly my friend Harry Tuft in from Denver. Within a couple of weeks we put together an album called The Things That Trouble My Mind. I came up with five original songs, some of which could only thinly be described as including social commentary. I added a complex banjo arrangement of the old folksong East Virginia, a condensed version of Dylan's song Hard Rain, a Woody Guthrie song and a couple of other songs by other composers. The sessions were fun, and went fairly smoothly. Josh Dunson, a music critic for Sing Out! Magazine correctly criticized my vocal performances. I wasn't happy about it, but I couldn't really disagree. As I anticipated, the album sold next to nothing. Judy Collins ended up covering the Medgar Evers song, and Gram Parsons, who was a big Journeymen fan as a high school student covered the mining song, They Still Go Down. Both of their recordings are still in print as CD's. I'm afraid my own record sank without a trace, although at this writing it ranks as number 1,580,570 best seller on Amazon in its original and only vinyl edition.

THE END OF THE JOURNEYMEN

By the time we finished the Troubadour engagement, it was clear that none of us had any enthusiasm for continuing the group. We played what college concerts had been booked through Spring, 1964, and tried to do the best shows that we could. We did one show at the University of Vermont where John never made it to the gig. Scott and I went up together, and did the show as a duo. One of our last shows was at the University of West Virginia. A student there taped the show illegally, and years later he sent me copies of the tapes. I dreaded listening to them, because I had heard some live tapes of the Kingston Trio which were really out of tune. Much to my surprise, our tapes, which have never been issued anywhere, sounded good. The student had a tape recorder in the men's bathroom, and there is one song that is accompanied by a flushing toilet.

THE JOURNEYMEN, R.I.P.

When we started the Journeymen, my objective was to save $100,000 so I could move to Colorado and go to music school. Musically, I wanted to bring some traditional songs to light that hadn't entered the pop-folk movement. I knew that the entire enterprise was going to be slicker and less spontaneous than the music that I cared about, but my objective was to be as true to the music as I could, given the obvious limitation that we were trying to create a presence in the pop business.

I think that on balance, apart from only getting to about a fifth of my financial goal, I was able to accomplish these goals. Scott was basically a solo singer. Although he did a fine job in the band, being a group singer was not his primary skill. As for John, it was another stepping stone for his vocal arranging abilities. His songwriting did not really blossom in our band, but I think it provided him with a foundation in roots music that he did not really possess when we started.

The contrast of our talents and personalities were intriguing to much of our audience, but we lacked the dynamism of the Kingston Trio. Certainly of the three of us I had the least saleable performing personality, and that probably was a bit of an impediment to our success. John tried to keep the Journeymen going for another year, replacing Scott with his wife Michelle, and me with Marshall Brickman. We never really talked about it, but my sense was that part of the reason John wanted to keep the group going was to receive the income from recording more Schlitz beer commercials. Schlitz declined to do that. Halfway through the year it must have become obvious to John that Michelle was not really cutting it as a vocal soloist, and John brought Denny Doherty of the Halifax Three on board. By this time not only had the Beatles hit, but the folk-pop movement was essentially played out.

John went on to start The Mamas and Papas. Scott sang at The World's Fair, and made couple of unsuccessful singles for Capitol and Epic. Later he re-united with John for one massively successful hit single. What I have done since Journeymen days follows.

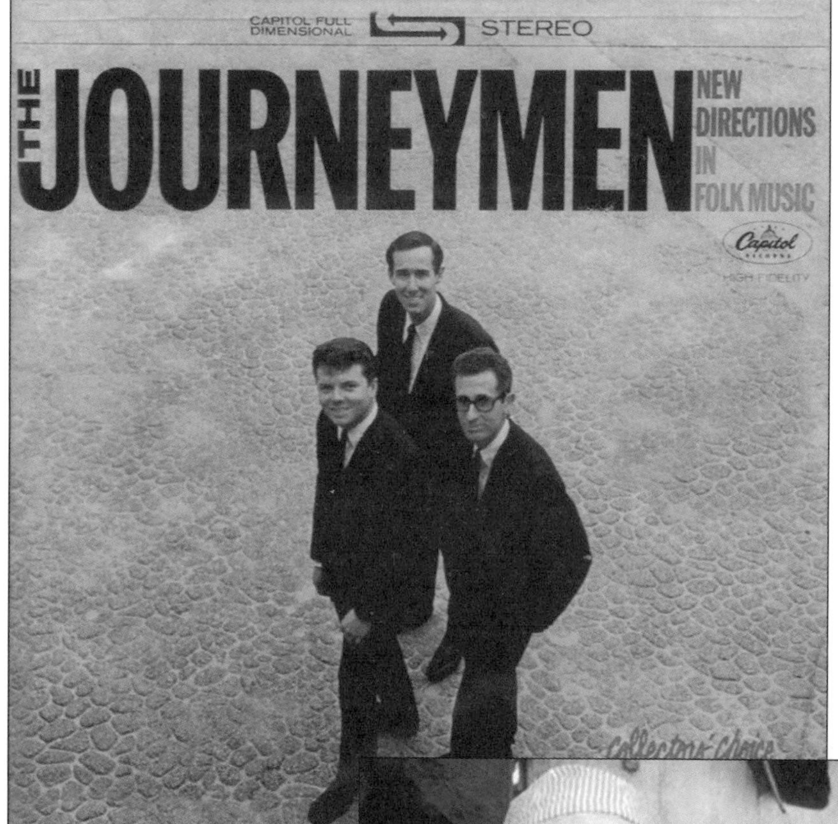

"New Directions in Folk Music" - the third and final release from The Journeymen.

When The Journeymen closed shop, John Phillips started a little group called The Mamas and The Papas.

Part 1 • Chapter 9

NEW YORK AND THE STUDIO WORLD

Just before the Journeymen broke up I found an apartment in Manhattan at 20th Street and 3rd Avenue. It was on the fourth floor, but this was a newly renovated building with an elevator. The block was an odd one. There were two attractive single family houses across the street, and next door to them was a five story tenement. Next door was the newly opening Police Academy, a training ground for future cops. I figured the neighborhood was safe!

My girlfriend Diane Deschanel came back from France, and a few months later we got married. Meanwhile, I pursued a career devoted to songwriting and studio work.

Three and a half years of constant shows left me with virtually no desire to continue performing. I began to think about producing records. I got a call from Dave Edelman, an A&R man at Cameo-Parkway Records in Philadelphia. He asked me if I wanted to co-produce an album with him. The label wanted to do a folk-pop album with Merv Griffin, the TV personality. I helped select the musicians, got my friend Dan Fox to do the arrangements adding additional musicians, and Merv even recorded one of my songs. I really didn't know what I was doing, but my familiarity with folk-pop music did contribute to the album. Merv was a capable singer, in a kind of 50's style, and he was fairly easy to work with. I'm afraid that the album did nothing commercially.

Shortly after that through The Journeymen's manager, Stan Greeson, who continued to manage me, I got a call from Artie Mogull at Warner Brothers, asking me if I wanted to produce a folk album with traditional folksinger Jean Ritchie. I was the sole producer on this project. I was paid $500 and appointed the leader of the sessions, which meant that I got double the union scale. I recorded the album at a studio on West 57th Street, with an engineer named Bill Schwartau, who became a close friend. Jean was writing songs, but because her family all sang traditional music and that was what she had build her reputation on, she attributed them to her "uncle." The songs were also somewhat political, because they protested conditions in the coal mining country and she realized that this might offend her family. Most of them were still living in Kentucky. Jean brought in two English vocalists named Jackie and Bridie, and I hired John Herald of the Greenbriar Boys to play guitar, Artie Traum to play some banjo, and Bill Lee to play acoustic bass. I played some banjo and guitar as well.

BILL SCHWARTAU

Almost all of my previous experiences with recording came from playing and occasionally singing on sessions as a hired gun. Being a decision maker in the control room was a new experience for me. Bill was absolutely fearless in the studio. He would literally try anything: various microphone placements, echo, whatever he felt would benefit a particular session. He once told me about a trio session with Duke Ellington, Charley Mingus, and Max Roach. As Bill told the story, there was so much rivalry and bad feeling in the room, that he turned out all the lights in the studio, so the players could not see one another. Appropriately enough the album was called Money Jungle. Over time, I would do a number of projects with Bill.

JEAN RITCHIE

I thoroughly enjoyed doing the recording with Jean Ritchie. It was a bit like stepping back into a purer version of the folk world that I had known so well before The Journeymen existed. I couldn't figure out why a large label like Warner Brothers wanted to do an album with a niche artist like Jean, but after a while I concluded that they wanted the publishing rights to her songs. In any case no one rushed me, and we spent about a week on the project. After the sessions were completed, Bill and I mixed the album, and he was just as innovative in the mixing process as he had been in the actual recording. The album sank quickly without a trace, but it was really my introduction into the world of record production.

SONGWRITING

Shortly after the demise of The Journeymen, I was signed to a staff songwriting deal by Al Brackman at TRO (The Richmond Organization.) This was primarily because of the success of my song Someone To Talk My Troubles To, which found its way into three albums that were in the top ten of the Billboard charts. These recordings were by the Kingston Trio, Glenn Yarbrough, and the Smothers Brothers. Eventually there were a dozen recordings of the song, but the only one that came through the efforts of the publisher was a French language recording. All of the other recordings came from artists or producers hearing the Journeymen's recording from our live performances, or from my own personal contacts.

When the deal was signed, I got really excited about songwriting, and wrote somewhere around a hundred songs in that year. I have to admit that most of these songs are ones that I would just as soon forget. A half dozen or so eventually got recorded, either by me or by people that heard me sing them. The bulk of the songs disappeared into the mist. TRO generously allowed me to recapture the rights to all of the songs that hadn't been recorded. The original deal paid me $6000 as an advance against future royalties, and a $1000 signing bonus. Basically I was on a weekly "draw" of $100 a week. Looking back on it, from a vantage point of forty years, TRO and I became frustrated with one another. They tried to get the songs recorded, and I tried to write "commercial" songs, but neither of us got very far. I wrote both the words and music to most of the songs, and also co-wrote a few songs with my friend Dan Fox. After about 39 years, the few songs that remained at TRO actually paid back the advance, and I started to receive small royalty checks. This income mostly came from Judy Collins' recording of the song about Medgar Evers, and Gram Parsons' recording of They Still Go Down. Over time I stopped trying to write songs for the pop market, and in my opinion, I became a better songwriter. I also focused more on composing instrumental music, and cut down on the number of songs that I was writing.

THE FOLK FREEZE

When I first left The Journeymen, the British rock explosion was just beginning. Consequently I was able to play on a number of recordings, including albums by The Brothers Four, the New Christy Minstrels, Connie Francis and a string of albums for Cameo Parkway Records.

Although folk-pop music as a style faded into near oblivion, I also broke into the more commercial aspect of studio recording. These were mostly sessions for jingles where I played bluegrass banjo. Unlike many of the folk sessions, jingles always involved playing from written music. Many of the arrangers didn't write out banjo parts, but simply would designate the appropriate chords. Although I had a basic knowledge of bluegrass, you could say that I am the only banjo player who learned how to play bluegrass in order to play on jingles. The written parts had their share of musical challenges. It was quite common to change keys, even in a thirty second jingle. Because I was playing bluegrass patterns, I would have to retune the fifth string so I could continue to play the patterns in a new key. Sometimes I would have to retune the fifth string in the middle of the jingle. The engineer would turn my microphone off for about four bars of music, maybe five seconds, and then turn the microphone back on. Since the orchestra might include anything from three to twenty other musicians, it was difficult to hear when I was in tune again. Later the fifth string capo came into general use, and the re-tuning became unnecessary. I would simply slide the capo on the fifth string up one fret, and the G would automatically become an A flat.

Another musical challenge was that music arrangers, the people who actually wrote out the instrumental parts, didn't understand the nature of the five string banjo. At first I tried to explain to them that if I kept a bluegrass pattern going, that the fifth string needed to be part of that pattern in order to maintain the flavor of the instrument. Many arrangers would hear this note as a mistake, not something inherent in the instrument itself. When I would try to explain to them that if I kept the pattern going I had to play that note, they tended not to believe me.

LEE BLAIR AND HANK DUNCAN

One night I played on a Brothers Four session at Columbia Records' 30th Street studio. This was a huge cavernous room, and with about six or seven musicians playing, it was the opposite of an intimate situation. To sum it up, the music was less than stimulating.

Since I only lived ten short blocks from the studio, I had walked there with my banjo and guitar. On the way home I had gotten about four blocks when I heard the sound of a ragtime banjo playing with a piano player. It was coming out of a small bar. There was no cover charge, so I went in and had a beer. Lee Blair was a banjo and guitar player who had played with Jelly Roll Morton and Hank Duncan was a ragtime-ish barrelhouse piano player. After a boring three hour pop-folk session, the music struck me as being refreshing and spontaneous.

When I left the club, I thought about what I had just witnessed. There were hardly any people there, and I imagined that the musicians would have been lucky to have made $25 for the evening. I must have made three or four times that much, plus pension contributions. I was acutely aware of how unfair this was.

GRAM PARSONS

I first met Gram Parsons when he attended several Journeymen concerts with his friend Paul Surratt and some other members of The Shilos, his teenaged folk-rock group. Gram worshipped the Journeymen, and the group even recorded a couple of my songs. After the Journeymen broke up, Gram appeared in New York, and I saw him several times. I had a Uher tape recorder and recorded some of his new songs. Later I took him to the Music Makers Studio, and Bill Schwartau recorded a half dozen songs. I played lead guitar on several of them. The songs I recorded were later released by Sierra Records, but I have never located the tapes of the session at Music Makers.

Gram had a complicated family life. His mother was a serious alcoholic, and his step-father, Bob, had a contentious relationship with him. Gram's family was quite wealthy, and owned a number of orange groves in Florida. Bob came up to New York and took Diane and me out to dinner with Gram and himself. He seemed to be very grateful that Gram knew a musician who was relatively sane and wasn't trying to take advantage of his step son. The dinner itself was unpleasant. There was a considerable amount of tension between the two of them, and Bob was playing the big spender role. He pretentiously tasted and rejected the expensive wine and was generally obnoxious. Years later Paul Surratt sent me a tape where Gram talks about the fact that I am some sort of unsung musical hero, and he is going to do his best to make me a star. After he left New York, Gram founded the Flying Burrito Brothers and was a member of the Byrds. Gram died under somewhat mysterious circumstances in Joshua Tree, California at the age of twenty six. Hearing this tape years later was a truly surrealistic experience.

JUDY RODERICK

I had met Judy Roderick during one of my Colorado vacations. Judy was a small woman who had a surprisingly big voice. She was an excellent singer, strongly based in the blues. By 1964 she had moved to New York City. On the basis of a strong performance at the Philadelphia Folk Festival she was signed by Columbia Records in 1964. Producer Bobby Scott saw her as a white Billie Holiday and accordingly, he recorded her with a number of swing and Dixieland musicians. Since there already was a Billie Holiday, and her recordings are still available, the need of various record producers to find a kind of parallel white artist has always mystified me.

In any case, the record wasn't a commercial success, and when Bobby tried to do a second album with Judy, they couldn't agree on a common musical direction. She was then signed by Maynard Solomon, one of the owners of Vanguard Records. Maynard was interested in doing an album that focused more on Judy's talents as a blues singer. I was called for a session, and went to the Vanguard Studios. Different engineers, producers and musicians have different notions of what a good sounding room is. The Vanguard studio was in an ex-bingo parlor with very high ceilings, and the control room was actually upstairs from where the studio was. Halfway through the session, Maynard asked me if I could do an additional session. It was then that I realized that I was actually auditioning for that gig. I found this mildly annoying, but I also realized that Maynard had obviously never heard me play before.

The album was called Woman Blue and it consisted of blues, a few jazz tunes, and a couple of my tunes. Maynard must have liked my tune Someone To Talk My Troubles To, because it was the first track on the album. It is still my favorite version of that song. Artie Traum played acoustic and electric guitar on the album, I played acoustic guitar, and studio musician Russ Savakus played bass. There were also several tracks with piano, bass and drums that didn't include guitar.

Judy sang her heart out, and of all the albums that I've ever been involved with, this is one of two or three that I really am proud of, and occasionally listen to. Unfortunately, the folk boom had ended, and this album came out a couple of years after the audience for it disappeared. I am happy to say that it was re-issued on CD in 1993, and is still available. Since Artie and Judy have both passed on, the music brings back many happy musical memories for me.

PARTYING WITH THE MAMAS AND PAPAS

In summer, 1966 the Mamas and Papas played a gig at the Forest Hills Stadium. John called me, and we met at Manny's Music Store on West 48th Street. John and Denny got the brilliant idea to buy a bunch of horns that they would play for a few seconds on the gig. John being John, he spent about $8000 in ten minutes, buying a trumpet for himself and several other horns for the other members of the group. We went outside the store, and encountered the daughter of Don Arnone and another teenaged friend of hers. I reminded John that Don had played on the Smoothies folk session for Decca Records. The two young girls were obviously star struck. John had a carriage with horses waiting outside the store, and he invited the girls to ride around Central Park with us. This was an innocent and generous gesture. When I ran into Don at a session, he made a point of telling me how much the girls appreciated it.

John invited me to attend the show at Forest Hills that night, and told me that he would put me on the guest list. I took the subway out there, but the box office personnel told me that there was no record of me being on the guest list. I was angry, and decided that I would skip the concert but attend the after-concert party at the luxurious St. Regis Hotel.

When I got to the party John met me at the door. There were two tables spread out near the entrance of the room. One had every conceivable sort of alcoholic refreshment. The other had a similar spread of drugs. John smiled at me, and said "I am the perfect host."

Since I am not a dedicated alcohol or drug user I settled for a beer. Meanwhile the Mamas and Papas' road manager and sometime violinist Peter Pilafian was walking outside the window of the room. He was stoned on something or other and he decided to climb the outside of the building. Peter was an experienced climber, but this was a bit much for me. I didn't want to see him self-destruct, so I left the party. I mused on the complexity of John's character, his generosity, his forgetfulness, and the ever-present demons of drug and alcohol that were ultimately destined to bring him to the brink of self-destruction.

THANKS A LOT, LOU ADLER

In 1967 Scott McKenzie's record of San Francisco (Wear Flowers In Your Hair) came out, and was an immediate hit. John Phillips and Scott had seemingly patched up their feud, and John had written this song as a sort of promotional vehicle for the Monterey Pop Festival. John and his record producer Lou Adler were in charge of that festival. Shortly after the record came out, the Mamas and Papas had to go to England and France for a tour, and John and Lou realized that they needed to get a Scott McKenzie album on the market as soon as possible to take advantage of the San Francisco song.

As far as I know, Lou had never recorded in New York before. In any case, John called and asked me to come play on the album. The sessions were booked at Columbia Records, starting at 11PM. Lou and John enjoyed doing all night sessions, but I had never been booked for a session starting at this hour. I had no idea what they were up to, but I knew that the sessions would be very lucrative, because the union rules decreed that by starting at that hour, the session was immediately in overtime. This meant that the sessions paid 1½ times the prevailing wage scale.

The first session ran until about 5AM. I played guitar and banjo, John played rhythm guitar, Scott sang, and there were no other musicians. By the time it was over, I felt as though I was mentally and physically dead. Lou asked me to come back the following night. On the second night, Lou touched the recording console. The Columbia Records engineers were unionized, and their rules specifically stated that if a record producer touched any part of the recording equipment, the engineer would turn off all the equipment, and issue a formal warning. The terms of the warning were that if the producer touched the equipment again, the session was officially over.

Lou was used to recording at independent studios in Los Angeles, where the staff was not unionized, and the atmosphere was extremely informal, to say the least. About an hour after the first warning, Lou touched the board again, and the engineer declared the session to be officially at an end. It was around 4AM then, and Lou told me that he would call me the next day, and tell me where we would be recording. He said that there would be two more nights of recording.

Sure enough, Lou called the next day, and told me that we would be recording at the studios of Atlantic Records. Atlantic's set-up was more like what Lou was used to, and the engineers were not unionized. Lou also asked me to book bassist Chuck Rainey and drummer Ted Sommer for the sessions. Both of these musicians were busy studio players, but because New York players rarely experienced all night sessions, they were available.

We continued to record on Wednesday and Thursday nights, again starting at 11PM. The rules of the musician's union stated that there had to be a half hour break between two sessions. Sessions were three hours long by union rules. Lou and John didn't take these breaks, because their philosophy was that you record until you get a successful take of a song. The union rules now had us in overtime on top of overtime.

I don't really remember too much about the sessions. It was fun to be temporarily re-united with John and Scott. Lou Adler was an interesting kind of producer. He wasn't a skilled musician, although he had some experience as a songwriter. His primary talent seemed to be in editing performances. On a number of occasions he would let me play anything that I wanted to, and then tell me that he wanted me to simplify or shorten a particular solo or instrumental figure. I knew both Chuck and Ted from prior session work, although I had never seen Ted play full drum set before. All the sessions I had been on with him utilized him on a variety of percussion instruments.

Lou was very complimentary about my playing, and told me that he'd love to get me to Los Angeles to play with Wrecking Crew bass player Joe Osborn. At the end of the last session he handed me the union contracts, and told me that I was the leader. He also gave me the name of his accountant, and told me to fill out the contracts and send them on to Los Angeles. I told him that I thought that John was the leader of the sessions, but Lou said that paying John to play was unnecessary. Since the Mamas and Papas were making plenty of money, and John as their primary songwriter was making money from his songs as well as their performances and record sales, I accepted this explanation.

The next day I filled out the contracts. Because of all the various ways that overtime had been accumulated this was a bit complicated. Because Lou had appointed me the leader, I was getting double union scale, so I didn't charge him for playing on the first two nights. I foolishly decided to be Mr. Nice Guy. I sent the contracts out to Los Angeles, figuring that we'd be paid in the three week window that record companies had before they paid musicians.

By this time Diane and I had moved to New Brunswick, New Jersey. She was getting a master's degree in counseling at Rutgers University, and since New Brunswick is about thirty five miles south of New York, it seemed logical to move there.. A couple of weeks after I sent the contracts out, the phone rang. It was about nine o'clock in the morning, and I was half asleep. I was greeted by an angry voice, saying "This is Jack Fidel from the union, you need to come in here immediately to discuss some illegal recording contracts you filed."

I dressed quickly and took the hour long bus ride to Manhattan, and walked in to Jack's office. He immediately read me the riot act, speaking at a deafening volume. He told me that I had recorded for a non-union company, and that I was going to be fined and expelled from the union. It seems that Lou's company, Ode Records, didn't have a registered union franchise. This seemed impossible to me, and I opened the pages of Billboard. At the time, Lou had three of the top five albums on the Billboard chart. There were two Mamas and Papas albums, and a Cheech and Chong comedy project. I showed Jack the list and he told me that he didn't care if Lou had five of the top five albums. For him, the only issue was that Lou didn't have a union franchise.

At this point, I didn't know what to do. I didn't know how to get in touch with Lou's accountant, and I knew that Lou had gone to Europe on tour with Scott and the Mamas and Papas. Since I was making most of my money from playing on sessions, the prospect of being fined and expelled from the union, threatened to put an end to my career. I turned to my manager, Stan Greeson, and he suggested that I go to Columbia Records, and try to find the person in charge of Ode Records. Lou's company was being distributed by Columbia, which is why we had recorded at Columbia in the first place. Contacting Atlantic would have been fruitless because all they had done was to rent Lou their studio as a favor.

A few days later I spent several hours at Columbia Records. I ended up talking to three people. The last person turned out to be the one who actually worked with Lou's label. His name was Ed Matthews, and he understood exactly what my problem was. The trouble was that he could do nothing about it. Lou was actually using Columbia's union franchise but Ed couldn't sign the contracts because Lou was in violation of Columbia's agreement with the engineers' union. Basically he told me that I was stuck.

I consulted with Stan Greeson again, and he suggested that I try to talk to Al Knopf, who was the VP of Local 802 in charge of recording. In other words he was Jack Fidel's boss. Al was a much lower key type person than Jack, and when we met he listened carefully to my sad story. He told me that he was going to make a special exception for me, that he would accept the contracts without a signature from the record company. The reason he decided to do this was that he concluded that I had made an honest mistake, and in fact Lou's accountant had indeed enclosed checks for me and the other musicians even though he hadn't signed the contract. I also realized that the union would only be able to collect work dues if the musicians got their checks. This was a relatively modest amount of money, probably about a hundred dollars or so for the three of us, but I still think that it factored into Al's thinking.

I never heard from Lou Adler again, and I regret that I never charged him for the first two nights of the sessions. It wouldn't have been close to constituting a sufficient payback for the problems that he caused me, but it would have helped.

ARTIE TRAUM

When I first met Artie Traum he was eighteen or nineteen years old. He mastered the guitar very quickly, and started playing professionally soon after this. I had used him on the Jean Ritchie session, and we both played on the Judy Roderick album. I liked his playing, and enjoyed working with him in the studio. I hired him to play on demos of some of my songs, and would run into him now and again at parties or in the Village.

Around 1967 Bob Dylan owned two homes in Woodstock, and Artie got a call from Dylan's then manager, Al Grossman, asking him if he wanted to house sit one of these houses, because Dylan was trying to sell it. Artie invited me up to visit Bob's mansion. The house had something like twenty two rooms. Artie beckoned me into a room down the hall from the living room. The room was covered with mailbags, filled with letters to Bob from fans. We opened several of the letters, which were typical of such missives. In an earlier book of mine called Which Side Are You On? An Inside History of the Folk Music Revival, I described a pitiful letter from a female fan in North Dakota who had apparently hung out with The Band when they were serving as Bob's back-up band. Who can tell what she had in mind. Did she think Dylan would invite her to another show, or did she want to date him? Neither Artie nor I could imagine how intrusive this level of popularity would be to someone's privacy.

At one point Al Grossman called Artie, and suggested that since he was not paying any rent for the house, maybe he could pay the heating bill. Woodstock is quite a ways north of New York City and has some bitter cold winter days. Artie pointed out that the heating bills for a twenty two room house would easily exceed the cost of the sort of house that he would have rented on his own dime. It was obvious that Al was so involved with "the hustle" that he could not stop himself from asking for any financial favors that were even remotely possible.

From time to time I would see Artie in New York, and later in Colorado and Oregon, while I was living in those states. Artie recorded with Eric Kaz in a rock band called Bear in the late 60's, had a duo later with his brother Happy, and recorded a number of albums. Some of them were jazz-influenced instrumental albums, and others were of his songs. He also wrote guitar instructional materials, and worked as a clinician for Taylor Guitars. Around 2003 he was diagnosed with melanoma of the eye. This is an extremely rare form of cancer. He was given the choice of having the eye removed, or using a new experimental laser treatment. Artie opted for the new treatment, which initially worked well.

In the fall of 2007 I met Artie at the offices of Hal Leonard Books in New York. He wanted to do a memoir, centering around his experiences in the Woodstock music community, and I had done several books for Hal Leonard's book division. At the time Artie told me that his eye was giving him trouble again, and he was going to have it looked at by his doctors at Bellevue Hospital. He told me that he was now reconciled to losing his eye, if the laser treatment couldn't be repeated. John Cerullo, who was the CEO of Hal Leonard Books was enthusiastic about the memoir, and a deal was made. Artie began to write the book when his doctors did some testing, and found that the melanoma had spread to his liver. Artie died in early 2008.

I really miss Artie's music, his wonderful stories, and his level-headed attitude. I consider his song The Hungry Dogs of New Mexico to be one of the best songs of social commentary of the late sixties. RIP my friend.

JIM CAMPBELL

While we were still living in New York City, my wife and I became good friends with Bill Schwartau. On a number of occasions we'd visit him at his brownstone in the West Village. Whenever I produced anything, I tried to do it at the Music Makers studio with Bill. He introduced me to a number of the people who were singing on commercials at the studio.

Studio singers were the elite of the studio world. The union contracts for singers were much more lucrative than the money that musicians earned for the same sessions. This wasn't so true of the money made from playing or singing on sessions, but it was important in terms of re-payments, called residuals. Singers could earn as much as $25,000-$30,000 from a single ad campaign. Singers were paid on the basis of how the commercial was broadcast. There were different re-payment schemes based on whether the broadcasts were in prime time, whether they were used on network or regionally, and so forth. Most musicians' payments were comparatively modest. Bill introduced me to a singer named Jim Campbell. Jim was an Alabama native who was not only singing on sessions at Music Makers, but also freelancing for various other accounts. Most studio singers were content doing what they were doing. They possessed a chameleon-like ability to imitate other voices and sounds. To put it another way, Mick Jagger has a very specific, recognizable sound. Studio singers utilize many different voices. They also may be called upon to sing solo parts, or be background singers for someone else's solos. The dozen or so top voices were making more money than many of the advertising agency people who hired them, so the singers never wanted to publicly emphasize their success. Jim told me that at one point he had commercials on the air for six different beer companies. Naturally he was not eager for any of these companies to know what competing products he was singing about. Another difference between studio singers and recording artists was that studio singers were not necessarily young or attractive. They were hired for their vocal skills, not as pretty faces.

THE IMAGINARY SPECIAL SOUND

One day Jim was doing a commercial, as I remember it for Pepsi Cola. The instrumental track had already been cut, so Jim was alone in the studio. In the control room was the creative director the ad agency, and the engineer, Alan Merchant. Many of the studio singers pump themselves up by doing little dance steps, kind of like the way a tennis player dances up and down awaiting her opponent's serve. Jim was a perfectly good looking fellow, but was a bit overweight at the time, and the agency producer kept finding fault with some aspect of his vocal performance.

Alan Merchant had recorded hundreds and hundreds of jingles, and he thought that the problem was that the producer was uncomfortable with the image of Jim dancing, even though this was not an on-camera commercial. Alan went into the studio and told Jim that he was going to fabricate a story for the agency producer, and that Jim should simply agree with anything that he said. Alan returned to the control room and told the producer that he was going to set up a baffle between Jim and the control room. He said that the producer would not be able to see Jim, but that a special sound would be created by the sound bouncing off the baffles into the microphone and on to the tape recorder. Jim agreed that this sounded like a good idea.

Alan set up the baffles, and they proceeded to record the jingle. The agency producer was beside himself with joy. He raced into the control room, threw his arms around Jim and said "that's the sound that I've been looking for." Alan probably smiled to himself. In fact he had changed nothing at all. Another day on Madison Avenue.

MUSIC MAKERS

Even though I was quite friendly with Bill Schwartau I had never done any jingle sessions for Music Makers, the company that owned the studio where Bill worked. Mitch Leigh was the owner of Music Makers, and he had a set crew of musicians that he used on sessions. Mitch decided to move into the record business by recording a duo that consisted of Jim and another studio singer named Bill Dean. Although Mitch was one of the top jingle composers in New York, he had other musical ambitions. He wanted to write and produce some records, and later he went on to compose the music for the hit Broadway show Man of La Mancha.

Jim and Bill prevailed on Mitch to use me and another guitarist named Sam Brown for their session. I got a call to play on the session, and asked the contractor what instruments he wanted me to bring. He told me to bring nylon and steel string guitars. I mentioned that I also played twelve string guitar, and he said I might as well bring that too.

I took an early morning bus in from New Jersey, planning to be at the studio by 9:30AM for a ten o'clock session. As it happened it snowed really hard that day. I arrived in the city right around ten. Now the reader needs to understand that part of doing studio work is that it is expected that musicians NEVER should be late for a recording session. Trying to get a taxi from the bus station to the studio was impossible. I walked as quickly as I could, and arrived at the session around 10:40. I found about fifteen musicians waiting around for me and for Sam Brown to arrive. Sam lived in another part of New Jersey, and he didn't get there until 11:00AM. We were both covered with snow, and there really wasn't much that we could say that wasn't obvious. I was really upset, because I imagined that I had blown my opportunity to ever get called to do a session for Mitch Leigh again.

We pulled out the music for the first tune, and I suggested that it might work well on twelve string guitar. Mitch agreed, and we did several takes, and then a break was called for the musicians. As a matter of form I called my answering machine. I was astounded to learn that Mitch had hired me for a jingle session the very next day. Apparently there was something about my playing that intrigued him.

This was the beginning of a long and fruitful musical relationship. I played on dozens of sessions for Mitch during the next few years. Many of them were for major clients, like American and Northeast Airlines, and the commercials often ran for months and even years. We were paid re-use fees for every thirteen weeks that the jingles were broadcast. I would go down to the union to get my checks, and I'd often get seven or eight checks, of which the majority were re-use fees.

GLEEM TOOTHPASTE: WE CAN'T USE YOUR BEST STUFF

Mitch had a legitimate musical education, with two music degrees from Yale, and had studied with the famous composer Paul Hindemith. Playing on his sessions provided me with a musical education that I had never before experienced. For example, many of his 30-60 second jingles had meter changes. You might be playing in 4/4 time, for example, and Mitch would throw in a bar or two of 5/4, before going back to 4/4. Nothing in my folk guitar days had prepared me for this kind of chart. I recall one session where there were no meter changes, and flutist Leon Cohen played an extra beat in two consecutive takes of the song. He looked up at Mitch and said, jokingly, "Hey Mitch, I've played too many of your sessions. I can't play in 4/4 time anymore."

One day I got a call to play from Mitch's musical contractor Marty Grupp to play twelve string guitar on a Gleem toothpaste commercial. It was a small orchestra that featured soprano sax and oboe playing in a kind of rhythmic counterpoint against a rhythm section of piano, guitar, bass, drums and percussion. Mitch had specifically scheduled the session to use Jimmy Abato, a renowned saxophone teacher and oboe player-studio musician Phil Bodner. Phil was one of those special musicians who played oboe, flute, alto flute, the recorder family, and the entire assembly of saxophones. Mitch had written an absolutely gorgeous piece of music, and all the musicians playing on the session were thrilled to be playing it.

After we had recorded a couple of takes of the tune, Marty called a ten minute break. Since the session was only scheduled for an hour, we were all a bit surprised at this. We could see Mitch and the advertising agency producer energetically discussing the jingle as we headed to the coffee machine. Ten minutes later Marty came out of the studio and told us to go home, but also said we'd be hearing from him soon. We were mystified, but the decision process wasn't part of our gig. About a week later, sure enough I got a call from Marty to play on another session for Gleem. For this session, Mitch had written three jingles that to be kind, were dull and pedestrian. One was even a bit of a rip off of Stephen Fosters' tune Oh Susannah. It was these jingles that the agency actually broadcast. It was abundantly clear to me that Mitch was thumbing his nose at the client. "If you don't like my best work, OK, I'll give you the junk that you prefer." If I had ever been in doubt about the musical taste of the advertising industry, this experience clarified it for me.

IMPROVISING IN THE STUDIO

Another producer called me to play banjo on a Kool cigarette commercial. The instrumentation was banjo, fiddle, guitar and bass. This was a bluegrass flavored jingle, with a fairly simple musical part. Unfortunately the fiddler was a classical violinist, and his attempts at country fiddle were truly lame. Towards the end of the hour, the agency producer pulled me aside, and asked me if I could play a country-Latin-bluegrass Eddie Peabody style of banjo. Eddie was a tenor banjo soloist, and the other musical styles don't fit together, in the least, so of course I told him that I could easily do this. Obviously he had no idea what he was talking about. He then asked if I knew someone who could play country fiddle. I recommended Arnold Eidus. Arnold was the music director for Gray Advertising, and had been a child violin virtuoso, who elected to give up a career as a touring violinist to stay in New York and live a more normal life. I had heard Arnold play some country fiddle on sessions and figured that this wouldn't be a problem for him.

A week later the same group of musicians with Arnold playing the fiddle came in to do the session. The arranger had not written out a part for the fiddle, just the necessary chords. Arnold asked if we could take a brief break. He then proceeded to write out a fiddle solo for himself. I was astonished. It had never occurred to me that someone could master a style, but be entirely unable to improvise in it. A few minutes later we all came out, and proceeded to record the jingle without much trouble.

MORE STUDIO STORIES

At one point Mitch Leigh used a black drummer named Bernard "Pretty" Purdy to play on a number of sessions that I was on. Bernard had played on a number of R&B and pop hits by such artists as Aretha Franklin. Purdy would arrive, set up his drums, and then set up a little promotional billboard claiming that he was the hit maker and if anyone needed him to call him at the listed phone number. Since whoever had called him for the session obviously knew his phone number, this little ploy always mystified me. I found Purdy easy enough to get along with and enjoyed playing with him. No one ever commented on Purdy's signs and he continued to use them during the four or five years that I ran into him in the studios.

I played on quite a few albums during my New York days. Generally they were business-like, and the music was professionally produced and performed. A few projects stood out, because of the unusual or bizarre nature of the sessions.

Two of the oddest recordings I worked on were produced or arranged by a fine piano player name Ron Frangipani. When Ron called me to play on a Townes Van Zandt album, I was really looking forward to it. I was aware of his reputation as an excellent singer-songwriter. Townes came to the studio with no music and not even any lyric sheets of his songs. This was fairly stressful for all of the musicians involved. He would simply start singing the songs, and we would play them. It didn't bother me that he had no written music, but I thought that he would have saved a lot of time and trouble if he gave us either chord sheets, or at the very least, had made copies of his lyrics. The entire experience was like a blur. The album was called Delta Mamma Blues, and about all I could figure out was that some of the songs involved real or imagined experiences with cough syrup. It was a relief when the week ended, and our part of the album ended. When the album came out it did not list any of the musicians who played on it, and the mix was so cloudy that I could barely remember anything that I played on the sessions.

Ron also called me to play on the soundtrack of a movie called Ned Kelly. Kelly was a famous Australian outlaw, and the movie was directed by Australian director, Tony Richardson. Richardson had a big reputation for his work directing such films as Look Back In Anger, Tom Jones and A Taste of Honey. The star of the film was Mick Jagger. We never got to see him, although he did sing a credible unaccompanied version of the traditional Australian ballad about Ned on screen.

The film consisted of a number of songs by children's author, songwriter and humorist Shel Silverstein. All of the songs were written in the key of A, and almost all of them used only three chords. The famous country "outlaw" Waylon Jennings was hired to sing the songs, but for whatever reason he and Richardson seemed to be constantly arguing. In fact in one of the sessions for the movie no musician played a note of music. Waylon and Tony sat in the control room arguing. After about an hour of this the drummer, Specs Powell, suggested that we go into the studio and jam on some blues songs. We half-heartedly played for about ten minutes, but no one was too enthusiastic about playing while all the arguing was happening. Ultimately Waylon sang only one song, and other singers were brought in after all of the tracks were cut. Of course we were all being paid for this down time, but I think all of us felt that this was a waste of our abilities and time. Being paid union scale didn't compensate for the commensurate boredom.

THE BLACK RHYTHM SECTION

At one point in the late 60's, a number of black musicians decided to form a "black rhythm section." The idea was that since they were the hippest players, they would demand double union scale as a group for playing on sessions. Purdy, guitarist Eric Gale, pianist Richard Tee, and several other musicians were part of this group. This wasn't an entirely goofy idea, because the LA session players called The Wrecking Crew were indeed getting double scale for their services. One of my studio buddies told me that the idea collapsed when producers wanted to call one or another of these players without the rest of them. When these players accepted the call, that was the end of the black rhythm section concept.

BUDDY RICH AND MARVIN STAMM

One day I was playing on as jingle at A&R studios. A&R had a bunch of studios, numbered as A1, A2, etc. I don't remember the product or the other musicians on the session, but the trumpet player was a fine young trumpet player named Marvin Stamm. For some reason bandleader-drummer Buddy Rich walked into the control room at our session. I presume that he had been doing something or other in one of the other A&R studios.

If you have never heard of Buddy Rich you should know that he was a notoriously prickly band leader. There are tapes of him screaming at his band on the band bus, and firing all of them. In the course of his drama-laden life, Buddy had had some run-ins with the IRS, and Marvin looked up from his music stand and said, "Buddy, how did that scene with the IRS work out?" I don't know whether Marvin had ever played in Buddy's band, or had simply done a few gigs with him, but this remark totally enraged Buddy. I should mention that Buddy was a rather small but very stocky fellow who was a judo master. He raced into the studio like a raging bull, and it took three or four guys to pull him away.

I was bemused by this incident. Here were a bunch of respectable musicians with coats and ties (except for me) and we were all making quite a bit of money playing this jingle, and suddenly this wild man came charging in like a furious rhino.

BENNY GOODMAN

It would be a close contest between Buddy Rich and Benny Goodman for an award as the world's least loved band leader. Anyone who ever encountered Benny Goodman has a story about his stinginess or his temper. Bucky Pizzarelli told me a story of his being fired from a gig at the Rainbow room in Rockefeller Center, then being re-hired a few days later when Benny fired his successor. But my favorite Benny Goodman story was told to me by Dan Fox.

Benny had a summer home in Connecticut with a complete recording studio in it. Though this is hardly unusual today, in the 1960's it was quite a big deal. Towards the end of his career. Benny liked to record whenever possible. A female singer who was a friend of Dan's was invited to go up to the recording studio with a half dozen musicians. It was winter and the studio was freezing cold. True to form, Benny did not make any attempt to adjust the thermostat. After about an hour the musicians took a break. The singer went up to Benny and said, carefully, that it was very cold in the studio. Benny looked at her and said, "you know you're right." He then went to his closet and put on a heavy wool sweater. The thermostat remained at the same temperature.

JOHN COLTRANE

I heard the jazz saxophone player John Coltrane perform on a number of occasions. I also had seen jazz guitarist Wes Montgomery play several times. During the Journeymen days Coltrane came to a club in the North Beach section of San Francisco immediately following a gig at the Monterey Jazz Festival. John had his regular quartet, but he added Wes and flute and saxophone player Eric Dolphy to the group. I had always enjoyed Wes' playing, but always felt that it was a bit more subdued than I would have preferred. At the time Coltrane had a jukebox hit with his version of the Rodgers and Hammerstein show tune My Favorite Things. The recorded version of the song was about fifteen minutes long, and featured John and pianist McCoy Tyner, along with Elvin Jones' drum parts and the bass of Jimmy Garrison. John played the song at this gig, and gave Wes a solo. Instead of his usual tasteful but under-stated guitar work, it seemed that Wes was on fire. I had no idea what he was doing, and I got so excited that I literally stood on a chair to watch. This was one of the most magical live music performances that I have ever seen.

A few years later when I was back in New York I went down to see Coltrane with his quartet at a club called The Village Gate. I went to the club after eating dinner, and it was well after 10PM when we got there. The entire audience was about six people, and that included me, Diane and my friend Morrie Schambelan, who was visiting from San Francisco. Morrie requested My Favorite Things, and Coltrane started to play. He would generally start by playing the melody, and the improvisations would then go for as long as he felt like playing. John had mastered the art of circular breathing, which meant that he didn't have to stop after say sixteen bars to take a breath. By now it was after 11, and the house sound man started to blink the lights. I would guess that he was thinking that there were only six people in the cavernous club, and if he could get Coltrane to stop playing, we could all go home. Coltrane was playing with his eyes closed. I could not tell whether he was ignoring the flashing lights, or if he was so off in his own musical world that he didn't even see them. He continued to play for ten minutes, and then the tune and the evening ended.

This performance had a very strong effect on me. It was obvious that John Coltrane was on a spiritual and musical mission, and if the audience was large or small he was still going to play his music with all the creativity and passion at his command. I had difficulty imagining too many other pop, folk or jazz musicians who would have that level of commitment to their art.

LUIS BONFA, EDDIE BELL'S GUITAR SHOP AND DAN FOX

There were several music stores where studio guitarists hung out between sessions, or to have instruments repaired. Eddie Bell had a store on West 49th Street between 7th Avenue and Broadway, and I bought strings and occasionally instruments there. The store was run by Eddie and his wife Paula, who managed the business. One day I walked into the shop and there was a smallish man playing up a storm on the guitar. In a few minutes about a half dozen other guitarists stood around, watching him play. It turned out that the man was Luis Bonfa, best known as the composer of Black Orpheus.

A year later I noticed that he was doing a show at a club in the Village, and Diane and I went down there to hear him. Luis' playing at the store was very relaxed and spontaneous, and he must have known that the people watching him play were all musicians. His persona in the club was entirely different. Every piece seemed to last less than two minutes. It would start out at a fast tempo, and accelerate throughout. I was extremely upset, and concluded that he had assumed that since Americans had a very short attention span, he would wow them with his speed and technique.

DAN FOX

There were several teaching studios at Eddie Bell's, and I became friendly with Dan Fox, one of the teachers. I ended up taking lessons from him in jazz guitar and in sight reading music for guitar. This was a necessity for doing commercial studio work, and although I had been reading music since the age of seven, I was not comfortable with reading jazz syncopations. Dan and I would have lunch fairly regularly, and became good friends. When Rene Cardenas was the manager of The Journeymen he arranged for our first album to be published as a music book by a legendary music business character named Charley Hansen. I introduced Dan to Charley and his then assistant Frank Hackinson. This began an entirely new career for Dan, as an editor and arranger of sheet music and instructional folios. Over the years Dan has probably written more such books than any other human being. They have ranged from easy piano arrangements to transcriptions of pop hits in the original recorded arrangements. Dan has also written so many instructional folios that he has occasionally used various aliases, like Roger Edison. There are probably less than a half dozen people in the music industry that I trust implicitly, and Dan is right at the top of the list. Over the years we have collaborated on instructional recordings for Music Minus One, and we have written dozens of instructional books for banjo and guitar. He started out writing classical music works like a string quartet and a symphony and later worked as a jazz guitarist. Like many musicians, he realized that none of these efforts alone would enable him to make a reasonable living.

CHARLEY HANSEN

Although I had very little contact with Charley Hansen, I can't resist sharing a couple of stories about him that Dan has told me. Most music publishers do not literally print music, but lease those rights to other companies. In the 1960's and 1970's, Charley Hansen was the leading print publisher, with affiliates in Europe. Charley was known to be extremely impulsive and to require employees to appear magically with virtually no notice. One of Charley's employees was a production manager named Phil Tannen. One day Phil went into Charley's office and explained that he was getting married the following week and was going to spend his honeymoon in Yugoslavia. Charley asked him how he could be reached by phone. Phil smiled, and said that the place where they were staying was on top of a mountain, and there was no phone service there. Charley then told him to at least leave the mailing address with his secretary.

A week later, the newly married Phil was relaxing in a mountain inn, where he and his bride had arrived just a few days earlier. He looked out the bedroom window. In the distance he noticed a man riding a bicycle up the mountain. A couple of hours later the courier knocked on his door with a telegram from Charley, saying, "be in Zurich tomorrow."

On another occasion, Dan was asked to go to London for a meeting with Charley and all his European affiliates. Everyone sat down to a sumptuous lunch, wondering when the business part of the meeting would begin. After about an hour, Charley banged on a water pitcher, and told the assembled executives that he knew they were wondering why they were all asked to attend the luncheon. He explained that he simply wanted to see everyone in the same room, and that he would be leaving for Switzerland in an hour.

Charley had a personal astrologer, and one day he sent a memo to his staff saying that on the advice of the astrologer, the company's lead artist Sam Cohen would now be known in the company as Glenn Cohen. The savant had told Charley that Glenn was his lucky name.

My last Hansen story involves Charley asking a music arranger who had just re-located from New York to Denver with his entire family to go from his Denver office to Washington, D.C., to deliver Charley's car to his sister in Washington D.C. The poor fellow drove the 1600 miles as instructed. As Charley's sister was thanking him for his help, she handed him an envelope from Charley. The note inside told him that he was fired. He then had to fly to Denver at his own expense to collect his own belongings and drive his family back to New York.

YOU CAN'T ALWAYS TELL A BOOK BY ITS COVER

Dan left Hansen to go to work for Warner Brothers' music print operation. He quickly became the chief editor, supervising a small staff. One of his young assistants was working on a Led Zeppelin folio which was supposed to contain all the parts of a particular album that were played on the record. He had some trouble transcribing one of John Paul Jones' bass parts, and Dan agreed that it was difficult to hear it clearly. It happened that the band was in New York on tour, and so Dan called their management office and asked if John Paul Jones could possibly stop by the office and show them what he had played.

Neither Dan nor his assistant knew much about John Paul Jones, so they fully expected a tortuous session where he would play the part and they would have to transcribe it. Jones arrived at the office, replete with long hair and rock star appearance. Dan told him what they wanted. Jones then asked if Dan had any manuscript paper, and told him that he realized that the mix made the bass part difficult to hear. Jones calmly picked up a pencil, and wrote out the bass part, in the bass clef, in a few seconds. The two arrangers looked at each other in amazement. They had no idea that John Paul Jones was a skilled studio man who had played on dozens of sessions in England, and who would later go on to write film scores.

BILL SCHWARTAU REDOUX

During the time I broke into studio work playing guitar at Music Makers, Mitch Leigh was writing the music for the show The Man of La Mancha. The show was in tryouts in Connecticut, and Bill was recording the shows while doing daily sessions at Music Makers. During this period, Bill was drinking too much and he became ill and had to stop working. I didn't see him for over a year. One day I was playing on a jingle for Music Makers. Mitch Leigh tended to use the same group of players in his rhythm section. We were running through that day's jingle when suddenly a rather disoriented and disheveled Bill Schwartau limped into the studio. All of us knew Bill and were startled. No one knew what to say to him. He told us that he was living on the Bowery, apparently in a flop house hotel. Someone came and ushered him out of the building. I always assumed that he died soon after that, but a couple of years ago his son Winn, who has pursued a career in forensic audio, told me that Bill lived in a nursing home in Brooklyn for some years.

This was one of my saddest moments in the studio. I felt completely helpless. I couldn't very well leave the session to run after him. I don't know what pushed him over the edge, but it was a great loss to the New York recording community. In his autobiography engineer-producer Phil Ramone has credited Bill with being a mentor, but very few people in the recording community remember him today.

Photo: Gen Fox

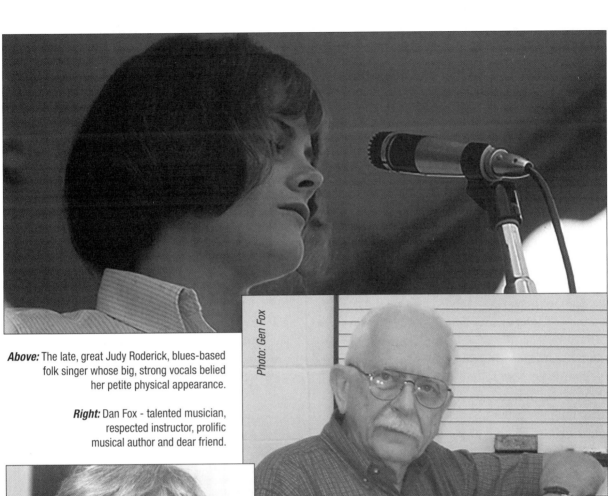

Above: The late, great Judy Roderick, blues-based folk singer whose big, strong vocals belied her petite physical appearance.

Right: Dan Fox - talented musician, respected instructor, prolific musical author and dear friend.

Left: Frank Hamilton - an extraordinary guitarist who is one of the co-writers of We Shall Overcome. He played on my Capitol solo album.

Photo by Caleb Deschanel, my former brother-in-law. His kids are Emily (Bones) and Zooey, who is also a TV and movie star and a singer.

Part 1 • Chapter 10

COMMAND PROBE RECORDS: BECOMING A STAFF PRODUCER

In 1968 my manager Stan Greeson arranged for me to meet with Joe Carlton at Command and Probe Records. This company was one of several companies that ABC Records owned, including Dunhill, Westminster, and ABC itself. I went to Joe's office at 54th Street and Avenue of the Americas. This was a large office building that also housed ABC radio and many other companies. Joe had a medium sized office, and festooned across the wall were gold records that he had accumulated during his career as a record company executive and producer. There was the immortal How Much is That Doggie In The Window by Patti Page, Kiss of Fire by Georgia Gibbs, and about a half dozen others. Joe had a sort of New York-thug voice, but he turned out to be intelligent and articulate. We got along well and he offered to hire me full-time. Since I was doing a fair amount of studio work, I suggested that I work afternoons, adding evenings when necessary, for a half-time wage. I wanted to reserve mornings for the jingle sessions that I was playing, and I didn't really want to give up playing. Joe accepted my argument that being involved with studio players on a daily basis would help me when I wanted to use these people on recordings.

Command and Probe were two very different labels. Command was a middle of the road audiophile label that had pioneered stereo recordings where the music traveled from one speaker to another. Probe was Joe's baby, and was intended to be a hip rock and pop label.

I was thrown right in deep water, co-producing an album by the so-called Glenn Miller band. Glenn himself had died in World War Two, but a band using his name soldiered on. I hadn't ever produced anything like that before. My job was to cue the engineer what solos were coming up, and to consult with the arranger about what take was the best one. This involved following the musical score, which I was not used to doing under that kind of pressure. In that period in the record business record producers were known as A&R (Artist and Repertoire) men. In fact almost all of them were indeed men at that time, with the sole exception, at least in New York, of Ethel Gabriel, who worked at RCA. A&R involved a variety of tasks. We were supposed to find talent to record, work with the acts on what songs to do, consult with the music arranger and mix the product. We were also responsible for the union contracts, which had to be filed within fifteen days of the session. By this time we were working in 16 track analog, so we had 16 tracks to play with. The studio that we used was Fine Sound, a studio housed in a hotel on West 57th Street.

My colleague in A&R was John Turner, who had worked in film in some capacity or other, and appeared to have more musical education than I did. Together we were assigned to produce a band from Kansas City called The Mystic Number National Bank. Joe Carlton had made some sort of deal with the band's managers which required them to sell a minimum number of albums in the band's hometown of Kansas City. The lead singer of the band was a big voiced singer named Glenn Walters. The band's piece de resistance was a lengthy version of the tune St. James Infirmary. The engineer at Fine Sound was a young man from New England named Russ Hamm, and we were really grooving on one particular take of St. James. About eight minutes into the ten minute arrangement, Russ looked up and realized that the recording light was not on. He had forgotten to turn the machine on, and I hadn't bothered to look either. The band finished the take, and we had to explain to them why they needed to do it again. Inevitably, that was by far the best version they did during the week we were recording. Every night we'd have them do the tune but it never really worked that well again.

During this period, I often went out to lunch with music publishers. Always at their expense, I might add. There were a string of restaurants on

West 56th Street between 5th and 6th Avenues, and I set a goal to try every one of them. Publishers wanted to place their songs with our artists, so they would ask what I was working on and ply me with demos of their latest songs.

FAT CITY AND FRUMMOX

I took the train to Washington D.C. to listen to a bunch of acts that a manager either was working with or knew about from friends of his. I signed a teen-aged Peter, Paul & Mary style group, who sang well, but whose record sank without a trace, and I also signed a duo called Fat City. Fat City was Bill Danoff and Taffy Nivert. They were good songwriters, and their demo was excellent. Their music was in a folk-rock vein, with a tinge of Mamas and Papas influence. We did an album, using a number of well-known studio musicians, and arrangements by a young arranger named Bob James. Most of their songs were originals, but I successfully pitched them one of my songs, called Wall Street, and a song by West Coast songwriter Jackie De Shannon called Holly Would.

The sessions were enjoyable, and we used a bunch of studio musicians who I knew, since Fat City didn't have a band. When the album was done, I listened to it carefully, and realized that they sang better on the original demo. I don't know whether they were more comfortable in the studio in Washington, or I had simply paid too much attention to the instrumental parts, and not enough to the vocals. It was a useful if painful lesson for me.

The song of mine that Fat City recorded was called Wall Street, and described an unincorporated town on a dirt road above Boulder, Colorado. We remained friends, and their first recorded song after the Fat City record was I Guess He'd Rather Be in Colorado. The song described me playing the banjo, and working in the ABC offices. It was recorded by John Denver, and later they collaborated with him on a major hit, Take Me Home Country Roads. A few years later they re-surfaced with a quartet they called The Starland Vocal Band, with a major hit song Afternoon Delight.

My friend Harry Tuft sent me a tape of a country-folk duo called Frummox. They were living in Denver, and playing in clubs there. I immediately wanted to record them, and was able to convince Joe Carlton to sign them. After Diane graduated from Rutgers we moved to a town called Roosevelt, a bit further south in New Jersey. The two principals in Frummox were Steven Fromholz, a Texas singer-songwriter and Dan McCrimmon, a native Coloradan. They planned to bring a friend of theirs, Travis Holland, to play bass.

I listened carefully to the tape, and decided that most of the album could be recorded with just the three of them. Both of them were capable guitarists, and Dan also played good harmonica. I knew that I could fill out the ensemble by playing banjo when that was appropriate, and I also decided to add occasional doses of nylon string guitar.

Since the company didn't have tons of money to spend, I suggested that they should come to my house, rehearse for about three days, and that we could record the following week. The rehearsals went well, and I immediately realized that some of the songs could really benefit from the addition of a fiddle. I called Eric Weissberg and he played fiddle, as well as adding occasional mandolin, pedal steel and electric guitar to the mix. The five of us were the core band that played on the sessions.

I love working in the recording studio, and some of the best music I have played or heard has been in that environment. It is challenging though, because you never know exactly what something will sound like until you hear it on tape. Some artists develop perpetual colds in the studio, others are unable to reproduce the feeling or even the sound that they have in a rehearsal situation, and sometimes the blend of personalities that comprise a finished recording doesn't come off. The Frummox record went almost flawlessly in the studio. Steve and Dan both sang and played at the top of their games, and because Travis was in effect part of the group, everything seemed to blend perfectly. Travis had an incredibly thick Texas accent, and we started to record a song called Loving Mind. Our New England-bred engineer Russ asked Travis the title of the song, and when Travis replied Luhving My-und, Russ called it Lavender Time, or something to that effect.

For the song The Man With The Big Hat, which was set in a barroom, we ordered in glasses filled with water from the hotel waiters and set up a barroom scene in the studio. (Remember that the studio was actually situated in a hotel ballroom.) We clinked out glasses together, made small talk, and even broke a glass or two. It was great fun, and set the scene for the song. Steve and Dan invited their friend Jerry Jeff Walker to the session, and he sang along on the chorus. When Russ and I mixed the album, it turned out that instead of singing the man with the big hat is buying, Jerry Jeff sang the man with the big hat is dying. Since the song and a good deal of the album was about the death of the traditions of the American West, I left Jerry Jeff's part in.

Most of the songs Frummox was recording weren't even remotely close to being material for a hit single, but there was one song, called There You Go, that I thought might work. Bob James came up with a really fine arrangement, adding drums, and a string section. We used Eric Weissberg for that session, and it was a treat to hear him play country fiddle backed up by an entire string section. I often wondered what the notoriously cynical but expert violin players thought about this. I hope they realized that none of them could have done it!

I consider myself to be a good record producer, but to this day I have very little interest in the technical aspect of recording. For this particular album though, I gave considerable thought to the way that I thought that it should sound. In the late sixties, many records used large doses of echo. Sometimes it was achieved through the use of an electronic echo chamber, and at other times it surfaced because a project was recorded in a very large room with extremely high ceilings. I wanted the brightness to come from the actual sound of the artists, and from the settings that we used on the recording console. In my opinion engineer Russ Hamm did a great job of equalizing the instruments and voices, and so we avoided the dated echo-y sound of many of the albums of the time. At the end of the week of session Eric Weissberg said something to the effect of "every five years I get to play on something that I really like." That alone was enough to make me feel that Frummox was worth recording.

THE COVER AND THE SAD ODYSSEY OF THERE YOU GO

The album had a double fold, with photos of Steve in the arid Texas dry land and Dan in the mountains on separate sides. I wanted the album title, Here To There, carved on a wooden fence as though it was the name of a ranch. ABC had three or four staff artists. The most inventive one was Bill Shepherd, but he'd been doing our psychedelic album covers, and I didn't think that he'd be the appropriate choice for this album. I went to two other artists, none of whom seemed to grasp what I was talking about. Finally I turned to Bill, and he came up with exactly what I visualized.

We issued There You Go as a single. It started to chart in Austin, and an important FM radio station there send us a telegram, telling us that it was the most exciting song that they had heard in five years, and they loved the song so much that they were going to keep playing it whether their listeners liked it or not. Unfortunately a minister pressured them to take the song off the air. It used the phrase, "don't give a damn," and in the minister's eyes this was sacrilegious. The station caved, and took it off the air. Later Dan pointed out to me that Billy Joe Royal had a big radio hit at the same time called Cherry Hill Park, about a girl losing her virginity in the back of a car. It did not, however, use any curse words.

The Frummox album became a cult favorite in Texas, and people talk about it to this day, 45 years later. Lyle Lovett later recorded the three songs that comprise Steve's Texas Trilogy in 1998. Rolling Stone did a rave review of the album about a year after it came out, but by that time Probe Records was out of business. Years later I played on a Frummox II album, but by that time the duo had become essentially a nostalgia act. Steve continued to perform and record, and appeared as an actor in several movies. He died in 2014 in a freak hunting accident when his gun fell out of a padded bag and discharged. Dan went back to college and taught high school for many years. These days he still writes songs, but performs rarely, and is building some really nice guitars, using the name Isle of Sky.

MITCHELL BRAITHWAITE: THE FAIRY TALE THAT DIDN'T QUITE COME TRUE

At Command and Probe our company policy was that if someone came in off the street and wanted to see one of our A&R people, if we weren't busy we'd make that happen. One day the receptionist buzzed me and told me that there was a young man named Mitchell Braithwaite who wanted to see an A&R person. I was sitting there reading the music trade papers, so I invited him into the office. He told me that he had a demo, and was looking for a record deal.

Most of the people that I signed or even saw perform came my way because a manager, a publishing company person, or a friend had suggested that I listen to them. Since I had never seen Mitchell before, I prepared myself for disappointing his hopes. I put his three-song demo on the record player, and was instantly hooked. I didn't care for any of the songs, but Mitchell had a very light and soulful voice. He didn't sound exactly like Sam Cooke, the great gospel-pop singer, but he had a similar vocal quality. I told Mitchell that I liked his voice, and enquired what his situation was. It turned out that he was on his lunch hour. His regular job was pushing clothing carts in the garment business. For any of my readers who haven't been to New York, there is a garment district of wholesalers and manufacturers that work on the west side in the streets just below 42nd Street. If you've ever tried to go from east to west in New York on 38th, 39th or 40th Street in a cab, you've seen dozens of young men pushing carts of suits, dresses or other clothing. That's what Mitchell was doing to make a living.

He also told me that the songs were all written by various members of the band Jay and the Americans, and that they had produced the demo. I told him that I liked his singing, but didn't much care for the songs, and that I'd get back to him after talking to my boss Joe Carlton. Joe suggested that I call Jay and The Americans office, and see whether Mitchell was under contract to them. When I made the call there was the usual show business bluster at the other end. Oh yes, if I liked Mitchell they'd be happy to produce him with their songs. I had nothing to lose, so I told them that I liked Mitchell but not the songs, and I intended to produce him myself. As a concession, I told them that I would be happy to consider any other songs they would send my way. Either Mitchell was not under contract to them, or they had given up on his getting anywhere, because they quickly acceded to my demands. I did listen to a number of the songs from Jay's office, but I didn't like any of them.

Joe suggested that we record three songs, and try to find a hit single. Mitchell was living close enough to the edge that he didn't have a phone. I had to call a relative who lived across the hall, who brought him to the phone. I told Mitchell what we wanted to do, and he came in and signed a contract.

Mitchell didn't write songs at this point, and so I went on a quest to find three songs for him. I listened to something between three and four hundred songs from various publishers. I remember visiting one publisher and listening to about fifty irrelevant songs. A couple of my other contacts yielded better results. Irwin Schuster who worked for Columbia-Screen Gems brought me a song called Long Time Coming, by the well-known writers Cynthia Weill and Barry Mann, and another publisher brought a song called My Woman Need Me. That tune was co-written by a young little-known writer at the time named Mac Davis, with Sharon Sheeley, who had written hit songs for Ricky Nelson, Eddie Cochran and other artists. For the third song, I decided to use the original lyric of This Land Is Your Land, by Woody Guthrie. It had some hard-hitting social protest lyrics, while the more popular version of the song is simply an exposition of the beauties of the American landscape.

I called Bob James, and we rehearsed for about six weeks with Mitchell, once a week. Sometimes I would play guitar for Mitchell, and when Bob had time he would come in and play piano. We booked studio time, using a great rhythm section with Bucky Pizzarelli and Billy Butler on guitars, Jerry Jemmott on electric bass, and Jimmy Johnson on drums. There were also three or four horns, and three powerful female back-up singers.

THE SESSION

The session began late, because the studio door was locked and the previous session ran late. When we started to do the session Mitchell seemed confused. It hadn't occurred to me how little recording experience he had under his belt. He thought that Bob and I would be the entire orchestra accompanying him. I didn't play on the session at all, and Bob was conducting not playing piano.

Despite its fitful beginning, the session turned out great. Mitchell was amazed at how quickly the musicians picked up the arrangements, and he in turn proceeded to shock Bob and me by coming up with some improvised harmony parts on Long Time Coming and a falsetto part on My Woman Needs Me. The back-up singers rocked This Land more than I ever had anticipated they would.

THE RECORD AND THE RE-RELEASE

The last step before a record is pressed is mastering. In 1968 when we were recording a 45 RPM single record, we'd go into a special mastering studio and do any final adjustments to the recording. A physical master of the actual recording was then cut, and that was shipped to the manufacturer. Joe Carlton would always remind me to make sure that the bass and drums were powerfully represented on the records. I went into a mastering studio owned by Mercury Records. The engineer there was particularly good at getting strong bass and drum sounds. I decided against using This Land, because much as I loved it, it was extremely shrill, and I couldn't see it getting much radio play. I thought that My Woman Needs Me had come out best, so we mastered it with Long Time Coming as the B side, and I went on vacation to British Columbia. When I came back, I discovered that as occasionally happens, there was a technical flaw in the master, and it had been re-mastered without me so that it would fit into the September release schedule.

The bad news is that the re-mastering job was lame. The bass and drums were on the weak side, and so the company went with Long Time Coming as the A side. Had I been involved in the re-mastering, this would never have happened. Although the Mac Davis song was a ballad, it had a great groove to it, and I thought Mitchell's performance was superb. The Probe promotion man at the time was a rock enthusiast who didn't especially "get" rhythm and blues. The record never got off the ground. Mitchell returned to his Garment District job, and I felt that we had lost a great opportunity.

JIMMY SHAW AND THE FAIRY TALE ALMOST COMES TRUE

A few months went by and Joe Carlton hired a new promotion man who specialized in black music. Jimmy Shaw dressed in orange suits, and had a flamboyant and excitable personality. The first day he was at work he came into my office. He looked at me, dressed in a flannel shirt and corduroy pants, and I could see his mind working. He figured I was another rock hippie in the record world. He asked me to play him something I had done. On a hunch, I pulled out Mitch's record and played my favorite side, My Woman Needs Me. Jimmy went nuts. He said, "That's a stone hit, man, a stone hit." I explained the situation to him, and he raced into Joe's office and told him that we had a hit on our hands and we didn't know it. I begged Joe to let me re-master the record but he told me that Jimmy was hot on it now if we had to wait a month for more records, he'd probably move on to something else. We re-released the record with

My Woman Needs Me as the side to be promoted and Jimmy worked his magic. He called a number of disc jockeys in the south, like Chatty Hattie in Charlotte, North Carolina. Meanwhile word began to spread in the office. Len Korobkin, the lawyer in the adjoining office, had met Mitchell and loved the idea of a total unknown making a hit record. He set Mitchell up with a New York booking agent who was ready to spring into action as soon as the record started climbing. The record charted in several southern markets and seemed to be about to happen. I saw Mitchell a couple of times and explained to him what was going on.

One day after work, I got into the elevator and a youngish black man looked at me, and said, "you're good, you're really good." I had no idea who he was, or what he was talking about. Later I found out it was Van McCoy, who had the huge hit Do The Hustle. I figured that someone must have tipped him off about Mitchell's record, because I didn't think the other things I'd done would have rung his chimes.

In several weeks it was all over. The record didn't spread past the few initial markets where it had surfaced. Jimmy moved on to other projects and the booking agent had nothing to work with. It was over. I never saw Mitchell again, but Long Time Coming has been re-issued twice, most recently as a track on a 2004 compilation CD called Goldmine Soul Supply (GSCD158.)

By googling Mitchell while writing this page. I discovered that he was only sixteen when we recorded him. He stayed in the music business in a vocal group called Chocolate Syrup, and became a freelance record producer and promoter, and wrote or co-wrote songs.

AMERICAN AIRLINES

One of the most lucrative jingles that I ever played on was an American Airlines commercial. I did five days of American jingle sessions, all written by Mitch Leigh. During one of the sessions, Marty Grupp, Mitch's contractor, came over to the musicians, and said "that was the one." He meant that that particular jingle was the one that would be the centerpiece of the campaign.

A few weeks later I went down to the union to get my check. Although the session had only lasted an hour, my check was close to $300. I gasped out loud in amazement. Eric Weissberg's aunt was a virtuoso flute player who worked in the recording department of the union late in her career. She gently explained to me that if I read the statement on the check carefully, I would see that the commercial had been sliced into various parts and I was being paid for each one of those parts. I thanked her for explaining it, recovered my equanimity, and ultimately enjoyed a ride of over $2000 for a one hour recording session.

THE MANHATTAN GUITAR CLUB, TOOTS THIELEMANS AND DJANGO

Around this time I was invited to join the Manhattan Guitar Club. Most of the studios had guitar amplifiers that the club had bought, so that studio guitarists didn't need to carry amplifiers with them. Membership was $50 a year, and included a key to the amplifiers, and an annual steak dinner.

Diane and I attended the dinner, which was very pleasant. I talked to a number of the people that I worked with on a fairly regular basis, but never saw outside the recording studio. One of the most interesting studio musicians in New York was Jean "Toots" Thielmans. Toots came to the United States from his native Belgium. He played harmonica, as well as a kind of folk version of jazz guitar. He also figured out a way to play the harmonica and whistle in unison with it. This resulted in his writing an all-time jazz standard called Bluesette. Toots saw me picking up some extra steaks and putting them in a box, and inquired about what I was doing. I explained that we had a dog named Django, and the steaks were meant for him. Toots then told me that the one major regret in his life was that he had been offered a chance to play with the legendary guitarist Django Reinhardt in Europe. At the same time he had a chance to play with Charley "Bird" Parker in the United States. Django was Toot's idol, but he thought that if he didn't accept the opportunity to go to America, that chance might never come. He turned down the gig with Django and came to the United States, where he has lived ever since. Toots then proceeded to go table to table, gathering a feast for my dog and his idol.

RON LOCKHART

I met Ron Lockhart, a young aspiring composer and piano player when he was working as Mitch Leigh's personal assistant. Ron and I had a similar sense of humor, and started to hang out together. After Ron was fired for sleeping late and not returning Mitch's car in a timely fashion, he got a job at the Columbia Record Club. Columbia and RCA both had record clubs at the time, and Ron was generous in letting me help myself to any of the new releases. I spent many happy hours on the floor of his tiny office, liberating some of these LP's for my collection.

Towards the end of his tenure at the record club, Ron started to write jingles. Ron was a pretty ballsy guy who played decent piano and taught himself how to arrange as his career blossomed in the jingle business. I did quite a few sessions for him, some under the aegis of Herman Edel, who had previously worked at Music Makers. Unfortunately I committed a foolish blunder while playing electric guitar on an imitation Johnny Cash jingle. I tried to imitate Johnny's guitarist, Luther Perkins' technique of muffling the strings, and as can happen in the studio, the more I did it the worse I sounded. That was the end of my relationship with Herman. Later Ron started his own jingle company, and I served as his musical contractor, calling musicians for these gig. For one gig I called four violin players who were all contractors themselves. Since it was an answering service that called them, they never did figure out who had called them for the session. They all played well, and Ron and I shared a good laugh watching their confusion.

THE CREAM DOESN'T ALWAYS RISE TO THE TOP

There are many people in the music business who live by the cliché "the cream always rises to the top." This is supposed to mean that anyone with talent and drive will eventually succeed. I've always felt that is one of the most pernicious myths in the music business. Some of the people who succeed are genuinely musically talented, other successes come from exposure and promotion. Luck and timing also enter in to the process. Similarly there are many musicians who don't ever reach any level of financial success or popular acclaim. Some of them are brilliant musicians with personal problems, some never develop an understanding of the music business itself, and some are simply too musically advanced for the taste of the broad public. Some musicians achieve a minor level of success, and become embittered because they assume that they are climbing the ladder of success. That ladder has many broken rungs.

I have known people who made superb records at a time when their record company was in turmoil or even going out of business. There are also the one hit wonders, who hit the jackpot once and never luck out again.

Overall I see little correlation between major success and talent. There are wonderful artists who have never gotten anywhere, and there are others who were promoted into stardom without a trace of artistry.

MORE STUDIO TALES

Generally speaking, studio musicians are very malleable and eager to please However, there are exceptions. Once day I was playing on an album for the Serendipidity Singers. George Barnes, a famous jazz guitarist, was playing electric guitar. Producer Bob Bowers had rented a tenor banjo for George to play. When we got to that particular tune, Bob asked George whether he would play tenor banjo on it. George looked up seriously without a second's hesitation and said "no." I thought that this was hilarious. Almost all of George's generation played tenor banjo before they switched over to guitar and I was certain George could either have played it, or tuned the four strings like the top four strings of a guitar.

On another occasion Eric Weissberg and Marshall Brickman were hired to play in a studio group called the Banjo Barons. It was not unusual for producers to create mythical groups who only existed in the recording studio. The 50 Guitars of Tommy Garrett and the Living Guitars were other such "ghost" groups. The producer for the Banjo Barons was Teo Macero, a composer and record producer best known for his work with Miles Davis. Apparently Teo knew nothing about the differences between the five string banjo and its cousin the four string tenor banjo. He was unaware that they are tuned differently, have a different instrumental range, and the tenor is played with a flat pick while the five string is played by the right hand fingers.

The session was a disaster, because the parts were unplayable on the five string. Eric and Marshall became increasingly frustrated because they could not possibly play the music as Teo had written it. Marshall got up, packed his banjo back in the case, looked at Teo, and said "Learn how to write for the instrument."

My final story came to me via the brilliant and little recognized banjoist Bobby Thompson. Bobby was the staff banjoist on the Hee Haw TV show and played on hundreds of recording sessions in Nashville. One day he played on a session with an excellent guitarist named Reggie Young. The session took place not long after the wah wah pedal was invented. Reggie had been asked to bring as many pedals as he owned. He came to the session with a paper bag filled with a half dozen pedals. After the rhythm track for the tune was completed, the producer told everyone to take a break while Reggie overdubbed the wah wah pedal. Bobby went out to drink coffee. After about fifteen minutes he peeked in the studio glass door. He saw that Reggie had all of the pedals laid out in a row on the floor. Just at that moment Reggie tried out the last of the six pedals. The producer didn't like the sound, and suggested that they start all over again. Reggie got up and packed the pedals back in his paper bag. As he went out the door he said to the producer "You called me, I didn't call you."

BARRY PUT A SMILE IN IT

Barry Galbraith was an incredible guitarist, in a city full of excellent studio players like Don Arnone, Tony Mottola, Al Caiola, Alan Hanlon, and another half dozen musicians who could read or improvise with equal facility. Barry got the call when you wanted a versatile jazz player, or someone who could sight read difficult parts on classical guitar

Barry developed some sort of shoulder and neck injury, and although everyone else still thought that he was playing very well, he elected to drop out of session work and start teaching guitar. I became one of his students. I had heard many stories about Barry from other musicians. Someone told me that he used to get up early to practice classical guitar before going to the studio. This was because when producers learned that he was playing classical guitar, they called him in preference to some of the well-known classical players in New York, none of whom could sight read as well as Barry did. Barry had been on staff for the David Frost show, which was the best job in town because as a syndicated show it paid according to the number of markets that the show was broadcast in. Network shows paid a set rate. Barry's protégé Howie Collins told me that he had asked Barry why he quit, and Barry said something to the effect that he became bored with playing chink-a-chink rhythm guitar.

Another Galbraith-ism was that unlike any of the other studio musicians, except for the folkie crowd that I ran with, Barry wore flannel shirts, rather than a suit and tie. He obviously didn't need the work badly enough to let a dress code dominate his work life.

Our lessons would start with the two of us reading Bach's two part inventions. Barry would play the left hand piano parts written on the bass clef and transpose them an octave at sight. Most of the guitarists I knew could barely even read the bass clef. Then we would play jazz arrangements that Barry had written or transcribed. I brought him an album by the Brazilian guitarist Baden-Powell and Barry transcribed it and taught me the piece that I particularly liked.

To try to keep up with my lessons I basically put

down the banjo, and was practicing jazz guitar three hours a day. My sight reading improved greatly, but at this point in my career I wasn't working enough studio gigs to really take advantage of those skills.

One day I mentioned to Marty Grupp, Mitch Leigh's musical contractor, that I was taking lessons with Barry. Like everyone else, Marty knew and respected Barry, although he didn't use him on the Music Makers' sessions that I played on. He told me that Barry had been fired from the Kate Smith radio show for not smiling enough! Some years later an arranger-producer named Dave Pell did some recording sessions with Kate, and called Barry for the guitar chair. Dave was aware of Barry's history with the radio show. The band did a take of the first tune, and Dave got on the talk-back microphone and said "Barry, that was great, but could you put a smile in it?" Everyone in the band knew the story, so they all broke out in raucous laughter.

My two years of studying with Barry was probably the highlight of anything that I learned in my years living in New York.. A few years after I moved to Denver, I sent him a recording of me playing the banjo. He wrote me a nice note and said that he really liked the record, and that he had never before thought of the banjo as a melancholy instrument.

SAM BROWN

Besides Barry, my other favorite studio guitarist was Sam Brown. Sam was an excellent classical guitarist who had studied with a well-known teacher in Detroit named Joe Fava. Sam's forte was finger style jazz, where he integrated classical and jazz guitar techniques.

Some people lead lives that never go as smoothly as they might have hoped. Sam enlisted in the Rangers, an elite unit of specially trained soldiers and served during the Korean War. When he returned he drove from his home town of Detroit to Baltimore. While he was eating at a restaurant, someone broke into his car and stole everything that he owned.

Sam drifted up to New York, where he was hired as Miriam Makeba's guitarist. For three years he traveled all over the world with her. At the time Makeba was a protégé of Harry Belafonte. Harry was a big star and wherever he traveled, Miriam was booked as well.

One day Sam was jamming in the dressing room with Harry's percussionist, who Sam described as a wonderful player but someone with little formal training. Harry's guitarist, who went on to become one of the busiest studio musicians in New York walked in, and joined them. Somehow when he joined in, the music died a slow death. The percussionist looked at this musician, and said, "man you are the most unmusical person I've ever seen." A bit later Sam walked in the room and found the guitarist recreating the scene. With his perfect, music school graduate ear he was re-creating Sam's parts, and the percussionist's parts as well. He had a thoroughly puzzled look on his face, as though he was trying to figure out what he had done wrong. I have always loved this story, because it shows the limitations of music training, as opposed to actually creating music. The two aren't necessarily contradictory, but the point is that they can be.

I periodically ran into Sam at various recording sessions. It was always a pleasure to hear him play. However, he was far from an ideal studio musician. Sam cared too much about what he was playing, and when a producer wanted him to simplify a part, he would shut down. He always wanted to do his best, and sometimes that wasn't what a producer required. In particular, Sam was badly suited to play on jingles, where musicality was not usually the prime motivation for executing the music. Sam produced and arranged a beautiful children's record with Carly Simon and her sister Lucy, called The Lobster Quadrille. He put together a small, almost chamber music style combo. He wanted some folk banjo and guitar parts and he was friendly with both Eric Weissberg and me, so he split the sessions between us. It remains in print, forty years later.

I hired Sam to play on an album of poetry and music by my friend Tom Glazer. I was playing twelve string guitar, and Sam was playing his classical guitar. When we recorded Dylan Thomas' poem Do Not Go Gentle Unto That Good Night, the overtones between the two guitars sounded like a third instrument. He was truly a soulful and remarkable musician.

Sam made quite a few jazz recordings, including some with Keith Jarrett, Gary Burton, and Charley Haden's Liberation Music Orchestra. There was a really dark side to Sam, that was visible to those of us who noticed these things. One day he and I completed a jingle session and two cops arrested him for parking tickets. Helplessly I asked him if there was anything I could do to help him. He said there wasn't. Singer Jim Campbell told me that Sam had twin daughters, one of whom had died at an early age. Sam was so poor at the time, that she was buried in a pauper's grave. Jim told me that Sam had confided in him that his inability to provide her with a decent burial haunted him.

After I moved to Colorado in 1972, I heard rumors that Sam was taking various drugs, and was going off the deep end. He was playing with the Monday night Thad Jones-Mel Lewis band at the Village Vanguard. Someone told me that instead of leaving the bandstand after the set ended he stayed up there and was mumbling incoherent things about Jesus.

In 1977 I was living in Colorado, and playing with a lounge band called The Main Event. Jim Campbell called me just before I had to go to work. He told me that Sam had committed suicide. Playing mediocre music after hearing that news made for a very difficult evening. I could barely play the endless electric guitar solos that the job required.

NIELA MILLER: DON'T TRUST THE ONE YOU'RE WITH

Niela Miller was one of a number of musicians that I had known in New York in pre-Journeymen days. She was writing songs early in the game. I must have met her around 1957. One of the songs that she often sang was Baby Please Don't Go To Town. When The Leaves and Jimi Hendrix recorded the melody under the title Hey Joe, I assumed that her songwriting efforts were really paying off.

I ran into Niela one day when I was working at ABC in 1969. I asked her how she was doing, and we talked a bit about the song. It turned out that her one-time boyfriend Billy Roberts, a twelve string guitar player who I also knew from my Village Days, had re-written the lyric and copyrighted the song. In turn Dino Valente also claimed the copyright and apparently Billy cut him on some of the royalties. Billy was getting most of the money for the song, with Dino getting some percentage of it. I asked Niela if she had tried to sue Billy. Since Niela had another career as a social worker and looked at songwriting as a hobby rather than a profession, she hadn't seriously considered this. I suggested that she come up to my office, and that we could ask ABC lawyer Len Korobkin whether he thought she had a good legal claim. Len opined that she had waited too long to take action, and that she probably wouldn't win such a suit.

If you enjoy reading about copyright, and have an interest in following the kind of muddle-headed comments that many internet habitués are apt to proffer, google your heart out on Hey Joe. Billy ripped the chord progression, which cannot be copyrighted, but he also basically stole the melody, and even adapted some of the words. The moral of the story if you're a cynic is, to re-position Stephen Stills, don't trust the one you're with.

Niela would have enjoyed receiving some money and credit, but she has had a long-term career in various aspects of social work. By the way, under the current copyright law (1976) each violation of a copyrighted song is subject to fines of up to $150,000 per song. If you do not copyright the song, you don't receive the damages, but you can recover the credit and the royalties.

THE END OF COMMAND AND PROBE: NOT WITH A BANG BUT WITH A WHIMPER

1969 was my second year at Command and Probe. By this time I had produced or co-produced the

Glenn Miller band, Dick Hyman's Concerto Electro, Frummox, Fat City, the Mystic Number National Bank, and singles by Mitchell Braithwaite, Doc Severinsen and actress Estelle Parsons. The way that ABC Records was structured was that the various companies each had a president, and they all reported to Larry Newton, the CEO of all the record companies. ABC started going into film, and Larry decided that he would leave the record division and head up the film operation.

Inevitably there was a power struggle for who would succeed him. Although Joe Carlton had plenty of executive experience, the most successful of the companies was Dunhill. Under Jay Lasker's rule, they had a number of hit acts. The Mamas and Papas were no longer really functioning, but they had Three Dog Night and Steppenwolf. Steve Barri was the hottest producer in the various companies, and he was tied to Lasker. Jay won the power struggle, and decided that the entire company would be housed in California. Every single person at Command and Probe was fired. Jay took pity on Charley Trepel, our national sales manager. He had worked there for twenty four and a half years, and Jay let him work out the remaining six months so that he could get his pension.

The company gave us a couple of weeks notice. We could phone anyone anywhere in search of a new job, and thankfully they paid the postage that I needed to send the huge number of records that I had accumulated to my home. One of my jobs for the company was to listen to foreign releases that might do well in the United States. I recommended that a song called The Witch by a German group called The Rattles be acquired for American release. It came out just as our company was disappearing. The Witch started to climb the Billboard charts, without any significant promotion from ABC. It got up to about number 40 in the United States but it was a worldwide hit. I was very gratified at this because it was a hard rock-electronic record, something that I would never have produced myself. It made me feel that I did indeed have some understanding of the pop music market.

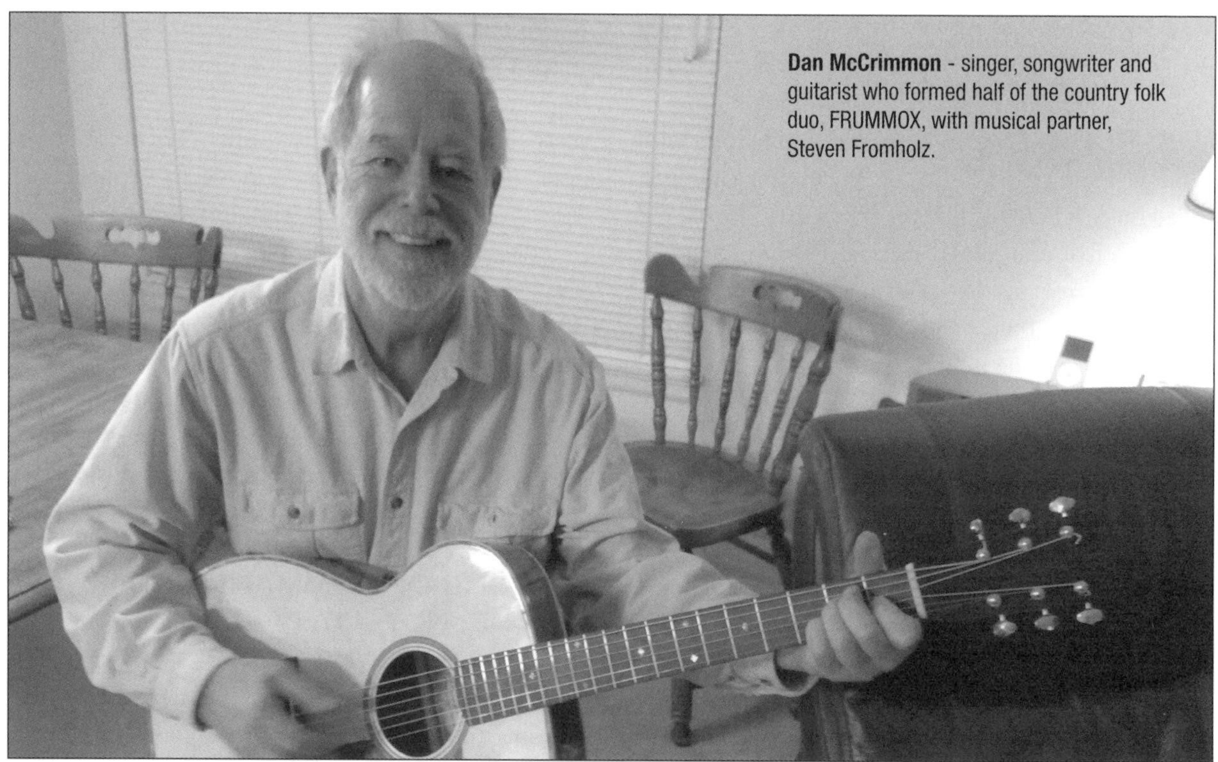

Dan McCrimmon - singer, songwriter and guitarist who formed half of the country folk duo, FRUMMOX, with musical partner, Steven Fromholz.

Part 1 • Chapter 11

FATHER AND SON AND THE URGE FOR GOING

In 1969, towards the end of my gig at Command and Probe, my father died. He had had a heart condition for eleven years, but continued to work far too hard. His identity was closely tied to his job as a hospital superintendent, and he never could find a way to lighten his work load.

During my years producing records, I had been working long hours, between my commitments to the record company and my freelance playing gigs. We lived an hour's bus ride from New York, and I went to work every day. Diane and I had some serious discussions about our lives, and we decided that we were ready to have children. Paul Jeremy Weissman was born in 1970, and our lives changed along with him.

I spent the next two years doing what studio work I could find, and was involved in several production projects that I was not able to sell. In 1970 my friend Ron Lockhart had made a connection with Muzak. He was writing some new tunes for them and thought that they might be interested in some new neo-folk tunes. Because Muzak played music over a long period of time, the resulting royalties from performing rights could have been considerable. At some point while I was thinking about the possible Muzak deal, I was also coming to the conclusion that a large segment of the record business was moving to Los Angeles. The majority of my work had come down to playing on commercials. I was in my mid-thirties and I couldn't imagine that I wanted to spend the rest of my life playing on toothpaste commercials. My original motivation for being in The Journeymen was to save enough money to go to music school, and to move to Colorado. My friend Harry Tuft had opened up the Denver Folklore Center in 1962. While vacationing in Denver in the summer of 1970 I picked up a flyer at his store from a school called the University of Colorado at Denver. The circular described a new program in music business education. I started to think seriously about enrolling.

THE NEON LIGHTS ALMOST ON BROADWAY

I was not getting much studio work in 1971 when arranger-composer Elliot Lawrence called and asked if I'd like to play in a Broadway-bound show called Prettybelle. Elliot was the music director of the show and I had played some sessions for him. He told me that it entailed going to Boston for a six week tryout, and then after a short interval the show would open on Broadway. The rhythm section in Boston would all be New York players and they would be augmented by local horn players. He invited me to a New York rehearsal of the show. I was pleasantly surprised to find that Howie Collins would be the other guitarist. I was hired to play banjo, with guitar on a few tunes. Howie and I went to the rehearsal and my reaction was that I thought the show was the worst thing that I had ever seen, but I realized that I knew very little about Broadway shows. At the time there was a hierarchy of musicians in New York. The bottom rung was people who worked in small clubs, just above that was the freelance club date market that consisted of gigs for weddings, bar mitzvahs and parties, then there were the theater musicians, and at the top were the musicians playing record dates, film scores and jingles. Most of the top level studio musicians scorned theater gigs. There were several reasons for this. First of all, the money wasn't as good. The basic Broadway scale at the time was four or five hundred dollars a week. Second of all, when you accepted a show it might well close in a day or a week, and then you would have to start over and look for another show. There was also the boredom quotient. If the show became successful and ran for five or ten years, most musicians would go absolutely nuts from the boredom of playing the same thing, night after night, with two additional matinees a week. On the other hand, there was actually money deducted for vacations, and if the show ran for a while there was also free health insurance.

In the case of Prettybelle the pay worked well for me, because I was doubling on banjo and guitar, I was playing a huge bass drum on one number, and appeared on stage in costume for some of the show. Each one of those things added percentages to my paycheck. I accepted the job, which included a stipend for a hotel, and went to Boston.

Prettybelle was written by Bob Merrill and Jule Styne, both of whom had quite a few hit shows under their belts. The director was Gower Champion, who had directed Bye Bye Birdie, and had a long track record as a dancer, choreographer and actor. The lead part in the show was played by Angela Lansbury. The more I looked at these credits, the less I trusted my own opinion of the show.

The show turned out to be quite lucrative for the New York musicians, because we were all on stage in costume, and it seemed that there were endless paid rehearsals. I had no concept of the logistics of Broadway shows. If there are, say, fifteen songs in a show, it is quite likely that the composer and lyricist end up writing twenty five or even more songs. When a song doesn't work in a show the director and the songwriters immediately come up with another song. An arranger writes the band parts, a copyist stays up all night, and the next day the band rehearses with the actors and actresses and that night the song goes in the show. Once I experienced this process, in later years I would understand why rock stars would have trouble writing successful Broadway shows. It is hard for me to imagine people like Bono or Sting working that intensively on songs, and adjusting to the fact that a director tells them that a song "isn't working." This doesn't mean the song is a bad song, simply that the director has deemed it isn't meeting the requirements of what is necessary to advance the action of the play.

The show opened to mixed reviews in Boston. Apparently there were conflicts between the producer and the director, and supposedly Angela Lansbury didn't feel the show was working out. For my part, I was having a good time eating in the restaurants on Newbury Street. There was one tune where I played guitar that I never ever played quite correctly. It was humiliating to me, but the fact was that although I could read music reasonably well, I didn't do well with the swing syncopations that were second nature to horn players, and for that matter to Howie Collins. On the other hand, I actually was getting to create some interesting banjo parts. It was also fun to play with Howie, who is an excellent guitarist.

The last two weeks of the run Diane and my son Paul, who was about a year old, came up for a short stay. Soon after that, the musicians and cast were informed that the show as closing in Boston, and we weren't going to make it to Broadway. Some ten years later a cast album of the show was recorded. This was long after I left New York so I wasn't involved in the recording, which was re-issued on CD in 1993.

JESSE JAMES HELPED ME BUY THIS CAR

It seemed as though 1971 was going to be the year of theater in my life. I got a call from Jim Keach, who is an actor and younger brother of the better-known Stacy Keach. For several years he had been working on a show about Frank and Jesse James and someone had suggested to him that I might be a useful addition to the team. There were already two other musicians who had written some tunes for the show, but I assumed that he thought I could add more of a folk element. A group of actors, writers, and the two other composers and the cast were all living together in New Hope, Pennsylvania, and were hoping the show could open at the prestigious Bucks County Playhouse in that town. Diane and I were not getting along at this juncture of our marriage, and occasionally I would stay over in New Hope.

Over the years the Bucks County Playhouse had often been used as a stepping stone for Broadway-bound shows, although that cachet has diminished. Jim's scheme was to mount a show that would so impress his brother, that he would join the cast. Jim wanted to play Jesse James, and he felt that Stacy could be influenced to play his older brother Frank.

Over a period of several months I wrote a half dozen songs for the show and played in the pit band with composer John Guth and several other musicians. The show played at the Bucks County Playhouse, and Jim indeed was able to persuade Stacy that they could re-write the show, add some new songs, and have a shot at opening the show on Broadway.

The show completed its run and I moved to Colorado in the summer of 1972, expecting that nothing further was ever going to happen. I got a call from Jim, some months after I moved to Colorado. Stacy was now on board, and they wanted me to come to New York and work on re-writing the show. They had arranged a production at the Bouwerie Lane Theater, off-off Broadway, and Stacy's then girlfriend, Judy Collins, had offered her summer home in Connecticut as a rehearsal space. I was going to music school at the time, but everything was going to happen during the summertime, so it worked for me. I contacted my friend Ron Lockhart, and he agreed that Diane, Paul and I could stay at his house on Long Island, and I enlisted him as the musical director of the show. It was never clear to me whether the other two composers weren't invited, or turned down the opportunity. I figured that while I was in town I would re-up with Radio Registry, the musician's answering service, and see if I could get some studio work while I was in town. That turned out to be a smart move, because I was able to do two or three sessions a week while I was in town. I also played in the pit band. Ron did a bunch of new arrangements, I wrote five or six new songs, and we were off to the races.

The cast was a good one. There were even some New York standbys like Tom Clancy, the oldest of the Irish folksingers the Clancy Brothers. The time in Connecticut was incredibly productive, and I even had the odd experience of actually writing one song in my dreams. I had heard of such things, but had never had that experience.

The show opened, and ran for a few weeks, and then we went back to Colorado. At one point the director of the prestigious Mark Taper Theater in Los Angeles supposedly told Stacy that he could either bring the show there, or he could play Hamlet. Not too surprisingly, Stacy opted for Hamlet.

I wrote it all off as one of those colorful but basically useless musical experiences that are common in the music business. In 1980, composer Christopher Allport called. He asked me if I had read that week's Newsweek. I told him that I didn't read that magazine. He suggested that I go buy it, and call him back.

I got the magazine, and learned that the Keach brothers were negotiating to turn their story about the James Brothers into either a TV series or a movie. As it happened, the Keach Brothers' lawyers had made the authors of the play and the three composers sign a contract saying that none of us could use any of the show in any way without everyone's permission. Christopher knew a lawyer who suggested that we might have a good legal case to share in the income from the new production. The play evolved into the movie The Long Riders. None of us were asked to participate, and the music was written by Ry Cooder, who probably had no knowledge of the original show.

The initial response of the Keach Brothers and the studio was that they would see us in court. A few months later they offered us a grand total of $3500 to go away. I called my brother-in law, cinematographer Caleb Deschanel, who was the only person I knew who worked in movies. When I told him what the offer was, he had a good laugh at the absurdity of the amount that the studio wanted to pay us. He explained to me that every movie has some sort of contingency fund that was used to pay off even the most frivolous claims that weren't worth fighting in a law suit.

Over time there were four offers. The lawyer advised us to accept the last one. He told us that he thought that we would win the case, but that it would take about four years to reach the California courts, and then there would probably be an appeal. He concluded that it wasn't worth the trouble or delay to pursue the case. Part of the final settlement was that I can't disclose what we received. I did consider buying a vanity license plate for my car saying something to the effect that Jesse James helped to buy this car.

In 1972, Diane's brother Caleb became engaged to be married. She and I had briefly separated, but got back together at Caleb's wedding in Los Angeles. I told her that I planned to move to Denver, and she agreed to join me there.

LEAVING BLUES

My last New York other session was a Pepsi commercial produced and written by Paul Evans. I was told to bring my five string banjo. In fact the session was in a Dixieland jazz vein. I took a flat pick out of my pocket, and played the banjo as though it was a four string tenor banjo. The orchestra was a twenty piece band, and it all seemed to work. My point here is that it seemed as though none of my professional colleagues had much of a clue as to what I really played. I was either playing bluegrass banjo, faking 1920's style Dixieland, or playing rhythm guitar. I wanted to go somewhere where I could play my own music for people who wanted to listen to it. I had received a thorough education in faking many musical styles, and learned how to produce music that I didn't necessarily like or understand at short notice and high dollar pressure. This was all very well, but I realized that basically it had absolutely nothing to do with anything that I cared about. To stay in New York would have been an inevitable path to a slow musical death. I felt that I was becoming musically stale and personally bitter and cynical. It was time to move on.

Scott McKenzie, my former bandmate, in the 1970s.

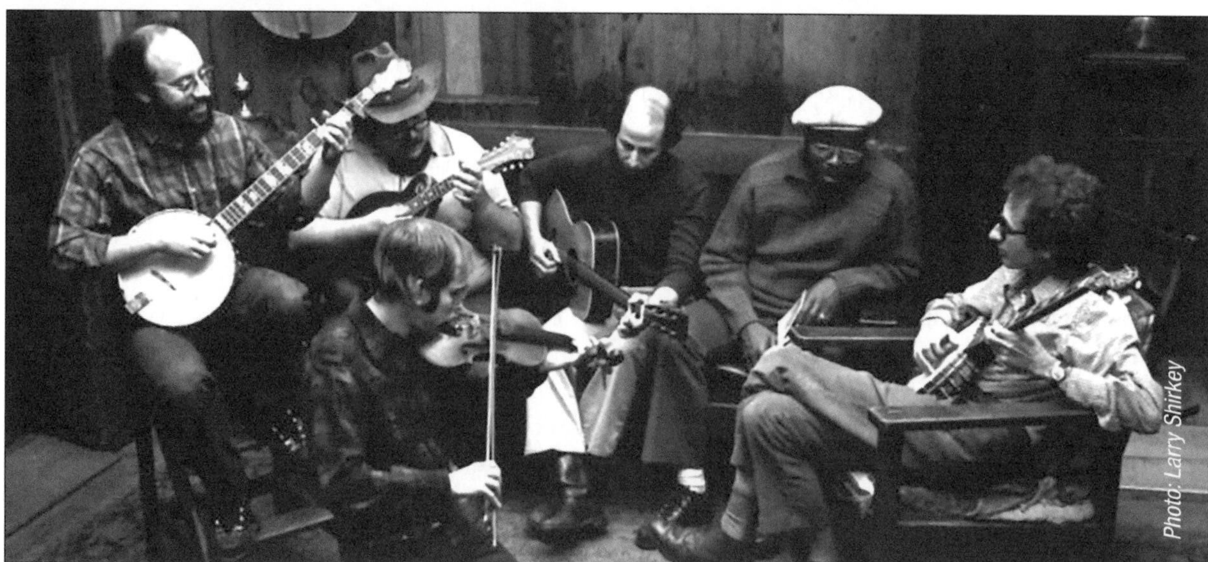

Photo: Larry Shirkey

Jamming at the Denver Folklore Center, 1975: Steve Weincrot - Banjo, David Ferretta - Mandolin, Larry Sandberg - Fiddle, Harry Tuft - Guitar, Wesley Westbrooks (listening), Dick Weissman - Banjo.

Part 2 • Chapter 12

THE COLORADO YEARS 1972-1983

I was in a manic state of mind during the two and a half days that I drove from New Jersey to Denver. I knew what I was giving up, in terms of potential opportunities in the music industry, but I focused on improving myself as a person and as a musician. I enrolled as a special student in the summer music program at the University of Colorado at Denver, and took a class in jazz history, and a ridiculously easy one called music fundamentals. I realized I wasn't going to learn anything new in music fundamentals, but I decided that by starting from the very beginning I could build a good foundation in music

A couple of days after I arrived in Denver, I had the car radio on while driving to school. I heard Mary Travers of Peter, Paul & Mary singing the new commercial for the state of Colorado. It was Bill Danoff and Taffy Nivert's song about me, I Guess He'd Rather Be In Colorado. It was a strange feeling to hear a song about me used as a commercial at the same time that I was the living example of what the song described.

HARRY TUFT AND THE FOLKLORE CENTER

I knew that in order to make a living in music in Colorado I would have to go back to teaching banjo and guitar and that I would need to play live music. There was a recording scene in Denver, but it was minute compared to what I had experienced in New York. Harry Tuft had opened the Denver Folklore Center in 1962. Originally a single store on a short block east of the downtown area, it had gradually expanded to include a concert hall, a record shop, the original music store, and a store that sold used clothes and beads called The Funk Shop. I started teaching banjo and guitar at the store, working about twenty hours a week, while going to college. At the end of the summer Diane arrived, and she briefly worked at the school as a secretary, managing lessons. Then, I enrolled in the music program as a full-time student.

UCD

I attended UCD from 1972 until 1974. The entire college was then housed in a single building in downtown Denver. The music program started in 1970, and was still quite small during the years I studied there. All of the classes were in the basement of the building, and actual degrees were granted by the mother campus in Boulder.

To enroll I had to get transcripts of all my undergraduate work. This was a bit complicated, because in addition to attending Goddard, I had gone to the New School and the University of New Mexico. I arranged all of this, and I was soon introduced to collegiate bureaucracy. I got a call from the admissions office which said that they had lost my transcripts. I suggested that since they had lost them, perhaps they could arrange to get new copies. This half-serious suggestion was greeted by silence, followed by a response something like "that's an interesting idea, but we won't do that." I sent for new transcripts and was admitted.

Because the school was so small, most procedures were more informal than the way colleges usually function. I was able to persuade the admissions people that I could study for a music degree without taking any other courses. My argument was that I already had a BA, and it didn't make any sense for me to be studying freshman English or biology. They accepted my argument, which is something I can't imagine would happen today, forty+ years later.

I studied at UCD for two years, and took 38 credits. At the time a BA in music was supposed to include 45 hours in music, but "extraordinary students" could graduate with 35 credits. I applied to graduate in the spring of 1974. My application was sent to Boulder to be processed. At the time, Boulder's music department had a secretary who had worked there for 25 years. She was a notorious tyrant, who ruled the department with an iron hand. She added up my hours incorrectly, and told Dr. David Baskerville, the head of the UCD Music Department that I had insufficient hours to graduate. Dr. Baskerville called me out of a class to discuss the situation with me. Since it was my life and my credits, I went over the hours with him and sure enough my addition was correct. I suggested that he call the secretary and have her rubber stamp my graduation. Dr. Baskerville turned red in the face and said, no, he would simply send her a new form. Like the entire music department in Boulder, he was terrified by this tyrant.

I was one of two people in the first graduating class at UCD, so it must have been obvious to this woman that she was reading the same application again. Nothing was said, however. As a result of these procedures, I graduated in the summer of 1974 instead of the spring. I went to Boulder to get my degree, and sure enough it was there. Without thinking about it, I blurted out, "this is the first time the university has ever gotten my paper work correct." There were about twenty students there, and they proceeded to give me the equivalent of a standing ovation. Obviously I wasn't the only one to have had some run-ins with the bureaucracy.

MOVIE MUSIC

I took classes in harmony, sight singing, counterpoint, took some guitar lessons, and played in the student jazz band. In my last year, I became especially friendly with two other students, Jim Cassell and Dave Menapace. The three of us lobbied the school to create a special seminar in composition. The school agreed, and two professors team taught it, all day Friday. The class met for about seven hours. In one class a professor named Paris Rutherford taught us how to write music for motion pictures and television. This was by far my most valuable class at UCD, and I quickly was able to make good use of it.

LEWIS FUTTERMAN, IMPROVISATION AND CRIPPLE CREEK

The jazz band at UCD consisted of students and a half dozen high school band teachers, who were taking the class for re-certification or graduate credit. Many of the teachers also wrote arrangements for the band, and I also decided to take advantage of this opportunity. I wrote a fairly elaborate arrangement of the old square dance tune Cripple Creek for fifteen pieces. I also included two banjo parts, one of which I would play, and the other one was played by Jim Cassell. My arrangement was only thinly based on the tune, and I included a trombone solo as well as sections of the piece in 5/4 time.

There was a trombone player in the band named Lewis Futterman, who was a young bebop enthusiast from Los Angeles. I gave him the music for his part, and told him that I wanted him to listen to what the banjos were doing, and under no circumstances to play a bebop solo. He nodded, and proceeded to play a bebop solo. I had been hoping that the professor, Roy Pritts would conduct the piece, since I was involved in playing one of the banjo parts. He was busy sorting the music for an arrangement that he had done from West Side Story, and told me that I should conduct. I found this really annoying, because I could hardly conduct while playing.

I tried to make the best of the situation, and through a half dozen performances, Lewis continued to play variations on his bebop solo. I finally gave up on him. Once again I had made some mistaken assumptions about the process of improvisation, just as I had done in New York with the fiddle player on the cigarette commercial. What I hadn't grasped this time was the concept that someone can be a good improviser in a specific style, but not be able to do so in musical genres that are unfamiliar to them.

I thought about this for many years, and in 2009 co-authored a series of music folios called Non-Jazz Improvisation, intended for people with Lewis' problem. I guess I should thank him for helping me to develop this concept.

COLORADO WOMEN'S COLLEGE

While I was attending UCD, Tom McCluskey, the head of the music department at Colorado Women's College (CWC) started to search the Denver area for someone to teach classes about the music business. Harry Tuft recommended me, and by my second year of music school I was teaching a class about the music business at the college. Tom was a percussionist and pianist, who was also the music critic for the Rocky Mountain News. The News was then one of two daily newspapers in Denver.

I had never considered teaching at a college, and felt a little strange teaching about music while attending music school, but I realized that my varied experiences in the music industry qualified me for the job. The music business at that time, and even today, is a strongly sexist industry, so the idea of training women to be in the industry was an interesting prospect.

After I graduated from UCD I started adding classes at CWC, and was hired as a half-time professor by 1979. My salary was the princely wage of $5000 for teaching three classes a year. Because I had never taught college and didn't even have a master's degree I didn't argue.

BOULDER

We decided to sell our house and move to Boulder, twenty five miles north of Denver. At the time our children were about three and seven, and we knew that the schools there were better. At that time the air in Denver was extremely polluted, and the air in Boulder was considerably better. Some unpleasant issues with our immediate neighbors reinforced our desire to leave Denver.

COLLEGES CAN GO OUT OF BUSINESS

CWC was in an odd financial position. A very successful local architect named Temple Buell had pledged to give his fortune to the school, and the school re-named itself as Temple Buell College in 1967. The terms of the gift were that the school would only receive the money after he died. Because the gift got so much publicity, other donations to the school plummeted. In 1973 the college took its name back, in an attempt to replenish its finances. The chair of the board of directors was an oil executive named Jerry Lewis, and he assured the college that it would remain financially viable. Lewis was the head of an oil company, but unfortunately the oil boom in Denver was turning south. He negotiated with a Christian organization called Young Life in an attempt to acquire the school. That didn't make too many of the free-wheeling somewhat progressive faculty happy, and the efforts of a fairly new president named Sherry Manning didn't pan out either. The faculty affiliated with the American Association of University Professors, a rather gentlemanly neo-union, but about all they could do was to place the college on an unfair list. In Spring, 1982 the school fired ¾ of its faculty, including me. It held on for a year, with department heads teaching all classes. In the summer of 1982 the game was over, and the school went out of business. The property was sold to the University of Denver, and all faculty left. I was out of a job, but I had applied for a grant from the National Endowment of Humanities, and received a one year fellowship that began in 1983. Temple Buell, by the way, lived until 1990. He was then ninety five years old.

For the only time in my life I filed for unemployment compensation, and received it for about three months. I explained to the employment counselor that I had a fellowship coming, and that I really couldn't accept another teaching job. He didn't say much, but told me that each week I needed to continue to fill out the paperwork, which said that I was applying for jobs. I actually did apply for a couple of positions, but essentially fabricated the rest of my job seeking. I didn't enjoy that, but I was indeed out of work, and needed the income to live on during this brief transition.

TOM MCCLUSKEY

Tom McCluskey had been kept on for the balance of the school year, as were all the department heads. After training as a digital tape editor in Salt Lake City, he moved to New York, and worked as a digital tape editor for RCA Victor Records. The studios at RCA were in midtown Manhattan, and Tom actually lived in the studio for some six years. He edited boxed sets of albums by Horowitz and Heifetz, and usually worked all night. He bought a futon, gave himself sponge baths, and took showers at his friends' apartments. Tom escaped detection easily, except for one incident where his boss wandered in just as he was getting up. He quickly folded the futon and hid it. Sometime after 2000 he moved to Durango, Colorado, where he does occasional gigs at piano bars and has some involvement with the local college.

GIGGING, MULTIPLE CAREERS AND THE MAIN EVENT

I knew that when I moved to Colorado I was not going to be able to make a living pursuing a single path, as I had done in New York. My work then had been built entirely around the world of recording. As soon as I got to Colorado I joined the Denver local of the Musicians Union, and was able to get gigs through them and from my connections to the folk community through Harry Tuft and the Denver Folklore Center.

In the mid-70's I got a call from singer Frank Richardson. He had a band called The Main Event. It was designed to play the many convention gigs that take place in the Denver area. I played electric guitar and banjo with the group, which included Frank on vocals and rhythm guitar, Gordie Meldrum on vocals, bass and occasionally trombone, and two female singers. After some false starts two women, Wanda Hine and Pam Van Ryan became fixtures with the group. The repertoire was country and rock hits of the day.

I played ALL the solos, except that Gordie usually did one trombone feature. In all the time that I was in the group, which was about five years I never actually learned any of their rock or country songs. I made up the solos on demand, and just followed the bass and rhythm guitar. The other members of the group could never understand why I didn't want to play the electric guitar parts from recordings, and I didn't bother to explain to them that I didn't want to waste my time learning this stuff, when it was a lot more enjoyable to make it up as I went along.

None of the other members of the group were full-time musicians. Frank worked for the state of Colorado, and then opened an early and successful computer business, Gordie sold trucks, and the two women had various office jobs and had spouses with full-time jobs. Gordie was the front man for the group, and he was entertaining. He grew up in Buffalo, Wyoming, and had sold trucks in Cheyenne until one day when the wind came up and blew all the receipts on the hood of his car away he decided to move to Denver. The music in the group was predicable, and generally boring to me, but convention jobs paid well as Denver music jobs went. I would usually get about $100 for each show, and we were playing three or four times a month. We played all along the front range of the Rocky Mountains, and even occasionally went to Cheyenne and Casper.

DOUBLE CONTRACTS

The agent for the group was a woman named Mary Mitchell. Mary was a bit of a devious hustler, and would often attend our shows. Mary was British, and had certain rules that her acts needed to observe if they wanted to play on her team. We were instructed never to eat any food at the events that we played, unless the sponsor of the event specifically invited us to do so. My favorite example of how Mary utilized this policy came in a gig that we did in Wichita, Kansas. It was a snowy day, our plane was late, and there was no food on the plane. (In those days planes customarily served snacks or even actual meals.) When we got to the gig Mary raced into the kitchen where we were dressing. Flashing a big smile she handed each one of us a tiny breakfast roll!

One night we were playing a convention gig for a group of cardiologists at a Denver hotel. The head of the events committee went up to Frank at the end of the gig, and asked if he could simply give him our check, rather than having to mail it from his home in Kansas. The check was in an unsealed envelope so Frank took a look at the check. It turned out that Mary was taking anoutrageous 50% commission for booking the job. Mary was a union franchised agent, and the union had a limit of 20% commission on one night gigs. I don't know whether Frank ever discussed this with Mary, but we were all horrified. It seems that Mary was filing a different contract with the union than the one she had with her client. Another member of the Denver union tried to bring Mary up on charges with the national union for this practice. He was not successful in this attempt. My guess is that he couldn't get any clients to testify about this situation. I would imagine that the attitudes of the clients were that they paid X dollars to get a band, they got the band and were satisfied, and whatever problems the band had with the agent were not something they wanted to be involved in solving.

Later I did some gigs for another agent in Denver who would always start the conversation with "how much would you charge for a three piece band to play for an hour at a wedding?" It was obvious to me that she jacked up the price to the client, so I would try to counter by asking what sort of budget the client had for the event.

THE END OF THE MAIN EVENT

I always looked at the gigs with the Main Event as a paycheck, not a musical endeavor. Early in the game it became clear to me that this was not a co-op venture. Frank appeared to be paying people different amounts for the same work. There was Frank, who was taking additional money for being the leader. I don't know what he was paying Gordie, but it was probably close to what he himself was getting. I was being paid $100, and the women something like $75 each. One night I was particularly irritated at Frank about something or other, and I told the women about this wage differential. They became very upset, and complained to Frank, and possibly to Mary Mitchell. From that point on, things went downhill. The gigs seemed to evaporate, and essentially I quit without formally resigning.

THE BROTHERS JOHNSON

Another one of my gigs was with an R&B-pop group called The Brothers Johnson. Although I hadn't heard their recording, I knew that it was arranged and produced by Quincy Jones. I really shouldn't have accepted this call, because I didn't have a suitable guitar or amplifier for rhythm and blues music. Nor, truthfully, did I have the right feel for the music. When I started to play, I immediately realized the error of my ways. I was fired from the gig, the only time this has ever happened to me, although there I played some New York recording sessions where I was clearly the wrong choice for the job. Later I discovered that the rest of the band was fired during the engagement.

Even though I generally believe in accepting musical challenges, this experience taught me that sometimes it is best to avoid situations that require you to do things that you really are not equipped to pursue.

AFTUH WE EAT

My friend Dan Fox often did casual gigs in the New York area. In New York and Los Angeles many of these gigs are quite lucrative, paying as much as $250-$300 for playing weddings, parties, bar mitzvahs or similar events. Dan had one of these wedding gigs in a New York suburb. The clarinet player, who I will call Edgar, was a well-known musician who specialized in avant-garde jazz, but like many musicians worked other gigs to feed himself. The band played for about ten minutes when the groom came over and invited them to share in the wedding feast. The musicians went to the table and chowed down. They all finished fairly quickly except Edgar, who went back for seconds and thirds. By the time he was working on his third portion, about a half hour had gone by. The groom walked back to the musicians and gracefully asked if they could possibly resume playing music for the event. Edgar looked up at the groom frowning and said in his best New York accent, "Aftuh we eat!

WRITING MUSIC

Right around the time I graduated from UCD I was given the opportunity to write music for several projects. A music editor named Dick Alweis contacted Harry Tuft and me and asked if we could write some folk-based music for a series of documentary films. John Deere Tractors apparently does events for prospective buyers where they show entertaining short films about various events that are in some way relevant to farmers. Using the skills I had picked up in my composition class, I did a summary of the events shown on the screen, with specific timings of how long each section lasted. We then asked Dick where he wanted music, and I wrote music for these sections. Harry functioned as an adviser and music producer, and I wrote, and often played a good deal of the music. I hired other musicians to play instruments like fiddle or flute. These films included one on Skunk Farming, and another called The Powder Man, about a man who was hired to blow up old buildings. This in turn led to writing music for a short film for Raincat Irrigation Systems.

One thing led to another, and I then wrote music for a half hour public television show celebrating the 1976 Bicentennial. This was an interesting project, because there was no script, just dance and music. We had a lot of freedom in creating the music for the dancers, and I thought how lucky I was that I had taken the composition class.

BARRY CORBET AND THE EDGE

It seemed as though I was really on a composition roll. Dick Alweis recommended us to a cinematographer named Barry Corbet. Barry was in the final stages of editing a feature film about extreme sports, called The Edge. We met with him, and the three of us immediately hit it off. Barry was an Olympic athlete who had suffered a spinal injury while filming from a helicopter. This left him paralyzed from the waist down. He had endured extensive rehabilitation at the famous Craig Hospital in Denver. Barry had a complete film editing facility in his house on Lookout Mountain west of Denver. We met with the director-writer, Roger Brown and a third partner, and quickly reached an agreement. Our fee was $10,000, which included studio time, my composing, Harry's supervision, and any other musicians and singers who we needed to hire.

Working on the music for this film was one of the most exciting experiences that I have ever had. The film was beautifully photographed, and included scenes of underwater sharking, freestyle skiing, surfing, white water kayaking, climbing expeditions and hang gliding. In Hollywood the composer of a film has all sorts of assistance with timings and scene breakdowns, but Harry and I did all the spotting of the film ourselves. I ended up writing five songs and about another fifty minutes of instrumental music. Most of it was recorded in Denver with engineer Richie Cicero. I met Richie in New York, where he went from being an assistant engineer to chief engineer. Shortly after I got to Denver I ran into him by accident, and he told me he was working at Applewood, a new studio in a suburb of Denver. Not long after that he left there to work as a freelance engineer, and we recorded the music for the film at several studios. I played many of the instrumental parts, and added a number of other musicians. Mike Phillips was a good solid drummer, and Alan Westrope played a number of wind instruments. Jerry Ricks had moved to Denver, and he and I did a whole series of enjoyable guitar over dubs on a song that went with the surfing footage, called We Can Follow The Sun. This song required an Allman Brothers style guitar ensemble, and Jerry and I did a total of six guitar parts on both acoustic and electric guitars. I needed a Beach Boys sound for the vocal, and couldn't find anyone in Denver who could pull that off. I flew to New York and used my friends Jim Campbell and Bill Dean, who did appropriate multiple vocal tracks in about an hour and a half.

The film lacked any commercial distribution, and Barry and Roger decided to four-wall it, present it themselves in rented theaters. There were a few showings, and then the film basically disappeared. A few films have succeeded using the four wall tactic, but it rarely happens.

BEASTS AND THE END OF MY FILM COMPOSING CAREER

The Edge was done in 1977, and didn't do a lot

of other composing work until 1982. At that point I got a call from a director-producer named Donald Hawks. He had a famous cousin, Howard, who had directed quite a few Hollywood movies. Donald had directed and produced a film called Beasts and needed music for it. The film was a thin, make that very thin, allegory about the relationship between beasts and bad human beings. The specific beast was a grizzly bear, and the bad person was a homicidal maniac.

The budget was very small, six or seven thousand dollars as I recall. Because the plot and acting were somewhat problematic, Donald kept asking for more and more music. Mid-way through the recording, he walked into the studio. The only musicians in it were Alan Westrope and I. Alan had several saxophones, flute, alto flute, clarinet and bass clarinet on a table. I had five and six string banjos, a nylon and steel string guitar, a twelve string guitar, an electric guitar, an electric bass and a rented keyboard. Donald was angry, because he thought that I was going to use a full orchestra. I was unable to make him understand that his budget would not have come close to paying twelve musicians at union scale. In any case, I wrote about two hours worth of music, including a song. Harry and I slaved over the film, trying to help make sense out of the script. Our contract specified that we should be paid for extra minutes of music. When we completed the project, we were still owed a few hundred dollars. Like the movie itself, that money disappeared. Both of us were happy to forget Beasts as soon as possible. Once in a while it still turns up on late night cable TV on local channels.

JERRY RICKS

Jerry Ricks learned to play guitar in a unique way. While working at the Second Fret in Philadelphia, he often invited the performers to stay with him and his wife Sheila. They lived very close to the club. Among the many musicians who stayed there were Mississippi John Hurt and Skip James. Jerry took informal lessons from these people, generally mastered their styles, and knew songs which they rarely if ever performed in public. Jerry was one of a handful of young black musicians who was interested in blues at the time. Taj Mahal was the best known, and Larry Johnson was a guitar student of Gary Davis in New York City. The older black musicians were delighted to pass on their knowledge and musical secrets to Jerry, who was friendly and helpful to an older generation of musicians performing for an almost entirely white audience. Doc Watson also stayed with Jerry and Sheila, and in the notes for one of his albums Doc credits them with sustaining his career when he was extremely homesick and questioning whether there was any point in continuing his extensive tours.

When I was in The Journeymen whenever I passed through Philadelphia I often visited with Jerry. He began to build a reputation as a guitar teacher, and taught dozens of people. Among them was John Oates, of Hall and Oates, and Jerry even played on their first album. We then jammed together I wrote a banjo tune called Mr. Ricks Rag in the mid 1970's. During the 90's I heard that Jerry was playing in Albuquerque. I drove down from Denver and surprised him. I ended up playing "his" tune, which resulted in a rare moment when Jerry was actually speechless.

After the Second Fret closed Jerry moved to Europe. I once saw a great picture of Jerry, wearing lederhosen and playing in an Austrian bluegrass band. Later Jerry formed a duo with an Austrian blues man named Oscar Klein. Oscar played harmonica, guitar and trumpet, and they made a number of albums and toured in various European countries.

One of the unusual things about Jerry was that he was equally fluent in blues and bluegrass styles on the guitar. Taj Mahal was the chosen keeper of the blues flame in the folk revival, and it seemed odd to me there wasn't really room for Jerry or Larry Johnson. Truthfully Taj was a better singer than Jerry, but I always felt that Jerry was a better and more versatile guitar player.

A couple of years after I moved to Denver, Jerry decided to move there. Jerry was a magnetic individual and he quickly built up an extensive teaching practice. He and I had a duo that performed in schools for Young Audiences, and we did recording projects together. Meanwhile Jerry studied jazz guitar with Dale Bruning. It seems as though there are certain key jazz teachers in every city that have a huge influence. Among Dale's other students over the years have been the versatile Bill Frisell and songwriter-multi instrumentalist Tim O'Brien.

Jerry couldn't seem to settle down. He lived in Toronto for a while, then moved to Mississippi. He finally made a couple of albums in America, but by that time there were quite a number of younger black blues musicians, like Keb Mo, Guy Davis, and a half dozen others. In the mid-2000's Jerry decided to go back to Europe, where he had achieved more recognition and success. He settled in Croatia, one of the few European countries without health insurance. In 2007 he developed cancer. The operation was successful, but subsequent hospital infection resulted in his death in 2007.

Jerry was tremendously influential to the musicians who studied or played with him. He is another example of why I hate the delusionary notion that "the cream always rises to the top."

THE BANJO INSTRUCTION BOOK

Before I left New York, Dan Fox had repeatedly told me that I should write an instruction book for five string banjo. At the time, the only widely distributed books available were by Pete Seeger and Earl Scruggs. Both of them were tough for a beginner to master. The week before I left town, Dan sat me down and showed me how to put together an instruction book.

Not long after I got to Denver I put together a very simple instruction book that showed students how to play basic Pete Seeger banjo. The emphasis in the book was on learning enough so that the student could accompany songs.

By this time Dan had edited dozens of instruction books, and his reputation influenced Herman Steiger at Big 3 Music to publish the book. Herman also knew about The Journeymen, and that was an additional selling point. It took quite a while for the book to make its way into print. It appeared shortly after the Deliverance movie came out. The film was soon followed by the hit record by Eric Weissberg and Steve Mandell. Because Eric's last name is a bit similar to mine, I am convinced that many people bought the book believing that Eric Weissberg wrote it. In any case, the sales were fantastic for about three or four years. It was a tremendous assist to my finances, as I was going to college, teaching banjo and guitar, and playing whatever gigs I could find.

THE HISTORY OF DUELING BANJOS

I don't know if even Eric Weissberg knows the entire history of Dueling Banjos. Most banjo players know that the tune was originally called Feuding Banjos and that it was recorded by Arthur Smith, who wrote it. He played tenor banjo on the recording, and Don Reno played the five string banjo. It happens that I had a banjo and guitar student when I lived in Manhattan named Ron Brentano. Ron was one of my best students. He moved to Portland, Oregon in the late 1950's, and formed a duo with guitarist Mike Russo. They played at a variety of clubs and coffeehouses in Portland. James Dickey was poet in residence at Reed College in Portland in 1963, and he heard Ron and Mike perform Fueding Banjos. At some later time he told them that his novel Deliverance was being made into a movie, and he wanted them to play the tune for the movie. The movie came out in 1972 and the duo were not chosen to play in it. To this day Mike is somewhat bitter about this, but Ron went on to a career as the chief field representative of the Oregon Historical Society.

Another odd part of the Deliverance story is that Bill Keith got the original call to play on the soundtrack, but he was headed to Europe for a tour and recommended Eric Weissberg for the gig. It is my contention that had Keith played for the movie, the tune would never have become a hit, because his style was complex and I doubt that he would have restrained himself sufficiently in order to create what is basically a simple arrangement.

Shortly before I moved to Denver, I ran into Eric on a session. He told me that he had just come back from Atlanta and recorded the soundtrack for Deliverance. He said that they made him play Dueling Banjos over and over, at different tempos and with different lengths. They then told him that they thought that it might be a hit single. Eric told me he thought that this was ridiculous, and he expressed doubts that the song would ever be released outside of the soundtrack itself.

The coda to this story is that Eric was never told that the record company was releasing the song as a single, and he had to hire a lawyer to get the record company to pay him royalties. The irony is that for some time both Eric and I had been trying to write and record a hit single. The one time that Eric didn't try, it happened for him. He also was not consulted on the authorship credits of the song. Arthur Smith's name did not appear as the composer, and he had to sue to get his share of the royalties. Since Eric knew many people in the bluegrass community, this was undoubtedly an embarrassment to him. When Arthur died in 2015, his obituary said that when people visited Arthur and asked him how the royalties worked out for him he would simply point at a photo of a yacht in the office of his studio.

THE FOLK MUSIC SOURCEBOOK

In 1965 Harry Tuft had put together something called The Folk Music Almanac. It was based on the old Farmer's Almanac, and Harry put it together with extensive editorial assistance from Phyllis Wagner and Boston folksinger Robert Jones. The book was intended to be a mail order catalog, but it actually functioned more as a folk music resource book. It contained woodcuts and brief reviews of recordings. In 1974 a friend of Harry's was at the offices of book publisher Albert Knopf, pitching a book of her own. She mentioned the Almanac, and the editors at Knopf asked her to have Harry contact them. The editors seemed quite interested in the project, but Harry was too entangled with the affairs of his store and his performing career to put a proposal together. I harassed him about this, insisting that it was a great opportunity. Finally Harry asked me whether I would do the book.

Writing a book is very different from writing a banjo or guitar instructional work, and I was hesitant about the project. I knew that the book would have to include reviews and lists of books and records. I asked Harry if he would let me contact Larry Sandberg, so that we could work on the book together. Larry was an excellent guitar player and briefly a student of mine. He was highly literate, with a classics degree from CCNY, and had completed most of a doctoral program at Yale in classics before transferring his interest to the music world.

Larry and I developed a proposal for the book, which included a series of articles by other people who were specialists in particular aspects of North American folk music, like American Indian and Mexican-American music, together with our reviews of books and records. Larry did 95% of the record reviews, and I dealt with most of the books.

Knopf enthusiastically accepted our proposal, and we spent the next year working in libraries, and writing to record companies and book publishers. Although we received a reasonable advance from the publisher, obviously we could not afford to buy all the available materials.

It took us about a year to write the book, guided by Knopf editors Bill Barich and then Kathy Hourigan. It was an all-encompassing task, and it involved a research trip to the Library of Congress and several days working in the Folksong Archive there. The book was published as a hardback and in a paperback edition. Larry and I were astounded at the number of reviews that the Sourcebook received. We were favorably reviewed in the L.A. Times, the New York Times, Rolling Stone and over thirty newspapers and magazines. We each went on a book tour, with Larry covering the eastern states, and I went to the West Coast. We did radio and newspaper interviews, and generally had a good time. There was a single negative review. Folksong purist Michael Cooney, writing in Sing Out! Magazine, was outraged that the book cost $6.95 in the paperback edition, while Harry's original Almanac was priced at $1.00. He also criticized the book for not having the charm and informality of the earlier work. I was amused at his first point, but agreed that this was a much more formal work than Harry's original work.

To our surprise, the book won the 1977 Deems Taylor ASCAP Music Critics Award. This included a plaque and a check for $500. Unfortunately, the sales of the book were a bit disappointing. Knopf had printed 25,000 books, and ended up selling 15,000. In 1989 Larry and I did a revised edition for Da Capo Press, but it received less attention and even fewer sales than the original work. By that time there were so many folk music books and recordings on the market that it had become a much more difficult book to write.

AUTHOR, AUTHOR

When I got the job teaching music business at Colorado Women's College, there were really only two books about the music business available. This Business of Music, by Sidney Shemel and Bill Krasilovsky was a detailed and well researched book written by two New York entertainment lawyers. When I tried to use it for my students, they found it unreadable for someone without an existing background in the industry. The other book that was available was by Lawrence Berk, the founder of the Berklee College of Music, and I found it even less useful. I decided that my next book would be about the music business.

I created a book proposal, and picked out three publishers to send it to. I felt that I needed a book agent to make the deal. I had a friend named Rick Abramson who was a great salesman. He knew nothing about selling books, but I found him to be an excellent record promotion man towards the end of my tenure at Command-Probe Records. He asked me why I chose someone who knew nothing about books for the job. I responded that I felt that his phenomenal sales skills would enable him to make the deal. Rick contacted three publishers. Two of them expressed interest, but one bowed out when a new book about the music business appeared in 1978. They felt that there wasn't room for another such book in the marketplace. This left us with Crown Publishing, an independent publisher that published a considerable number of non-fiction books, and even had a book that was similar to mine about the movie business.

I worked on the book with editor Philip Winsor. I told him that my family and I would rent a place in Woodstock, New York in summer, 1978, and complete the book in six weeks. He undoubtedly thought that I was living in fantasy land, but in fact we rented a house in Woodstock, and I did research in New York, and completed the book in six weeks. I wanted to call the book The Music Business: Self Defense & Career Opportunities. The Crown promotion people flipped the title, pointing out that in such book outlets the book would get filed under judo and karate books if we used my title.

Crown was a very different sort of company than Knopf. When the book came out there was no promotion tour, only a small ad in the New York Times. They quickly sold out of a limited hardback edition, and the paperback was issued simultaneously. Sales started slowly, but they soon picked up. The book eventually went through three revisions, the last one in 2003. Phil Winsor left Crown not too long after the book came out, and a senior editor named Brandt Aymar called me out of the blue a few years later. He had no particular interest in the book, but computerized printouts indicated the need for a revised edition. About that time, Crown was sold to Random House, and the sales and distribution of the book immediately improved. Over the years the book has sold over 100,000 copies and has been translated into Japanese. It is probably the single most commercially successful endeavor that I have undertaken. Sometime during the 70's I was in New York City, and wandered into the Schirmer Music bookshop. They had some forty copies of the book displayed on a table in a solo display. I was so stunned that I didn't tell the sales people that they were displaying my book.

Over the years I've written or co-written twenty two books, counting this one. In teaching about the music business I have concluded that in today's complex and truncated music market, anyone wanting to pursue music as a career should pursue multiple tasks and income streams. This is what I have done ever since moving to Denver in 1972. I would like to say that this has been the result of excellent planning, but the truth is that I have simply pursued what opportunities have been available to me. That is still what I am doing 45 years later.

THE AMERICAN FEDERATION OF MUSICIANS

When I came to Denver I was still a member of the New York local of the Musician's Union (the American Federation of Musicians.) A few weeks after I arrived I joined the Denver local. I quickly realized that working conditions for musicians in Denver had little in common with the world I had been living in. I would get calls to do recording sessions or commercials for a fraction of what I was used to getting paid. I didn't accept these gigs.

Tasso Harris, the president of the union, was a trombone player who had moved to Denver from Los Angeles. He was an interesting character, charming, often self-serving, and confident. A reform ticket under the leadership of another trombone player named Carl Johnson won the next election. Carl's main tactic was to form committees to study everything. I got on the recording committee, and came up with the concept of creating a lower wage scale for playing on records that were manufactured in small quantities. The union sent me to new York to the pre-negotiations for the next recording agreement. My concept was based on the notion that all over the country musicians were making records that were essentially being sold in a local market, rather than albums recorded for a major label with national or even international distribution.

When I presented this idea, the participants in the negotiations were truly shocked at this concept. Al Knopf, the Vice President of the New York local who had saved my butt in the fiasco over the Scott McKenzie recordings looked at me and quite seriously said that if my proposal were adopted it would ruin the music business. Dennis Dreith, the youthful head of the Los Angeles studio musicians sub-group the Recording Musicians of America and I ended up in a shouting match. Dennis represented the interests of studio musicians in Los Angeles, Nashville and New York, and initially he found my proposals threatening. Of the nine or ten people in the room, no one even gave me a glimmer of hope that my proposal would be adopted.

A couple of years later Dennis changed his mind. Consultations with some of his members indicated that some of them were playing on chamber music records that were pressed in small quantities. These musicians welcomed a change in the rules, so that they could do more of this work. By 1980 the federation adopted my proposal with one modification. Instead of classifying records by the number of albums pressed, they changed the criterion to the budget for the record. The scale that they adopted was basically about 1/3 less than the scale for recordings made with major label-style records.

WESLEY WESTBROOKS AND THE NEH

One of the first people I met in Denver was a black gospel music composer named Wesley Westbrooks. Wes was a friend of Harry Tuft, and had put together a local group to perform his music. The group had strong male and female lead singers, Cliff Young and Bobby Malone. I was captivated by the singers, who really tore it up when they performed at the Denver Folklore Center Concert Hall. I named the group Roots and Branches and produced a session where we recorded three songs. I stirred up some record company interest, but was never able to come up with a deal. Meanwhile I became very friendly with Wes, and he gradually told me the story of his life.

Wes was born in Arkadelphia, Arkansas. His grandfather was a self-taught genius, who was a janitor at the local white college. He actually tutored white students in history and French, even though he himself had never even gone through grade school. Wes' father was also a janitor at a local college and also sang and played drums, though not professionally. Wes was born in 1920, and although this was the era of segregation, lynchings and poll taxes, as Wes told it, life in Arkadelphia was generally peaceful. When Wes was in his early teens he got a job working for a dairy, delivering milk. He became friendly with the white daughter of the owner, who would occasionally give him ice cream treats on hot summer days.

One night a friend of Wes' father came to the house and told him that his son needed to leave town immediately. It seems that there were rumors spreading in the town that Wes and the girl were having some sort of illicit relationship. That night his parents placed Wes on a train to Kansas City, Kansas, where his Uncle Fred lived. Wes was told that he was being sent up there in order to get a better education. It was years before his parents told him the real story.

The more Wes told me, the more I thought that his story would make a great book. I applied for a National Endowment for the Humanities College Teachers Fellowship in 1982, while I was working at Colorado Womens College. I was concerned that the book was not really related to the things I was teaching, but when I called the endowment they said that this was not a problem. I wrote the grant and after getting some important feedback from a professor at another local college, Pam Metz, re-wrote it. I was absolutely astonished when I got the letter of acceptance. The grant was for $18,000 plus some additional travel money. This was more than three times my salary at the college.

Just before the grant period began I was fired from the college, which soon went out of business. I made plans with Wes to do some travelling and interview people who were important in his personal and musical life. This was easy for Wes to do, because his day job cleaning airplanes for United Air Lines gave him flying privileges.

The grant was supposed to start in January, 1982. Wes was diagnosed with liver cancer in the summer of 1981. It became obvious that he was not going to be able to come with me on my travels. I immediately dropped everything, and started taping hours and hours of interviews with him, when his condition temporarily improved and he got out of the hospital. I had planned trips to Arkadelphia, San Francisco and Los Angeles to meet Wes' relatives, and trips to New York and Kansas City to meet close friends and musical peers. He called all of these people to introduce me and to explain what I was up to. Without exception they were incredibly helpful and supportive.

Wes had led a complex and eventful life. Charley Parker had been a schoolmate of his. After high school he had moved to Chicago, and sat in with various bands. He spent World War II in Tunisia and Italy, and played in an army band. After the war he had taken advantage of the G.I. Bill and gone to music school in Chicago, studying trumpet and arranging. Since New York was the center of the jazz universe, Wesley moved there. He brought a heroin habit he had picked up along with him. Part of the time he lived in the subway and then slept during the day at the apartments of friends who had day jobs. He also participated in some robberies of white tourists who came to Harlem to pick up black women.

He studied with famous trombonist arranger J.J. Johnson, and decided that he didn't have the talent or the drive to become a bebop trumpet player. When his friend Fats Navarro died, Wesley realized that he needed to leave New York and quit his heroin habit. He took a bus to the drug rehabilitation center in Louisville but was too timid to go in. Instead he went on to his parent's house in Arkadelphia. He told them that he was sick, and needed to be left alone.

During the next three days he kicked heroin on his own. He then enrolled at the University of Arkansas at Pine Bluff. He ended up finding his real métier as a singer in the school jazz band. He became close friends with George Joiner (who later changed his name to Jamil Nasser) the leader of the school's jazz band.

Wesley ended up in Denver when his wife Alleze

decided that she had enough of Kansas City. He got a job with United Airlines, and also became a gospel and blues music disc jockey on radio station KDKO. That led to his meeting the Staples Singers, who eventually recorded four songs that Wes had written, or co-written with Roebuck Staples. He Don't Knock was also recorded by the Kingston Trio, and Hear My Call Here was recorded by the English folk group Pentangle. The song Why Am I Treated So Bad was a big success for Cannonball Adderly.

This is only the tip of the iceberg of the story that I hoped to tell. I spent the entire year travelling, interviewing Wes' associates and relatives and writing what I hoped would be a book. Wesley passed away just after Christmas in 1981, before the grant even formally began.

My grant year brought me some of the most cherished experiences of my life. In Los Angeles I met a cousin of Wesley's who was a high school principal and was the family genealogist. Among the people I visited with were his cousin Bob in San Francisco and various relatives in Arkadelphia. Among the musicians I interviewed were Jamil Nasser and saxophonist Clifford Jordan in New York, and Wes' close friend bandleader Oliver Todd in Kansas City. Everyone remembered Wesley with great warmth and they all had stories about him. Clifford Jordan told me that his band had played in Denver, and now there are "a bunch of musicians in Brooklyn going around talking like Wes, who don't even know how they got to talk that way."

I put what I thought were the finishing touches on the book and started to send it out. By this time it was 1983, and we were in the midst of the Reagan era. Suddenly it was as though black Americans had disappeared from the scene. Even well-known black non-fiction authors were having trouble getting their books published. I used two different agents, and basically got no nibbles.

Outside of one check for $1500 Wes never made much money from his songs. In many ways he was his own worst enemy. When Roebuck Staples asked Wes what he wanted for his work on Why Am I Treated So Bad, Wes had a small bill on his desk for something like $50. That's what he asked Staples to send him, and that was the payment that he received. Wes' name sometimes appears on the credits of He Don't Knock, and sometimes it doesn't. I was taken aback that Greg Kot's recent biography of Mavis Staples, I'll Take You There includes no mention of Wes or his songs.

As I explained earlier, I have now written or co-written twenty two published books about roots music and various aspects of the music business. I still have the Westbrook manuscript, which is called A Good Time In Hard Times: The Life of Wesley Westbrooks. The title comes from one of Wesley's cousins, who told me "we had a good time in those hard times in Arkadelphia." I don't think it will ever be published. I guess the bottom line is that he simply wasn't famous enough. Sort of the cream falls to the bottom!

Harry Tuft (left) with the late Manny Greenville (center) and his son Mitch. Manny was Joan Baez's manager, and booked or managed a number of acts, including Dave Van Ronk, with his company Folklore Productions. The company still exists, run by Mitch and his son Matt. The photo was taken at the Folk Alliance meeting in Washington DC, sometime around the late 1980's or early 90's. Manny was one of the too-few truly honorable people on the business side of the folk music revival.

Left: Harry Tuft and Wesley Westbrooks. Wesley was a good friend of mine, and was the subject of my National Endowment for the Humanities grant, and the only book I've ever written that never found a publisher. This picture is from around 1980.

Right: Tim O'Brien in the recording studio. Tim played and sang, with his sister Mollie, on my first solo CD, New Traditions. The song they sang, Soon You Will Be Coming Back To Me, was later used in the NBC TV series, *My Name Is Earl.*

Below: Taken in the late 90's, when I was VP of and host for the Music & Entertainment Industry Educators Association in our annual meeting in Denver. Far left: Me. My University of Colorado at Denver colleague Frank (Dr. J.) Jermance, and Jim Mason, Colorado Institute of Art instructor and free lance record producer. (They are the 4th and 5th people from the left.)

Part 2 • Chapter 13 

1983-1990 GRADUATE SCHOOL IN OKLAHOMA

1983 and 1984 were bad years for me. I was invited to apply for a teaching job at the University of Colorado at Denver, and submitted several of my books and a resume. The books were returned to me, and I was informed that they could not hire a full-time professor who did not have a master's degree. The excitement of the Westbrooks project had turned to serious depression. After a year of the most exciting research work that I had ever done, I was unable to sell the book.

On a personal level things were equally rocky. The honeymoon that had peaked with the birth of our daughter Janelle in 1974 had gradually withered away. Our goals and aspirations seemed to be moving in different directions. I wasn't sure what I wanted to do, and I began to consider going to graduate school, in an effort to expand my employment horizons. After some years of not committing to a specific career, Diane found a one year program at Creighton University in Omaha that would provide her with a career as a registered nurse. She took a few part-time pre-requisite courses at a local community college, and was admitted to Creighton. She left in the beginning of 1983, and was gone for a full year. During that time we drifted further apart. We had some serious conversations about what a one year separation entailed, and realized that it might mark the beginning of the end of our marriage. Diane went off to Omaha, and I stayed in Boulder. In the fall of 1983 our daughter Janelle went with her, but she did not like school in Omaha, and missed her friends in Colorado. She returned to Boulder almost immediately. That turned out to be a wonderful thing, because Janelle and I became much closer. Meanwhile Paul went to high school, and then spent his junior year as an exchange student at a high school in France. I vacillated between getting a masters degree at the University of Colorado music school in Boulder and enrolling in an unusual graduate program at the University of Oklahoma. The Oklahoma program was called an MLS degree, a Master of Liberal Studies. It did not require long-term residence in Oklahoma, but involved three different sessions there for a total of seven weeks. Because the Colorado program involved studying a number of things that didn't interest me, like opera history, and the hours required seemed to increase every time I met with the professor who was running the program, I chose Oklahoma.

I was really surprised that a relatively conservative school like the University of Oklahoma would have such an innovative program. It dated back to 1939, and was available for undergraduates as well as graduates. The time spent in Norman involved seminars with various professors from the university, and one of the seminars was designed to help students understand the process of writing a master's thesis. The students came not only from Oklahoma, but from various parts of the United States. Some were enrolled in the program because they were teachers and getting a graduate degree would increase their salaries. One older gentleman was retired from a job supervising engineers in the North Sea for Phillips 66. He told us that he enrolled because his friends were idling away their days in rocking chairs, and becoming ill or their brains were rotting away from disuse.

The program required students to do all of their written work at home. The first seminar was spent on campus in Norman. Students chose three professors from the UO faculty to work with. Two of them involved the student's major field of study, the other had to be in another field. I worked with two sociologists and tried my hand at short story writing for my elective course.

At my second seminar we began by introducing ourselves. Because every one works at their own pace in this program, there were quite a number of people who I hadn't met in the previous session. One fellow student worked at a ten minute oil change company, and when he found out that I was a musician and a songwriter, he asked me whether I could write a jingle for the company. Using one of my fellow students as a singer, I wrote and recorded this jingle. It paid $500, which easily covered my weeks of living expenses in Norman.

I thoroughly enjoyed my course work in Oklahoma. Unfortunately although the program still exists, they no longer offer an MLS in Humanities with an emphasis in social science. They do offer a number of other masters degree programs, however.

THE WINNIPEG FOLK FESTIVAL, BROWNIE McGHEE AND NEW TRADITIONS

Canada has a number of folk festivals that take place during the summer. Two of the largest ones are in Winnipeg and Vancouver. I had the honor of playing the Winnipeg festival three times during the middle 80's. One of the times that I played there was while I was going to graduate school in Oklahoma. I got permission to take a couple of days off, and flew up to Denver from Oklahoma City to get a connecting flight to Winnipeg. I saw Brownie McGhee and Sonny Terry in the airport, and sat down to talk with Brownie, who I hadn't seen in years. Since Diane was staying in our house at that time, rather than go back to Boulder, I decided to wait at the airport.

I ended up talking to Brownie for eight hours, literally. He was a bright and articulate man, and he told me all sorts of stories about growing up in Tennessee. One of the stories was about a town in the mountains where inter-racial marriage was common. Brownie explained that this town was isolated and protected. Since it was in a remote place, hardly any strangers would ever pass through the town. I knew that there were towns in the South that favored the union side in the Civil War and that most residents in the Appalachians never had slaves, but I had never heard this story before.

Brownie told me that someone was working on a biography of him. He didn't tell me any details, but it's now twenty five years later and no such book has appeared. I have always regretted that I didn't have a chance to write that book. I have always felt that Brownie's contribution to the blues as a songwriter and guitarist have been under-estimated. Possibly his sophistication and intelligence didn't fit some of the blues fan's obsessions with the blues as a "primitive" art form.

Playing at the Winnipeg festival was probably the best experience I have ever had playing music live. Festival volunteers met you as you passed through customs. They took you to the hotel and the next day drove you to the festival site. All day long there were workshops and brief concerts by Canadian, American and world music artists, and the festival director, Mitch Podolak, was a genial and energetic host. The festival was held in a large provincial park. If you wanted to go to a workshop, volunteers ferried you in a golf cart to that part of the area, and picked you up when you wanted to leave.

One of the years that I was there, I played my early banjo suite, A Day In The Kentucky Mountains outdoors in the rain. Folksinger-storyteller and radical agitator Utah Phillips stood in the rain and listened to the whole piece, and told me how much he enjoyed it

To this day I am grateful to Mitch and Winnipeg for the opportunity to play extended pieces that I rarely performed in public, because they are too intense a listening experience for audiences that are used to three minute songs and instrumental pieces.

BRECKENRIDGE & MARV MATTIS

In 1980 I taught at a one week summer workshop on songwriting and the music business in Breckenridge, Colorado. The workshop was held at Colorado Mountain College and led by Nashville songwriter Jud Strunk. He died in October of 1980, and coordinator Tom Hart asked me to organize the three day 1981 workshop. This started a ten year association with the workshop.

THE EXPERTS WHO DIDN'T HAVE THE ANSWERS

In 1983 my alma mater, the University of Colorado at Denver sponsored a two day seminar on the music business for its students in its burgeoning music business program and the general public. I attended the workshop, and listened to various music business luminaries discourse on what it takes to succeed in the music business. Among the participants were Bob Crewe, producer and songwriter best known for his work with the pop-rock group the Four Seasons, and Los Angeles record producer Eddie Lambert, and a VP of Columbia Records. After two days of being constantly bombarded by the panelists about the need for creating hooks in hit songs, I raised my hand and expressed my appreciation for all of the music business information that was being given to us. I then said, "How do you explain the success of Windham Hill Records?"

Windham Hill practically initiated the notion of New Age instrumental music. It was started by accident by a guitarist and carpenter named William Ackerman when he made a recording as a Christmas present to a number of his friends. The record found its way to Seattle radio, and received an extremely positive reception. When listeners called, they invariably asked where the record was available. After dozens of such calls, station DJ Jeff Heiman called Ackerman and told him that they loved his record, but if he didn't get it into record stores, they would have to stop playing it. Ackerman then founded Windham Hill Records. His own record proved successful, but when he produced a piano solo album by George Winston, Windham Hill became a very viable company. That record, which cost under $1000 to produce, sold over 500,000 copies. Another stock in trade of the company was black and white scenic album covers on all of their releases.

At any rate, when I asked these music business gurus about Windham Hill, their response was silence. None of them had ever heard of Windham Hill. Almost instantly a BMI representative named Marv Mattis who had sponsored the seminar leaped on stage, and explained what Windham Hill was. He asked the members of the audience, mostly between the ages of 20 and 30, how many of them were aware of Windham Hill. Unlike the panelists, close to half the audience knew about the label. Marv then looked up, and told the audience that he wanted to talk to the person who had asked that question.

Marv and I became good friends. He was instrumental in the success of the Breckenridge Songwriter's event. Under his guidance, BMI paid the cost of getting hit songwriters like Paul Overstreet and Stewart Harris as well as various music business insiders like John Braheny and Dennis Dreith to come to Breckenridge.

THE BROKEN WRIST

In the summer of 1985 I tripped and fell on the main street of Breckenridge while going to lunch. I broke my wrist in four places. I had an operation, wore a cast on my arm, and I was very concerned that I would not be able to play again. I did physical therapy for about eight weeks, and gradually began to play again. The only permanent effect on my playing was that at the base of the guitar, I have some difficulty playing barre chords. These are chords that require the player to extend the left index finger across all the strings. Since I lost about 5% of my radial motion in the left hand, this is difficult for me. Because the banjo has fewer strings, the accident has had virtually no effect on my banjo playing.

I continued to do my course work for the Oklahoma degree with my broken wrist, and my son Paul taught me enough computer skills so that I could write the thesis on my computer. My subject was the difficulties that mid-career musicians confront in playing their original music in public, as opposed to performing songs already known to audiences. I interviewed nineteen musicians. They were of various sexes, ages and races. After a couple of re-writes my thesis was accepted, and I received my MLA degree.

DIVORCE AND A NEW CAREER

By 1984 Diane and I had divorced. She moved back to Denver and quickly got a job as a nurse in as local hospital. For a year, we kept our house in Boulder. We each rented apartments, mine in Boulder and hers in Denver. We alternated weeks in the Boulder house. Our thinking was that the children didn't cause the divorce, it was our choice, so why should the children have to move? After a year of going back and forth, Diane decided that the children could live in Boulder in the house, and she could see them on weekends.

When Paul had come back from France, he really had turned from a boy into a young man. He was much more self-confident, considerably taller, and ready to start considering his choice of a college. Janelle was finishing junior high school, and had a strong group of friends, many of whom also came from divorced families.

SENIORS AND MUSIC

In the mid-80's I got a call from an agent in Philadelphia named Charlotte Britton. She told me that there was a small circuit of gigs playing for seniors in eastern Colorado, southern Kansas and southeast Kansas. Later I learned that these gigs were the remnants of what had actually been a national tour.

The tour involved three gigs a day at a combination of senior centers and nursing homes, with the one in south central Kansas including high schools. The pay was about $900 for 7-10 days, but it involved between a hundred and a hundred fifty miles of driving a day, AFTER you got to the central location.

I quickly discovered that playing for seniors is very different than playing abstract banjo pieces for a friendly audience of music fans. I quickly worked up a repertoire of old time songs like You Are My Sunshine, Redwing and Goodnight Irene. At the senior centers the audience was active and ambulatory, but the nursing homes were another story. The residents were often strongly medicated, and it is certainly the only time I ever have seen someone fall asleep while I was playing the banjo within ten feet of where they were sitting.

In one of the Kansas gigs there was a man who was a decent harmonica player. He would play along for a verse or so and then he would literally fall asleep. Five minutes later I would again hear the sound of the harmonica. The strangest experience while playing for seniors occurred in one of the nursing homes in eastern Colorado. I was singing the John Denver hit Take Me Home Country Roads when a very agitated woman got up and started screaming "Take me home, I don't want to be here." It turned out that she had just been placed in a nursing home against her will, and so what I thought would be a nostalgic happy go-lucky song really upset her. It made me marvel at the many shades of meaning a specific song can have, depending on an audience member's personal situation.

Years later I did a half dozen or so performances at a nursing home in Portland. This facility was a low residency private home with about five residents. One day when I arrived I was told that one of the residents had just died. The manager of the home asked me to keep playing as two attendants removed his body with a stretcher, so as to distract the surviving residents. I suppose it was my chance to play a solo New Orleans funeral.

SUSAN

In the summer of 1986 I got a job teaching music in a summer arts program at Clayton College. Clayton was originally a school for orphans that was in a period of transition. The students were an interesting cross section of arts-oriented kids from Denver, and the teachers were similarly from various backgrounds. By mid-summer I was dating the art teacher Susan Planalp, and we quickly became close.

Meanwhile since I now had my masters degree I started to send out resumes to every place that I could think of. One resume went to NARAS, the National Academy of Recording Arts and Sciences. This is the organization that presents the Grammy show. At the time, they were looking for an educational coordinator, to interact with the various educational programs in their regional chapters. The organization had a new CEO, Joe Smith, who had been the CEO of Warner Brothers Records, among many other jobs in the industry. He left after about six weeks to take a job as CEO of Capitol Records, but apparently he was one of the people who chose me to as a finalist for the job.

I flew out to Los Angeles, and had a good interview with Richard Ranta, who was basically spearheading the organization's educational and scholarship programs. After about a week I was offered the job and accepted it. Before I even started work, the organization flew me out to attend the Grammies. I struggled through finding and wearing a tuxedo, and witnessed an electrifying performance by Ladysmith Black Mambazo, who were singing and dancing behind Paul Simon. Otherwise I found the event dull and lengthy.

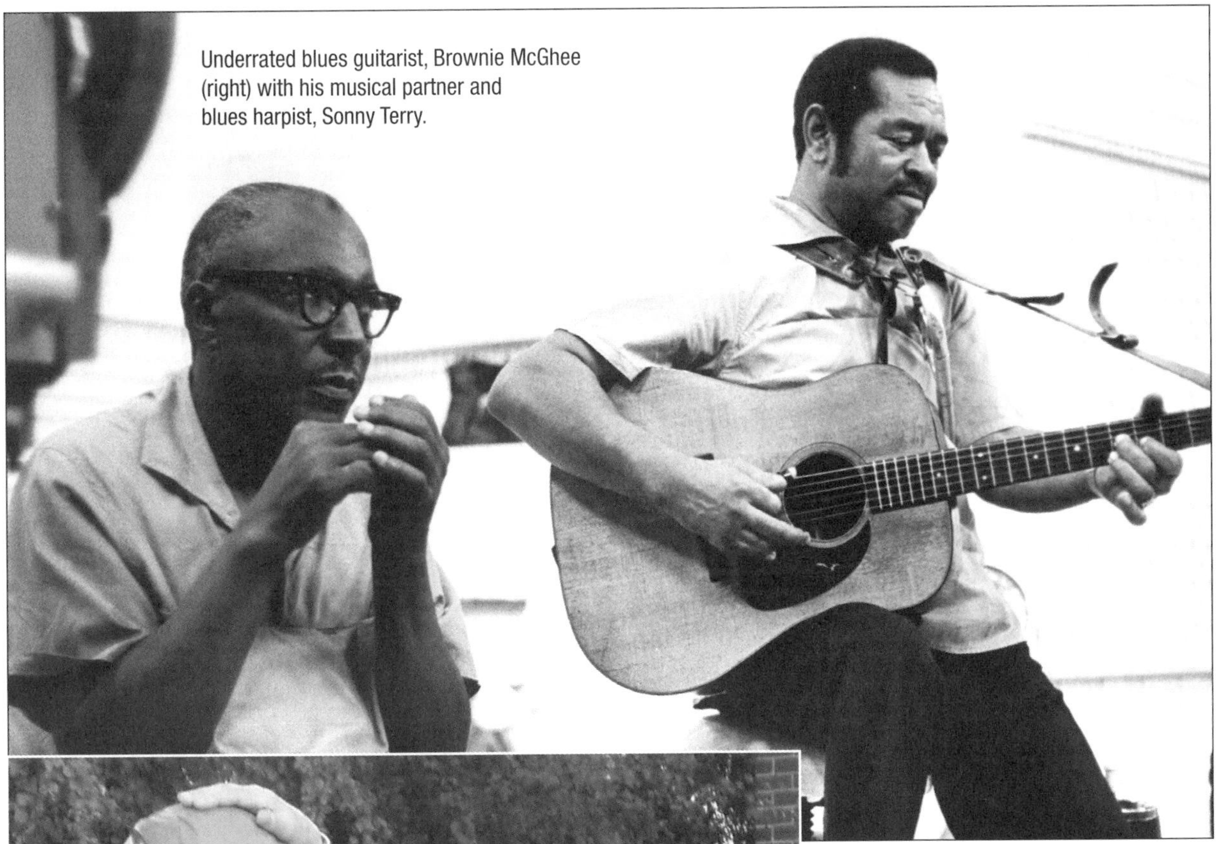

Underrated blues guitarist, Brownie McGhee (right) with his musical partner and blues harpist, Sonny Terry.

Photo: Dick Weissman

Art teacher Susan Panalp, whom I met while at Clayton College in 1986. We have been married for almost 29 years.

Susan Panalp

Part 2 • Chapter 14

I DON'T LOVE LA

In 1988 it seemed that everyone was leaving Denver. The area was going through one of its occasional bust cycles, while the oil shale industry was in tatters. From a personal point of view the timing wasn't great for me. Susan and I had been seeing each other for about six months, and we both really wanted to be together. She had a job teaching art in the public schools, and couldn't join me right away. I flew out to Burbank, and after about a month was able to find an apartment not too far from NARAS national headquarters.

Looking back on my 14 month job at NARAS from a twenty five year vantage point is amusing. When I went to Los Angeles, I feared that I would be an old fogey in an office where I assumed everyone would be listening to hip hop and heavy metal music. After all, I was over fifty years old by then. As it turned out most the employees were middle aged women. They loved Barbra Streisand and Neil Diamond, and my roots music tastes were extremely left wing to them.

The editor of the Grammy magazine was Ian Dove. Ian was a sarcastic Britisher and a fanatical jazz lover. The huge benefit of working for NARAS was that for some reason record companies and artists submitted multiple copies of recordings, far more than the organization required. Ian and I were dedicated LP and CD scavengers, racing off with numerous extra copies for our collections, or to trade in at record stores on Melrose Avenue.

NARAS had two organizational components. There was the paid full-time staff, and there were elected officials from the various regional chapters. This included a national president. After Joe Smith's resignation, Christine Farnon, a long-time employee was restored to her position as the head of the office. Christine was an intelligent, self-educated person who had worked her way in the industry up from being a record company secretary. She was extremely well-organized but a difficult boss. Sometimes Christine seemed more like the house mother at a dormitory than a CEO of a major music business organization.

Susan joined me in Los Angeles after her school term was over, and we got married. She immediately applied for many school jobs and found opportunities to do art workshops in various suburbs of Los Angeles. She accepted a job at an exclusive private school that had many celebrity students, including the daughters of record producer Quincy Jones and the sons of movie maker John Hughes. The non-celebrity parents were wealthy two parent career families.

Only a few months after I got the gig, I got into some fairly serious trouble. The payoff to the people who constituted the volunteer component of the organization was the annual trustees meeting. I made the mistake of expressing an opinion at at a trustees' meeting in Jamaica. It seemed that staff were never expected to have opinions, only to carry out the directions of the trustees. I came close to being fired, and Christine absolutely shunned me on the plane ride back to L.A.

THE RETURN OF MARV MATTIS

About the only thing I liked about L.A. was that I bought a folding bicycle, and about ¾ of the time I would bike from my house to the office. Susan was doing well in Los Angeles. She had a gallery for her work, and her workshops were lucrative. I was struggling. I hated my job, which mostly consisted in parceling out the small scholarships that the chapters gave to colleges. I have an unforgettable memory of my work situation. The woman who worked in back of my cubicle listened to classical music all day, and the woman across the way favored 70's hard rock. Dueling musical styles, with my desk in the middle.

I took to having lunch with Marv Mattis in Hollywood. That was almost an hour's drive from my Burbank office, going through Laurel Canyon. I cherished the times out of the office. When we started meeting I'm afraid that I chewed Marv's ear off with my complaints about NARAS. The last few months of my time in LA the situation got reversed. Marv was one of the two major executives of BMI in Los Angeles. The national chair of the organization decided to get rid of his cohort, Ron Anton. She asked Marv to fire him. Although they weren't especially close, Marv did not have it in his heart to insert the corporate knife. The result was unexpected. Ron was indeed fired, but Marv was given the shunning treatment. He was not invited to certain meetings. He found himself in rooms with two people talking about something and totally ignoring him. He began to realize that BMI had decided to force him out as well.

Shortly before he was unintentionally retired, he got a salary increase. It was as though the company was expiating its guilt for firing him by increasing his pension. That sum was based on his highest wage level. During this period I became Marv's counselor, instead of the other way around. Maybe it partly made up for all the times he had helped me. He ended up moving to Santa Fe, New Mexico, and later to Crestone, Colorado. He is one of the rare truly honorable people I've known in the music business.

MARV AND SANTA FE

Shortly after Marv moved to Santa Fe he decided that he needed some window blinds. He went to a hardware store on a Friday around 4:30 PM. The proprietor rustled around in the back, looking to see if he had the right size. He came back to the front of the store, where Marv was anxiously waiting. It turned out he didn't have the size. By now it was after 5. Marv quickly asked if there was another store where he could go to get the blinds. The proprietor looked at Marv and smiled. He said "Manana, isn't that what you came here for?" Hollywood meets Santa Fe. Santa Fe 1, Hollywood 0.

LEAVING LOS ANGELES IN THE BROAD DAYLIGHT

I wasn't much of an LA enthusiast. My children were in Denver, and I tried to visit them every two weeks. I was also paying child support for them. Between the child support and the trips, I was always broke. My NARAS salary was $26,000, not much in LA, even in 1988. When I didn't go to Denver, we would often spend weekends in Santa Barbara or Ojai. It was kind of a relaxing alternate reality for me. Soon it became a question of how long I could tolerate the job.

After I had been at NARAS a little less than a year, they decided that they needed to hire a new CEO, and to leave Christine Farnon as the office manager. After several interviews of people who were active on the volunteer side of the organization, they hired Mike Greene. Mike was a failed singer-songwriter who had worked himself up to a high level position at a post-production TV and film facility in Atlanta called Crawford Communications.

Mike was a smooth and articulate fellow who was ready to bring the organization into a modern world of contemporary business. The day that he was hired Ian Dove drew a cartoon with Mike landing on the moon. The caption was "the ego has landed."

Although I agreed that the organization needed some re-thinking, I intuitively felt that I could never work for Mike. During this time, one of my ex-students at the Colorado Mountain College Workshop called, asking what I knew about a school called the Colorado Institute of Arts. She told me that they were starting a music business program. I immediately called Bob Yablans, the director of the program, and he offered me a job teaching there full-time in the fall of 1988. I accepted, even though the $18,000 salary was less than I was making in Los Angeles. Susan was ambivalent about leaving, but her ambivalence was overcome by her sympathy for my working conditions.

Part 2 • Chapter 15

BACK TO COLORADO

I called in sick for a couple of days, and drove one of our two cars to Boulder, where I rented an apartment. I flew back, gave notice, and two weeks later we drove to Mendocino, where Susan was doing a workshop. Bob had told me there was a faculty meeting I should attend, so while she was teaching, I flew back to Denver. I walked into the meeting, and he looked at me, and said, "what are you doing here?" That was a great way for me to sense what sort of job I had accepted.

THE COLORADO INSTITUTE OF ART

There are a number of two year vocational school programs in the United States. CIA, which is now called the Art Institute of Colorado, is one of a number of schools that offer diploma, AA and BA degrees in various aspects of the visual arts, culinary arts, and video production. The program that I taught in was a two year AA degree, which is the same degree that community colleges offer.

Please note that I am writing about my experiences with the school in 1989, because I have had no contact with the school since that time. If you go on line, however, you may interpolate that the conditions I am describing still exist. The way that the school was organized reminded me of a factory. Classes were four hours long, with morning and afternoon classes, and there were also programs offered in the evening. From the school's point of view this meant that most classrooms were effectively used at all hours of the day, and into the evening hours. The students themselves were truly a motley crew. There were some who already had degrees from a four year college, and decided that they wanted to learn about the music business. Other students had dropped out of college at an earlier time, and there were some students who hadn't ever attended college before. The standard for admission was basically covering tuition, rather than fulfilling a particular grade point average. Recruiters were paid commissions for each new student, so when they talked to prospective students they tended to inflate the chances of a student getting a lucrative job after graduation. Most of the students were being partly financed through Pell Grants from the federal government. This didn't pay the full cost of tuition and books. Many students graduated with debts that would follow them around mid-way into their careers.

I found that teaching four hour classes was generally absurd. Students would troop in late, leave early, or even be half asleep in a class. It was difficult to take this personally, because keeping a class going in a positive and up-beat way for four hours at a time was taxing to anyone teaching there as well. The skills and qualifications of the teachers paralleled those of the students. Some were surprisingly qualified for such a low level institution, with real practical experience in the business. Some were winging it, barely staying ahead of the students from lesson to lesson. On the positive side, the school had a recording studio, and had enough budget to have occasional guest speakers.

I never met a teacher in our program who believed that teaching four hour classes was a good way to educate students. Drew Armstrong was a teacher in the program who taught classes on venues and concert promotion. Drew was from Louisiana and had a strong southern drawl and a laid back delivery. We used to joke that Drew was the only one who could successfully teach a four hour class, because he talked so slowly that he could deliver an hour and a half's worth of material in four hours.

In the early 90's the Art Institutes headquarters in Pittsburgh undertook a study that concluded that there weren't sufficient jobs in the music business to justify continuing their music business programs. The Seattle school continued their program for some additional years, but the other schools quickly phased out music business as a course of study.

There is considerable controversy about vocational schools that has brought about some inquiries by the federal government into the practice of paying recruiters commissions for each student admitted. For my part, I couldn't wait to get away from the CIA and towards the end of my one year tenure, that opportunity arose.

BOBBY THOMPSON

CIA decided that the music business students should take a trip to Nashville. Drew Armstrong and I both knew people in the industry there. Drew set up a meeting with an important Nashville entertainment attorney and manager, and I arranged a lunch with songwriter Guy Clark, and later invited banjo players Bobby Thompson and Vic Jordan to yet another gathering. I don't think any of the students had ever heard of Bobby. The chances are good that the readers of this book know little or nothing about him, which is really a shame.

There are certain musicians who are known as musician's musicians. This means that other professionals respect their unique abilities, but these talents are not universally known. One of the most interesting musicians that I have known to fit this description was the late Bobby Thompson. Bobby was a five string banjo player who played with the bluegrass band Jim and Jesse and then moved to Nashville to become a studio player. When Bobby was considering moving there, a friend of his advised him to master the art of rhythm guitar playing. In those days a typical recording date in that town included three songs in three hours. Bobby's friend explained that most dates would only feature banjo on one tune, so that if you wanted to get hired, you needed to play something else. An added bonus was that playing banjo and guitar entitled you to what the union calls doubling fees when you play two different instruments. For record dates that bonus was 20%.

Bobby bought a metronome and practiced rhythm guitar until he became an excellent timekeeper. Once he moved to Nashville he became part of the A team, the elite studio players who often did three sessions a day, five days a week. Bobby also became the staff banjo player on the Hee Haw TV show.

Bobby was one of the first, if not the first, banjo player to play in the so-called melodic style. This entailed breaking down the three finger patterns that Earl Scruggs had perfected in order to play specific melodies, as fiddlers do. I did an article on Bobby for Frets Magazine, and he told me that he came up with this style when Jim and Jesse's fiddle player taunted him, asking him whether banjo players ever actually played melodies.

Expanding on his work, Bobby came up with some elaborate banjo solos. When he played them at Jim and Jesse's shows, he was greeted with shouts of "play Foggy Mountain Breakdown." That was the Earl Scruggs signature tune that also was used in the movie Bonnie and Clyde. Disgusted with this reaction, Bobby abandoned these experiments.

Meanwhile a New England banjo player named Bill Keith experimented with some of the same melodic concepts, and was hired by Bill Monroe, known as the father of bluegrass. Fueled by Monroe's endorsement, the style caused a sensation among banjo pickers.It is difficult to be sure who invented the style, but it is clear that Keith has received the lion's share of the credit due to Monroe's importance.

In 1969 Bobby joined a new group of younger Nashville session players to form the group Area Code 615. This new generation of studio players were influenced by rock and jazz music and they recorded everything from Beatles tunes to Mason William's Classical Gas. This album was way ahead of its time, and caused great excitement among forward-thinking country music aficianados.

One night I was idly flipping channels on my TV set, and I encountered a banjo duet on Hee Haw between Bobby and Roy Clark. Now Roy is a good guitarist, and an excellent entertainer, but he is a rather average banjo player. Bobby had a beard and was dressed in overalls. He had a stovepipe hat that almost covered his entire face. Roy was animated, and as is his usual style, was making the most grotesque "this is really hard" expressions while playing a really basic banjo part. Bobby's hands were moving like an express train, but his face showed no expression. I thought to myself that 95% of the people watching this think that Roy is playing the really intricate stuff, and Bobby is just backing him up. That's what I mean about Bobby being a musician's musician.

In the early 70's Bobby started to experience some problem with his hands. Doctors assured him that is was all in his mind. In 1985 he went to a session where he was unable to move his right, picking hand. A doctor immediately diagnosed him as having MS (multiple sclerosis.) Bobby never played professionally again, and he died in 2005.

Since Bobby and Bill Keith started their melodic banjo styles many other players have imitated these techniques, and some, like Bela Fleck, have expanded them. To my ears, the special quality that Bobby possessed was his ability to maintain a strong rhythmic base, no matter where his melodic inventions took him. I have never heard another melodic banjo player who had that sort of rhythmic solidity.

Left:
Bobby Thompson - unsung hero of the banjo, musician's musician, innovator of melodic banjo, session player, and staff banjo player on Hee Haw. His style has been adopted, imitated and expanded by some of today's top players.

Below:
Current photo of Nashville, TN.

Part 2 • Chapter 16 

NIGHTS IN TUNISIA

Mid-way into my year at the CIA, Susan and I decided that we needed to take a break and go to some place exotic that we knew next to nothing about. We considered a trip to Morocco or Tunisia, and even discussed going to both of them. That idea was quashed when we found out that the State Department was recommending that Americans not go to Algeria. Since the train from Morocco to Tunisia passed right through Algeria, that was the end of that notion.

We finally selected Tunisia, partly because we knew so many people who had been to Morocco, but Tunisia seemed to be a destination unknown to most Americans.

We decided to go across the desert with a group of other tourists. There were three four- wheel drive vehicles, and we set out for Tamerza, a town near the Algerian border. We arrived at our cabin and went to dinner. A group of musicians was playing, including two percussionists, a lead singer, and a shenai player. The shenhai is an Arabic version of an oboe. This player was very skillful, and he would alternately use a bagpipe attachment to get additional sounds out of his horn. The lead singer was a Jimmy Cliff imitator who also "played" bongos. The lead percussionist at one point imitated what "Jimmy" was playing with one finger. It was a very enjoyable evening, and showed me that even in relatively remote part of the world, musicians were listening to all sorts of sounds.

By the time dinner was over, the rain had intensified. A small stream below the cabins had turned into a raging river. We went to our cabin and tried to sleep. Water started to seep in through the ceiling and the badly fitted windows and under the door. At midnight there was a knock on the door. I opened the door and a Tunisian asked me in French if we were all right. Using my high school French I told him we were fine.

The next morning we were told at breakfast that the trip had been suspended, and that a large percentage of Tunisia was flooded. When some of the tourists asked where we would stay that night, our Tunisian guide told us that we would be taken care of. About 4PM we were escorted to cabins that were further up the hill and were not flooded. There weren't enough cabins for 25 of us, so we doubled up. Our co-inhabitants were a Belgian tourist and his wife. She was recovering from a serious operation, and she asked the guide whether we would be OK. He responded that we would all be fine, if Allah willed it. I doubt that she found this response too re-assuring.

The next day we were told that the trip was reinstated. We piled into the four wheel vehicles and literally drove through the waters. Our four wheel drive Toyota was the only one that made it out without being stuck in the water.

Our destination was an army barracks. The commandant told us that our trip was over, and that we were to stay in the barracks until further notice. They gave us blankets, and we all slept on the floor. Since many of our fellow tourists were smokers, the air was so thick that it was hard to breathe. The TV was turned on, and I was fascinated by the Tunisian music that was playing. It featured the fretless oud, along with a western orchestra

Someone told the commandant that Susan was an artist and I was a musician. He concluded that she would do a mural of the great Tunisian flood, and that I would write an epic symphonic work celebrating this tragic event. I did in fact write a neo-Tunisian banjo piece, played with a slide on the left hand. The slide is able to simulate the various non-scale tones that a fretless instrument is capable of delivering.

The next day our tour was magically reinstated, the flood subsided, and the tour ended at a Tunisian resort frequented mostly by British tourists. On the way there we stopped at a small town and dined at a restaurant that was so small that the proprietors sent their kids to bring in chairs and bags of spaghetti from neighboring houses. Their hospitality was touching.

When the tour ended, Susan and I stayed at a fancy seaside resort for a couple of days. One night a waiter objected to my whistling as I walked into the room. "No whistling in Tunisia," he told me.

I was able to buy some Tunisian cassettes in the marketplace, which also had bootleg cassettes of Madonna and LL Cool J for about $2 each. What I remember about Tunisia is the friendliness of the people, and how every child seemed to be rhythm crazy, beating time on benches or anything else available.

PROVINCIALISM

Americans often get a bad rap for provincialism by Europeans. On our Tunisian journey, most of our fellow tourists were Belgians. One of them was the traffic controller at the Brussels airport. He asked me whether all Americans drove Cadillacs. I asked him what gave him that impression. He told me that all the people on the TV show Dallas drove them. I said that maybe all Texans drove them, but it certainly was not true of all Americans. I'm certain that he didn't get the sarcastic aspect of my remark.

My son Paul had gone to college with the daughter of the American ambassador to Tunisia. Paul told me before we left that if I had any problems that we could call the ambassador. I made the mistake of telling one of the Belgians about this while we were staying at the army barracks. By the end of theday the rumor had spread that The American Marine Corps was going to helicopter in and save all of us.

Left:
The Shenhai - an Arabic version of The Oboe.

Below:
The ancient and beautiful land of Tunisia.

Part 3 • Chapter 17

1990-2002
THE UNIVERSITY OF COLORADO AT DENVER

One of my acquaintances who became a good friend was Frank Jermance. He was an excellent jazz guitarist who got tired of performing, and settled into a career teaching music business and guitar at the University of Colorado at Denver. In fact, he was the one who got the job that I had been invited to apply for some years earlier. Frank told me that his colleague Don Gorder was leaving, and there was a job opening for Fall, 1990.

Since I now did have a master's degree I applied for the position soon after we came back from Tunisia. I was still working at the Colorado Institute of Art, but I thought that UCD represented a far better opportunity. At the same time I applied for a job at Middle Tennessee State University in Murfreesboro, Tennessee. Murfreesboro is thirty five miles from Nashville, and I thought that it was possible if I got the job there I could also pick up some session work in Nashville.

I went through the application process at both schools, and soon heard from UCD that I was one of three finalists for the position. I had worked at CWC and CIA, but I really had no clue what it was like to be interviewed for a position at a large state university. I gave a one hour lecture on the international music business. It was attended by students and faculty, and I also answered a number of questions from both groups. I was interviewed by a hiring committee, by the full music committee, the dean, and the chancellor of the school. Since I lived in the area this was all accomplished in a single, rather stressful, day. The other two candidates came from out of town, and their interviews were spread out over two days.

Seven faculty members voted on the candidates, and then this decision had to be approved by higher level administrators. I later found out that I won by a single vote. Candidates are not supposed to know who they are competing against, but of course the information was eventually leaked to me. Two of the people who voted against me favored a candidate who was a flautist but had made mistakes in her music business lecture. From everything I was told later, she had little experience in the actual music industry. She was however a woman, and these two opted for the addition of another female colleague. The third person who voted against me did so because I played the banjo, and as he put it, "the banjo is not a musical instrument." Furthermore, he was a composer and she played the flute, and he thought it might be nice to have a flutist around for whom he could write music.

All of these deliberations took a few weeks, and then the dean offered me the job, a tenure track full-time job with a salary of $31,000 plus benefits.

The very next day I got a call from the department chair at Middle Tennessee. He told me that it had taken a long time for them to decide on their finalists because they had a hiring freeze due to an affirmative action lawsuit. He said that was now over, and he invited me to be interviewed. I had already accepted the other job, but I thought I'd find out more about what he was offering. As he was talking to me he was clearly reading my resume. He told me that I "only" had master's degree so I would not be eligible for a tenure track job, and my rank would be that of an instructor. I then told him that the reason that Middle Tennessee interested me was that they had an excellent folklore collection and an archive of popular music, and these were both things that fascinated me. He immediately snapped that if I got involved in those areas I would have to do it on my own time, because they had nothing to do with my teaching duties. Since I had the other job in hand, this whole conversation amused me. At state schools there is a kind of hierarchy. For example, in California UC in Berkeley and UCLA in Los Angeles are considered the top schools, and then the hierarchy goes down to the many campuses of UC and the California State University colleges. Without being too insulting, Middle Tennessee wasn't exactly at the top rung of the Tennessee college system, and yet they wanted someone teaching music business to have a PhD. Notwithstanding, mind you, that there are no PhD programs in music business to this day. I thanked the gentleman for calling me, and told him that I had already accepted the job at UCD, and informed him that it was a tenure track job.

UCD: THE EARLY YEARS

A few years after I graduated from UCD, the school moved into a new campus a few blocks away. The campus is called Auraria, and is unique in the sense that three different institutions share the facility. The other two are the downtown campus of the Community College of Denver, and Metropolitan State College. The latter school initially did not offer graduate courses, but after its expansion in the 21st century it began to do so, and its name has been changed to Metropolitan State University.

The three schools actually share classroom facilities. Because the campus is always crowded, the fight for space between Metro and UCD in particular is childish, time-consuming and bewildering. The schools are not supposed to offer similar programs, but similar foundation classes are often taught in both schools. For example as a UCD student you might be taking music theory, while across the hall Metro students would be taking a similar class.

My first semester teaching at UCD, I was assigned two new classes on the first day of school. One was a class in Arts Management, which I was barely qualified to teach, and the other was a class in Music Appreciation. I spent my first month trying to prepare for these classes as though I actually was qualified to teach them.

Early in the game I discovered the joys of faculty meetings. At my other schools these were basically non-existent. The chair of the department might call one meeting a semester. At UCD the meetings were sometimes once a week, once every other week, or occasionally once a month. It usually depended on who the chair of the department was, and how much responsibility he or she wanted to delegate to other faculty members.

TEACHING LOADS

Teaching loads at different colleges vary greatly. A full-time professor at UCD taught five classes a year, three in one semester, two in another. Business professors only taught four classes a year. At the mother campus in Boulder professors taught four classes a year. When I worked part-time at Portland Community College after I left UCD, a full-time course load was sixteen hours a quarter. Most classes in the music department were four credit classes, which included a lab. Full-time professors taught three quarters. So a full-time professor at PCC taught approximately as many classes in a quarter as UCD professors taught in the entire academic year. The trade-off was that since UCD is what is called a B research university, there were expectations that the professor do research and/ or creative work. I'm not certain what sort of research work my colleagues were doing, but I wrote more books during my time at UCD than the other nine people in the music program together. I guess I would have to conclude that the research expectations were more abstract than real. Some professors indeed did performances or wrote music, and a few wrote occasional journal articles.

The sticking point in college teaching comes in the sixth year when professors apply for tenure. (Not every college follows the tenure system, but most of the ones that you have heard of do so.) During this critical sixth year, the professor submits an extensive dossier that lists all their research or creative work, as well as the evaluations that students submit after each course Student evaluations are a whole other matter. Some students are fair and scrupulous in their evaluations. Others treat evaluations as a popularity contest. "Al was a very funny professor," so he gets a good evaluation. I knew one professor who appeared to do little in the way of teaching. Because he gave all students an A he generally got excellent evaluations.

TEACHING AND KEEPING THINGS FRESH

Some professors use the same textbook for years. When their class comes up, they take a cursory look at the latest edition of that book, and essentially use the same syllabus and notes that they have used before. To avoid boring myself and the students, when I got through a class, I tore up my notes and the syllabus. I felt that this would ensure that my lectures weren't simply the same tape in a different year. When I came up for tenure, this actually got me in a little bit of trouble, because some of the professors wondered if I bothered to do syllabi. During my teaching days there were two evaluations that preceded tenure, but that has been narrowed to a single three year pre-tenure evaluation.

DEANS

During my time at UCD we had three deans. The deans rode herd over the music, theater and art departments. All of the deans during my years at UCD came from the theater area, even though this was by far the smallest program in the school of the arts. The first one had only spent two years at UCD when he was hired by Wayne State in Detroit. Laura Cuetara, the next dean, came from our theater department. She was deposed after a couple of years because of a feud with the art department. A few months before her return to the regular faculty, she visited each professor in the entire school of the arts. The university had passed a one class liberal arts requirement of a course dealing in some way with multi-cultural diversity. I came up with a class called Social and Political Implications of American Music. The intent of the class was to examine social and political aspects of non-classical American music by examining music by and about Native Americans, African-Americans, Spanish speaking groups and women. There also was a segment on songs written to bring about social change, including what I referred to as "the music of hate." By the music of hate I am referring to American neo-Nazi music, and songs that favor segregation.

When I put the course proposal together I realized that there wasn't a single book that covered all these bases, although many books had been written about each of these subject areas. I decided to write a workbook for the class, and then to try to sell it to a publisher, both as a textbook and a work that would be of interest to the general reader who had an interest in American music and politics.

THE ONE YEAR CU FELLOWSHIP

I knew that writing a book of this kind would entail doing a tremendous amount of research. I also expected that it would prove difficult to do that level of serious research while teaching. Fortunately for me, the University of Colorado had a one year fellowship program for exactly this sort of research. Inevitably that this would be a very competitive situation, because the year rewarded the winner a full year of pay, while normal teacher sabbaticals only gave professors half pay for a full year, or full pay for a single semester. When I was awarded the fellowship I was told that I was the first professor that anyone remembered who won the fellowship before getting tenure.

The year that I spent on this research was very rewarding. I read a large number of books and did write the workbook that I was able to use in the class a year later. I spent only occasional days on campus, checking on mail and email, and meeting the new dean of the College of the Arts.

TENURE

I applied for early tenure, which means that I applied during my fifth year rather my sixth year. For the non-academics reading this book, the tenure process is usually attempted after six years of teaching. The candidate must assemble a lengthy dossier that describes his or her work, a record of research or creative work that has been undertaken, and a complete set of student evaluations. The candidate also includes books, articles or any creative work that has been done during the six years.

The benefit of obtaining tenure are that it is an extreme form of job security, and almost always results in an upgrade from Assistant to Associate Professor, and in a variety of ways it gives the professor status and a higher level of input into the scheduling of classes. The up-grade in rank includes a sizeable wage increase. In my case that was a 10% bonus. This is far more than typical academic yearly increases, which run from 0 to a high of about 3%, depending on the financial situation at the college. It is very difficult to fire a tenured professor. Usually only the firing of an entire academic department or a really horrendous act like coming to classes drunk or stoned or charges of sexual harassment can result in a tenured professor losing a job. The latter is not an unknown situation, but one that rarely occurs. From my point of view the primary reason for tenure is that administrators might fire a professor for political views or behaviors that are perfectly acceptable but that don't conform to an administrator's ideas. Someone who is denied tenure becomes a lame duck. Since the decisions are made near the end of the academic year, the professor is giving an additional one year terminal contract and then must relinquish the position.

Various schools treat tenure as being easy, difficult or impossible to achieve. At schools like Harvard or Yale a professor must secure a reputation as being a top scholar in their field or they don't get tenure. They are indeed informed of this before being hired. An acquaintance of mine was denied tenure at Yale, but immediately got a job with tenure at a state university. From their point of view it was an honor to hire a professor who had taught at Yale!

Many people oppose tenure. For the reason I have discussed above, I support it. I do believe that the five year post-tenure review process needs to be transformed into a serious review, instead of the rubber stamp that it often becomes. In any case, while in my fellowship year, I was awarded tenure and promoted to Associate Professor.

MARK HECKLER

Mark Heckler, the new dean, also had a theater background. He was energetic and ambitious. Every semester we would have a meeting of all the various departments in the School of the Arts. The one that I remember best was early in Mark's career. We all filled out a number of sheets with the heading SWOT. This stands for strengths, weaknesses, opportunities and threats. During my years of college teaching I became suspicious of this sort of exercise, because somehow administrators always seem to find a way to manipulate the results to justify whatever programs that they have in mind before the exercise begins.

Mark was always looking for ways to promote our programs. He made over forty trips to China to set up a student exchange that the administration ultimately abandoned. He set up a number of important promotion tools, like web sites and in general fought to increase the budgets of each department. I will have more to say about him and educational administration when I discuss the period of 1999-2000 when I became head of the music department.

OREGON

My children had some savings from money given to them by my parents. During Jimmy Carter's term as president (1976-1980) interest rates escalated to the high teens. Since my children's accounts were in bank CD's this inflation provided them with a huge cushion of college money. My son decided to go to Lewis & Clark College in Portland, Oregon. On a visit to see him, I ended up driving around the entire Oregon coast. Two small towns particularly interested me. Bandon in Southern Oregon has a long, wonderful, and relatively isolated beach. Astoria is in Northwest Oregon, across the Columbia River from Washington border and is 90 miles from Portland.

It was wonderful to be in places that were very green and cool in the summer. Over time Denver has developed hot summers, and because there is usually relatively little rain, the grass usually turns brown in mid-July. Susan and I took a trip to Oregon in the summer of 1991, and checked out both towns. We even looked at houses there. Our thought was to find a summer home, and eventually move there when I

left UCD and Susan gave up public school teaching. Bandon at that time had a population of around 2200, and although we loved the beach, the town seemed too small for us. We also envisioned having to drive 140 miles to Eugene for dental or medical services. It didn't seem to be a realistic choice.

Astoria had about ten thousand people in 1991 and it had doctors, dentists and even a hospital. This was partly because the town had a Coast Guard facility. Astoria is located at the mouth of the Columbia River, where it feeds into the Pacific Ocean.

The town has quite a number of imposing Victorian houses and we contacted a realtor while we were there. We didn't find anything suitable, but the minute we got back to Colorado, she called with a house that sounded interesting. The college year was just starting, so Susan flew back there without me to check out the house. It was a three story Victorian, with a large basement and a huge amount of space. It had an outside balcony on the second floor where we could sit out without being visible to people in other houses or on the street. From 1991-1999 we spent every summer in Astoria, and we moved there in 2000.

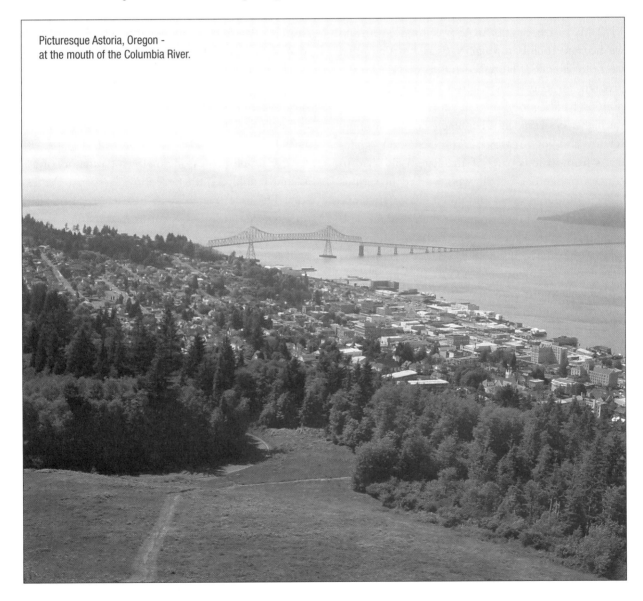

Picturesque Astoria, Oregon -
at the mouth of the Columbia River.

Part 3 • Chapter 18

1996-2000 THE END OF THE UNIVERSITY TEACHING TUNNEL

After my fellowship ended, I returned to regular teaching at UCD. I had served on one college-wide committee before I was awarded tenure, so I had some concept of college bureaucracy The following are two specific examples of the collegiate politics and procedures. The first one occurred when the Grammy organization decided to do a Colorado segment of their Grammies in the Schools program in 1992. My successor at NARAS was Ron Bergan, and we became friends through various functions that we both attended. He asked me to coordinate the program for its two day visit to Colorado. The organization had begun to present educational programs for high school students. I contacted numerous high schools and got a reasonable representation of students from various parts of the state. I also had to contact presenters, people who worked in various aspects of the business and could talk to students. NARAS in turn at the last minute presented me with a nationally known guest speaker and performer, who sat in with some high school bands. Their choice was the famous vibraphone player Gary Burton.

Because of the convoluted nature of the Auraria campus, janitorial staff worked for three sets of bosses. Getting the parking for school buses was something of a nightmare, but it all worked out. I had carefully reserved the facility in which we were holding the event, which was an old church that was actually on campus. I got there a half hour before the event was to begin. As I had feared, the doors were locked. I made call after call to the facilities service, always leaving messages on answering machines. Fortunately a passing theater professor happened by, immediately grasped the situation, and physically went down to where the facilities people worked, and insisted that someone come back with her and open the door. It all worked out, and the rest of the day was almost an anti-climax. This inevitably led me to the old joke along the lines of "how many calls does it take to get facilities managers to open a door?" I guess the answer is one more than you are able to make.

THE SALARY COMMITTEE

For three years I served on the campus-wide salaries appeal committee. Each of us were given a loose leaf book which contained the salaries of everyone working at the college. As a music professor I realized that we were going to make less money than those in the engineering department, but I had no idea of the breadth of that disparity.

The members of the committee came from various departments of the school, including physical sciences, humanities, business, and so forth. No one in the music department in 1992 was making as much as $50,000. Not even our full professors. Full professors, or simply professors, are the top category of academic employees, the rank above Associate Professors. The exact hierarchy is: Instructor (not usually on a tenure track.) Assistant Professor (on a tenure track but not tenured.) Associate Professor (achieved with tenure.) Full Professor- (usually attained from six or seven years after the associate rank is given.) As the professor goes up the academic ladder, each bump comes with a liberal dose of prestige and power and an approximately 10% wage increase.

The exact function of our committee was to serve as a sort of appeals court. For example, an Associate Professor of Chemical Engineering gets bumped from $76,000 to $77,000 and appeals on the basis that everyone else in the department has gotten a 3% raise. We would read the appeal, request a response from the department chair, and then try to mediate between the opposing factions.

Many of the requests were childish or frivolous, and the increase requested seemed almost humorous. It also involved us in departmental politics. An example of this might be that professor X has written more books than Professor Y, but the latter is head of the department. Professor X thus attributes her small salary increase to Professor Y's jealousy.

In many cases we found ourselves unable to unravel departmental politics, and the entire process seemed like a waste of time. What I did learn from this experience was that music and art professors were definitely at the low end of the financial totem pole

WHY ARE YOU TALKING TO ME?

One day a student came to my office to talk with me. He was a finance major who was doing brilliantly in the business school, but his real passion involved audio engineering. He entered my office hesitantly and seemed reluctant to speak, even though he had made an appointment with me. I asked him what was wrong. It turned out that no one teaching in his major field of study had ever been willing to meet with him. Apparently they regarded students as a distraction. One professor kept making and cancelling appointments with him, because she was always "too busy." Once again I confronted the reality of academic life. In certain areas of the school students were definitely an impediment to the professor's real goals. They were either research projects that would build their resume, or consulting jobs that would add to their income.

DON'T GIVE UP THE SHIP: TALKIN' 'BOUT A REVOLUTION

I tried to sell my book on American Music and Social Change for several years after getting tenure. It was rejected by a number of publishers. I began to think I was re-living the Westbrooks research project situation, and would never sell the book. The problem was that at the time there simply weren't enough college courses that involved all of the multi-cultural groups that I covered in the book. The project had something of a happy ending, when in 2009 Hal Leonard Books agreed to publish the book, which was published a year later, with a few revisions.

THE RETURN OF SCOTT McKENZIE AND JOHN PHILLIPS

I hadn't seen John Phillips or Scott McKenzie in years. My last communication with John was in the late 60's when he called to ask me to come to California to play on a new Mamas and Papas album. He said that he was sending me airline tickets. When the tickets didn't arrive, I tried to call him a week later, and was unable to locate him. I decided that I had had enough of the Hollywood star syndrome.

In 1970 Scott's album Stained Glass Reflections was released by A&M Records. We happened to be in Swarthmore, Pennsylvania one weekend on a family trip, visiting my first wife's mother. Walking downtown I saw posters placed all over town about a free concert by Scott at Swarthmore College. I went to the show, and sat in the back of the room where Scott couldn't see me. He was singing well, but he refused to sing either his San Francisco hit or the failed follow up Like An Old Time Movie. About San Francisco, Scott told the audience, "I don't sing amphetamine music." Referring to Old Time Movie Scott said "I can't sing a song that uses the word groovy." Later in the show Scott asked permission to read a poem. In general his performance was distant and unfocused, and I'm sure it puzzled the students, who had come to hear him do his hits.

After the show I spent a little time with Scott. It was obvious to me that he was entirely unaware that Swarthmore is one of the top academic colleges in the United States, and that he hardly needed permission to recite a poem. He told me that he was performing the next night at West Chester State Teachers College. I looked at him and smiled, and suggested that asking permission at that school might not be a bad idea.

Scott was friendly but a bit distant. I had the impression that his feud with John had gotten even worse than it had been in Journeymen days. He told me that he had spent some time living in Virginia Beach, and occasionally doing jingles in Washington, D.C., but that was about as far as our conversation got.

By 1980 John had become a pitiful drug addict, and was busted in New York. After going through rehab and doing anti-drug speeches for teenagers, he formed the Mamas and Papas Revival band. The first revival group had Denny and John, and the female parts were sung by John's daughter McKenzie and Spanky McFarlane, of Spanky and Our Gang. They came to Boulder, and I went to see them at the Boulder Theater. When I went backstage, John asked me how they sounded. I told him that I thought the vocals sounded really good, but the band was so loud that I had trouble hearing the words. John turned to the band and immediately lectured them about playing too loud. He asked if I wanted to see a performance the next day in suburban Denver, but I declined. He said it sounded just like me to turn down the invitation. We started talking about various things, and John smiled and told me that after twenty years he felt that we could simply pick up our old conversations without explanation or delay.

It would be another ten years before I saw John again. In 1992 I was in Los Angeles on some other business, and spoke to Paul Surratt, Gram Parson's old band mate. He told me that John was getting a liver transplant at UCLA. I met Paul at John's bedside at UCLA. He had been operated on the previous day. He looked like a ghost. His skin was yellow, and he looked as though his weight was down to not much more than 100 pounds. The operation was very lengthy, and John was in severe pain. We talked briefly, and I was glad that I had visited him. He was generally in a good mood, considering how sick he had been. He shared a couple of amusing details about his hospital stay. He said that the surgeon had played his harmonica during part of the operation. He also said that Scott had been there, and that the doctor had offered to give him a complete examination when he surmised that Scott had a drinking problem. According to John, always the storyteller, Scott had fled in terror.

In 1993 I got a call from John and Scott. John was living in Palm Springs, and he asked me to come out and play on a new solo album that he was working on. I had the sense that this was Scott's idea, but we didn't discuss that. It was the middle of the semester at UCD, and I had to get permission from Franz Roehmann, the head of the department.

When I got to Palm Springs the band was already there. John (Kito) Buonamassa was the piano player and had put the arrangements together. John was then using the name Kito, since no one seemed to able to spell Buonamassa. Phillips called John "Chart Man" for his ability to write a musical arrangement in a matter of minutes. Scott played acoustic twelve string guitar and sang, and Kenny Brescia played lead guitar. Percussionist Robin Daniels from New York covered the rhythm.

During the first day of recording, John seemed tired and mentally removed from the recording. On the second day, John and Scott suggested that since all three Journeymen were present, that we sing a few Journeymen songs. I was not excited at this idea, but I figured that anything that lifted John's spirits was a worthwhile undertaking.

We sang three or four songs together. Everyone was in a state of shock. It was as though we were well-rehearsed and had returned after a short vacation. Someone was taking video of what we did, and I only wish that I could watch that video now. Along with so many other things, it has disappeared into the mist.

None of us said anything about the impromptu Journeymen reunion. That day we recorded three songs, and the rest of the recording went very well. That magical moment seemed to have transformed the entire project

We had the sense that Paul Gilman, the producer of the sessions, and his engineering assistant Alex were also out of their comfort zone. Many tunes had false starts caused by engineering problems. When the recording was completed, it proved next to impossible to mix. Because we were all in a living room with no sound baffling, everything spilled onto other people's performances. A wonderful week of John and Scott's vocals, with some really nice guitar parts by Kenny Brescia, and some of my own best work were in vain.

John originally had hoped to release the album in 1996, and when my fellowship came through, we talked about my touring with him. Neither the album or the tour ever happened. I did play a half dozen gigs with the Mamas and Papas Revival Band. Scott had entered the band as the fifth vocalist, and eventually he replaced Denny Doherty, when he didn't want to tour.

We played a couple of stadium concerts for well over 50,000 people in Denver. These were rock and roll oldies shows, with acts like The Beach Boys, Chuck Berry and Martha and the Vandellas. My main reaction was the sort of thing that Linda Ronstadt talks about in her autobiography. I was terrified that I was playing out of tune, and there was so much audience noise that it was difficult to follow the rhythm. The other gigs that I did with the band were casino gigs. Knowing that my temperament and ideology were about as far removed from the world of casinos as anyone could possibly be, John found it amusing to include me on those gigs. This included stints at Reno, Las Vegas, Lake Tahoe and Cripple Creek, Colorado. They were always on weekends, so they didn't interfere with my teaching.

In 1997 Washington's World Folk Music Association arranged for a Journeymen reunion concert at their annual festival. By this time John had slowed down, and he decided that he couldn't make the trip. Shortly before the event Scott bowed out as well. He cited various physical ailments. I called Dick Cerri the head of the organization, and asked him if he still wanted me to perform there. Since both John and Scott were from Washington and I wasn't, I didn't see much reason to go. Dick assured me that I was welcome.

When I arrived, I saw that the cover of the program was a Journeymen photo. I think that my presence at least indicated to the audience that we really had accepted the gig. I did a set with several other people sitting in, including Bill Danoff. We played his song I Guess He'd Rather Be In Colorado together. My banjo pieces were well received, and I was left wondering whether we would have been able to re-capture the magical moments that had occurred at John's recording session.

John died in 2001. I was in New Orleans at the time, at an academic conference. I didn't attend his memorial, because it would have been difficult to arrange at the last minute, and also because I didn't relish being at the confluence of his various wives and girl friends. Scott told me that it all came off relatively peacefully. I guess I felt that I had said my farewells to John prior to his actual death. He was certainly one of the most interesting and complex people I have ever known. I only wish he had found more peace in his life. I'll discuss Scott further in the next section of the book.

PROTEST MUSIC AND THEATER MUSIC

In 1991 I worked on the music for a play about the Ludlow Massacre with professor Larry Bogard of the Metro Theater Department. This event, which had been celebrated in song by Woody Guthrie, took place in 1913. A multi-ethnic group of miners went out on strike against a Rockefeller-owned coal mine. Two women and eleven children were killed, as well as an additional dozen strikers in what became known as the Ludlow Massacre.

When I met Larry Bograd he was using period music for the play, but I convinced him to let me write a final song after the breaking of the strike.

This led to making a connection with several leaders of OCAW, the United Coke, Chemical and Atomic Workers Union. Under the guidance of Phyllis Olmacher and the sponsorship of union president Bob Wages and long time union official Tony Mazzochi I wrote the music for the union's national convention, and Larry Bograd wrote the script. Among the songs was one about Karen Silkwood. Silkwood worked at the Kerr-McGee uranium plant in Oklahoma, and was a member of OCAW. She died in a mysterious automobile accident in Oklahoma while on the way to meet a New York Times reporter. Her intent was to disclose the company's unsafe labor practices. My song, and additional discussions between Larry and the union led to his writing a play called The Half Life Of Karen Silkwood. The former dean of UCD presented it at his new school, Wayne State University in Detroit. Larry ended up using only one of my songs, in the play, Dancing In My Dreams.

Part of the union's motivation for doing the play was that Meryl Streep and Cher had starred in a fairly successful movie about Silkwood, and the union felt that she had been presented in a somewhat unfavorable light. The song used in the play attempted to explain why Silkwood left her husband and three children in the middle of the night, and moved from Texas to Oklahoma. As far as I know, the short run in Detroit was the play's only performance.

Through the 90's I did music for two of the OCAW national conventions, as well as writing music for the Labor Party convention in 1996. The Labor Party was an attempt to form a political party that would represent the interests of the labor movement and working people in general.

I also produced and wrote all of the songs on a cassette that OCAW funded. The songs were basically a compilation of all of the work I had done for the union in the 90's. The union then did a video of the songs and script used at their convention.

After the initial convention, I did all of the music, and worked on a script with the help of union cultural leader Phyllis Olmacher. These projects were very gratifying and because a union was sponsoring them the budgets were reasonable, and everyone was fairly paid. In 2002 the union, which was suffering a decline in membership, united with the Paperworkers Union, which in turn was absorbed by the United Steelworkers Union. Tony Mazzochi died in 2002, and his dream of the Labor Party was never really fulfilled. Some ten years later I recorded several of the OCAW songs on an album called Four Directions.

ENGLAND

Once you have a university job, and in particular, if you have gained some notoriety through writing books, or doing some sort of creative work like painting or writing music, opportunities come up through either careful planning or someone encountering your work. I have known a number of art professors, for example, who do guest lectures at other colleges including exhibitions of their work, and then in turn hire professors who made these opportunities possible to do similar things at their school. There is something that makes me uncomfortable about such arrangements. Kind of you scratch my back and I'll scratch yours. Some of these situations involve people doing excellent work, and others are more like people who are career oriented finding other professors with a similar bent.

Out of the blue I received a call in the late 90's, asking whether I wanted to do a week's residency at the Liverpool Institute of Performing Arts in England. Apparently the school had contacted me on the basis of an administrator seeing several of my books about the music business. This was a school teaching music business and performing skills that started in London, but moved to Liverpool when it received some financial support from Sir Paul McCartney. The school was actually located in the facility where Paul had attended elementary school.

Because of the McCartney connection the school was able to get such guest lecturers as George Martin, the Beatles' record producer, and Mark Knopfler of the band Dire Straits. I was thrilled at the opportunity to teach in England, and using frequent flyer miles Susan went with me.

To this day I have never seen anything like LIPA, as the school was called. The energy level was so high that each day was exhausting. The school had experienced some administrative changes, so each day I would go there and not know what I was being asked to lecture about. I ended up talking mostly about the American music business. I really enjoyed relating to the students, who came from all over the world. It was interesting to me that they were thoroughly puzzled by American life. For example, England actually has programs for re-training unemployed youth in musical pursuits. The students were entirely puzzled when I explained that America didn't have such programs, and was unlikely to develop them. We managed to spend some time in London on the trip, and I came back to Colorado exhausted but mentally refreshed.

JAMAICA

A similar call resulted in my going to Jamaica to discuss the music business for the Jamaican Trade Board. This was in late summer 2001. The second morning that I was there, I was watching morning television when the planes hit the World Trade Center in New York. The reactions of my Jamaican students to 9/11 varied widely. Some were horrified, and other took the sort of Malcolm X position that the chickens had come home to roost. To some Jamaicans, America was a crazy wealthy colonialist paradise that deserved this punishment.

I ended up being stranded in Kingston for three days after the conference had ended. My host, Marjorie Scott-Anderson and her husband entertained me as best they could during this involuntary hiatus. They took me to an amusing play, whose dialogue I found difficult because of the extensive use of Jamaican patois. I tried to walk the streets of Kingston where I was offered numerous drugs and other possible recreational opportunities before deciding that an American white boy walking the streets of Jamaica was an extreme version of a black man walking in Beverly Hills. I also went to one music store. It turned out that most Jamaicans bought their instruments in Atlanta or Miami, and the stock of instruments was pitiful.

I returned for two more years and taught at two songwriting boot camps, also run by Ms. Scott-Anderson. It was really interesting to interact with aspiring songwriters. Many American singer-songwriters are deeply ensconsed in writing what I call "me" songs, songs about their own personal lives. By contrast Jamaicans were examining political or religious themes in their songs that did not necessarily reflect their personal experiences. One of the best songs I heard was a catchy reggae-based tune called Dr. Jesus. There was also a wonderful song written by a young woman who was actually an art student. The song was about child abuse, and was called Only A Fly On The Wall. It was a brilliant and touching song that described the singer as being a fly on the wall, and witnessing the horrors that the song described. It reminded me a bit of Suzanne Vega's song, Luka, and was possibly even better than that.

COLLEGE GRANTS

One of my most rewarding accomplishments was bringing little known but interesting musicians to the UCD campus. At the time the school had no performing arts facility, so we were compelled to use classrooms of various sizes. Most universities have some sort of grant programs, and I was able to get four grants to bring artists in from various places. Len Chandler was a singer who I knew in Greenwich Village. He was one of the few black singers who performed regularly in the Village. He was arrested over fifty times in various Civil Rights demonstrations. Len told me that one time he was in jail with Nazi Party chief George Lincoln Rockwell. Despite Len's obvious color, Rockwell insisted that he couldn't possibly be black, because he was too intelligent! Len had a master's degree in oboe performance, and became interested in folk music when a white college professor played recordings by Leadbelly in a class. He quickly took up guitar, and with his fine voice and intriguing guitar style he was a dynamic performer.

Besides bring Len to the campus, I also brought a Native American artist named Vince Two Eagles and an American Indian rapper named Julian B. to the campus. Peggy Seeger also came to the campus, and performed at several other events in Denver. Peggy is Pete's half-sister, and the wife of the late English playwright-songwriter Ewan MacColl.

THE URBAN UNIVERSITY AND THE DENVER CHILDREN'S HOME

In the late 90's UCD started to focus on its role in the urban metropolis of Denver. I got a grant from UCD to work at a lock-up facility for emotinonally disturbed children called the Denver Children's Home. My program was designed to help the students write songs. I then integrated the program with a record production class that I was teaching at UCD. Each DCH student was assigned a UCD student as a producer. The Children's Home was an alternative to jail for kids who had experienced some trouble with the law, but who the courts determined were salvageable without jail time.

I went into this program with a small amount of experience in a similar facility in suburban Broomfield, Colorado at a place called Wallace Village. I had spent one day a week at Wallace Village working with a somewhat similar population there. The difference was that Wallace Village had a combination of white and Mexican-American kids, and DCH had a predominantly black population with a sprinkling of whites and Mexican-Americans.

At the end of the DCH program, usually about six weeks after we started, we took the kids into a professional recording studio, and each student recorded one of his or her songs. After we finished the studio edited the songs onto a single cassette, and each student got a copy.

I had a number of remarkable experiences at both facilities. At Wallace Village I had one student who started writing extremely violent songs about killing his relatives. After he came up with the third one, I became very concerned, and told his regular teacher what was going on. It turned out that he was not taking his medication. He was very angry with me for ratting him out, but it is quite possible I prevented a serious crime from occurring. Another Wallace Village student was a vivid and serious songwriter. He came to me at the last class I taught at Wallace Village, and told me that his songs were no good, and he had torn them all up. He then proceeded to sing me a new song, which was truly wonderful.

Dealing with a population that consisted of what many people would call misfits or even juvenile delinquents was a powerful learning experience for me. At DCH I had one student who didn't say very much during the class. I had donated a Casio keyboard to the school, and he was absolutely brilliant at coming up with new sounds and rhythms. I mentioned this to the principal of the school. He told me that this student had a testable IQ of 70. My response was to say that maybe the test wasn't a realistic way to test his particular talents. Another student wrote excellent rap lyrics. He was quite prolific, and not a class went by without a new song. The night before the recording session he ran away from the school. In his case what that meant was that he simply ran around the city block several times until he was caught. Since the school practiced behavior modification therapy, a form of psychology that rewards good behavior and punishes bad behavior, he was not allowed to attend the recording session. Apparently the pressure to actually record his music was too much for him.

I was told by the counselors at DCH that the best outcome that they could hope for was a 20% adjustment to the "real world" upon graduation from the program. I'm certain that a number of my students ended up in prison, or even were killed on the streets. One of the most rewarding parts of the program was pairing the kids with the UCD students. Many of the DCH students never had experienced a single positive interaction with young white people, and very few of my UCD students had ever dealt with a population like the one at DCH.

By the time I left UCD in 2002, I had done the DCH program four times. The days of the urban university were over, and in 2001 our dean would no longer give me release time for one class for working at DCH. I was unable to find anyone else on the music faculty who wanted to continue the work. It was a powerful learning experience for me, and the songs that the DCH kids wrote were often more interesting than the songs that came out of my songwriting classes at UCD or the summer workshops at Colorado Mountain College.

A few days before I wrote this section of the book I received a phone call from someone who had been a student at the Wallace Village program. Thirty five years after the fact he thanked me for the classes he had taken there. He told me that he had been teaching English as a second language in Germany for the past ten years, and had called me on a whim.

Part 3 • Chapter 19 

OREGON SUMMERS

From 1991-1999 we would drive to Astoria from Denver every summer. During our six week stays we would walk on the beach with our dogs, drive across the river to state parks in Washington, and hang out in Astoria.

Astoria has many of the characteristics of a small town, with some odd twists of its own. The primary industries that supported the town were fishing and the resultant canneries, and lumber. Both of these industries have suffered a steep decline. What had been several dozen canneries in Astoria and directly across the Columbia River, had degenerated into a single cannery. The city has made a strong attempt to replace these industries with tourism. Astoria has a rich stock of historic Victorian homes and is also the place where the Lewis and Clark expedition ended. There are various nearby sites that celebrate the expedition, and Astoria has a tower called the Astoria Column which provides views of the Columbia River for those who have the energy to climb the 164 feet to the top.

The original settlers were Scandinavians, especially Finns. There is still a Finnish gift store on the main street, but the population has seen an influx of aging hippies, Mexican-Americans, and regular old solid business folks. David Crabtree, a musician friend of mine who is a bamboo farmer, likes to say that people in Astoria are "hiding out." For such a small town there are a number of part-time artists, musicians and writers.

During our summers in Astoria I would sit in at the Uniontown Café in town, play at Monday night jam sessions at the smoke-filled American Legion in Cannon Beach, and do occasional gigs. None of the local gigs paid very well, so there were virtually no full-time musicians living in Astoria. For a while I played with a Dixieland band that did occasional out of town gigs and I also joined a local swing band that specialized in tunes of the 40's and 50's.

Susan exhibited at two contemporary galleries, one in Astoria, and the other in Cannon Beach. We both realized that pursuing the arts in Astoria meant reducing one's expectations and scope, because the city was simply too small to support a major art community. The trade off was very cool summers, and proximity to ocean beaches. Boulder is hot in the summer and essentially land-locked. Colorado gets year round sunshine, and the predominant color in the sky in Astoria is gray, but after some twenty years in Colorado it seemed like a reasonable trade off. One of my most vivid memories of Astoria is a July 4th cookout on a downtown pier. It was so cold that we were wearing winter coats and it still felt cold.

As the nineties went by we decided that it was time to think about leaving UCD and Colorado and making a permanent move to Oregon.

LAST YEARS AT UCD, AND THE MOVE TO OREGON

At the end of each summer we would return to our Boulder home with the sort of feeling that you get when after a Sunday night party you have to go to work the next day. Susan got a master's degree in special education during the 90's and worked for three years in the Boulder County schools. As is the case with many special education teachers, she found the work exhausting and depressing. After three years she began working as a full-time painter.

THE REALITIES OF THE ART WORLD

I am the last person in the world to say that making a living as a musician is an easy life. However it is pretty straightforward compared to being a painter or a craft person. Art schools turn out an ever-larger group of would be professionals. Finding an art gallery is difficult, and when an artist is able to do so, galleries now get 50% of the retail price of the artist's work. Artists must pay for their own framing, and some galleries require them to pay part or all of the costs of promoting a show. When an artist is able to affiliate with a gallery, it is unusual to have no more than one show every two years. When a gallery finds than an artist's work doesn't sell, the artist usually is fired by the gallery. Artists also must now compete with low priced foreign arts and crafts. There are co-op galleries where artists band together and share all the costs of operating the gallery. These are certainly laudable efforts, but if you have thirty artists, each one has to wait his or her turn to get a show. Basically there is no equivalent for the kind of one-off gigs that musicians play. A musician does the gig and then gets paid. There are also instances where gallery owners delay on paying artists. Because of all these factors, many artists end up teaching college or public school. Because school budgets vary, art and music are generally the first subjects that are cut.

It's a hell of a way to make a living. Writers, by the way, don't have it much better. I have read that the average income of a writer is under $5000. Amazon squeezes publishers for better discount rates, which result in lower advances and even lower royalties to writers. Writers also turn to teaching, and there are dozens of summer workshops that employ writers who are making a bare living at their craft, teaching wanna-bees who dream of writing best sellers.

This leads us to the world of theater. In most middle sized or even larger towns, there is only one full-time theater company. The many little theaters pay actors and actresses little or nothing. They turn to the world of television commercials and voiceovers, but this is also a limited market.

All these professions seem like a party compared to the world of dance. A dancer's career has a similar level of longevity to a professional athlete. Knees, feet and backs wear out and by the age of 35, professional dancers, who rarely make a decent living in the first place, are out of work.

What I am trying to say here is that the options available to professional musicians seem varied and comparatively lucrative relative to what other practitioners in the arts experience. So the next time you or your friends complain about the music scene, think about becoming a professional dancer, writer, artist or actor.

THE BANJO PLAYER BECOMES THE HEAD OF THE MUSIC DEPARTMENT

In spring, 1998 the position of chair of the music department at UCD became vacant. In general, the head of the department needed to be a tenured faculty member, and Dean Heckler asked if I wanted to assume these responsibilities. The good news was that I would move out of my cubby-like office without a window into a more spacious room, and I would teach four classes a year instead of five. I also was offered a good salary bump, going from the low $40,000 level to just over $50,000. The bad news was that I would be responsible for departmental budgets, I would have to attend meetings of the College of the Arts that included the chairs of the art and theater department and the dean. I would have to supervise departmental budgets and classroom scheduling, and I would also have to mediate the frequent turf wars between our various divisions. This included the audio, music performance, scoring and arranging and business areas. Fortunately Holly Allen, the secretary of the School of the Arts was an invaluable resource. She had worked at the school for some years and seemed to be familiar with every budget and every person that could actually answer a question in the entire university.

We had hoped to hire a new department chair and head of the music business program at the end of 1998, but for a variety of reasons that didn't occur, and I reluctantly agreed to stay on for another year.

REFLECTIONS ON THE CHAIR, AND MY LAST UNIVERSITY GRANT

The university created a grant program that was intended to fund innovative initiatives in combining technology and current music programs. I applied for the grant, and we were awarded about $90,000. I talked to all of the faculty, and tried to distribute the money in a fair way. It seemed as though everyone had something that they wanted to do with the money. I ended up buying a $30,000 piece of equipment for the audio department. A few years later, I discovered that they had never actually used it. A few students took it out of the box and assembled it. By that time, like almost any "hot" audio item, it had basically become outmoded.

The dean and I had a frank conversation about my future. I told him that Spring, 2000 was going to be my last semester at UCD. He then informed me that at that time the school had two options that I might want to consider. In the first option I could continue to work half time but get full-time benefits. Since I was now old enough to go on Medicare I didn't find this option attractive. As I was just about to conclude the conversation he offered me another alternative. I could work half-time, every other semester if I wished, and draw my full salary minus what it would cost to replace the courses I normally taught with part-time faculty. As I explain below, I was quite aware of how little part-time faculty were paid, and I realized that by accepting this deal in a sense I was becoming part of the problem. On the other hand, if I had simply left, I would have been replaced by another tenure track professor.

PART-TIME FACULTY WORK: ACADEMIC SHARECROPPING

Most colleges employ as many or more part-time professors as they do full-time faculty. The way that they are treated can only be described as shameful. At state institutions, even today, for teaching a three credit class the average pay scale is between $2000 and $4000. At community colleges it's near the bottom of the scale, while at flagship state universities its closer to the top of this scale. Part-time employees get no retirement benefits or health insurance. Unless they are specialists who have some extraordinary level of experience or knowledge, their schedules are determined by the department chair.

What is truly shameful about this is that many full-time faculty are generally disinterested in this inequity. Rarely will a full-timer fight for their part-time colleagues. The expression "academic sharecropper" comes from the fact that part-time professors who rely upon teaching for the bulk of their income often teach at three or four different colleges. Many colleges also limit the number of courses that part-timers teach, lest they fall into the category of half-time or full-time employees. The most extreme example of part-time sharecropping that I know about was in a newspaper story a few weeks before the time that I was writing this section of the book. The story profiled a professor who lived in New York City, and taught in Providence, Rhode, Island, Hartford, Connecticut and Boston. Surveys of part-timers have revealed that a quarter of them are actually living on food stamps. To further aggravate the lives of part-timers, they are often treated in a patronizing manner by the regular faculty. When I was chair of the department, I actually attended classes taught by part-timers, as well as reading their student evaluations. As far as I could tell, no chair had done this before. It was as though these people were sub-humans.

By the way, another subject is the use of graduate students to teach classes. We did not have graduate students at UCD, so we didn't follow this practice. From talking with professors at other colleges, graduate music students often prepare and grade tests, and do any tutoring that students may require. They also sometimes actually do class lectures for the regular professors.

My retirement agreement came with the stipulation that I could choose to teach for one, two or three years. I didn't think that I could handle three years and one year seemed not to be worth the trouble. I elected to pursue this path for two years.

THE OREGON COMMUTER

From Fall, 2000-Spring 2002 I taught only in the spring semesters. Susan stayed at our home in Oregon, I rented an apartment in a student rental complex in Boulder for four months, and lived in Oregon the rest of the year. During the first year I followed my usual custom of working four days a week. I had long ago reached an agreement with the various deans that I would work Tuesday-Friday, and take Monday as my research day. Since I was writing books all during the time I was at UCD, no one ever argued with this arrangement. Typically I worked Tuesday-Friday, from 10AM to about 5PM. I had several hours of office hours by appointment, but when I was in the office and not in class, I kept my door open.

The first year of this arrangement went by without incident, but in the second year the dean abandoned his support for the program at the Denver Childrens Home. During my new half-time role, I observed that a number of people in the department, including the chair were barely working two days a week, which I found appalling.

As part of the grant I had received, we started a record label called CAM (we were then called the College of Arts & Media.) We started by recording student projects in a sampler format, with each student recording one tune. On the first couple of records several faculty members also recorded one tune. I knew that I was going back to Jamaica to teach in the summer of 2002, so I dreamed up the notion of bringing some singers from the Jamaican Songwriters Bootcamp back to Colorado. I would then teach a special advanced record production class and appointing my UCD students to be their record producers. I came back for three weeks in Fall, 2002 to teach that class.

Together with Marjorie Bennett-Anderson I chose three Jamaican songwriters to come to Denver to record. I was able to pay for their accommodations with the grant money, and we rented a professional studio. I hired several faculty members to play on the recordings, and they were also paid with grant money.

It was a great learning experience all around, and we recorded enough tunes for a CD. On one tune none of the faculty, including me, were able to play a suitable lead part for a reggae-based tune, and one of our students ended up playing the part. It was a great example of students teaching the professors.

PART-TIME OREGON

We had never been through an Astoria winter. To put it concisely, it rains, often in buckets, from around September through May. I am probably the least handy person in the universe, and our Victorian house needed consistent and expensive care. Some of the town residents in the winter basically shut themselves up in their houses, and drank or smoked themselves half way to oblivion. We began to wonder about our choice of "retirement" community.

Part 3 • Chapter 21 

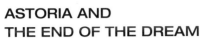

ASTORIA AND THE END OF THE DREAM

Although Susan lived in Astoria for three years, because of my buyout at UCD I was only a full-time resident for about a year. We met some interesting people in Astoria, but the town began to have too many limitations for anything we attempted. Susan quickly found that although she did have a few places to exhibit her art, most of the tourists who bought art in Astoria wanted pictures of boats or pretty landscapes.

I formed duos first with fiddler Gary Keiski and then with David Crabtree. Gary described himself as an improvising fiddle player. He is a person who chooses to live on the edge, and is willing to pay the price so that he can devote as much time as possible to his music. For a couple of winters he stayed in our house in Boulder while we were gone. Gary is an honorable person who had overcome many obstacles since childhood.

We had fun playing together, and he was willing to rehearse for long periods of time. Because he never had any money he never really had an instrument that was worthy of his talents. We made one album together that included a nice guitar tune that he had written, but by and large Gary was an improviser and not a composer. After a couple of years we broke up as a duo. Because of his reticent personality and general shyness, I had to assume all of the business load of our duo, and I realized this would not change. I'm writing this paragraph around 9AM in Denver, thinking that Gary is probably having his first coffee of the day at the Bald Eagle coffee shop in Cannon Beach.

CRABO

Everyone called David Crabtree "Crabo." A well educated idiosyncratic fellow who was a classical guitarist, had fished in the Bering Sea, and also lived in Europe. Settling on the fringes of Astoria Crabo became a bamboo farmer. He had many colorful stories about his life, like the one about a fishing boat sinking in the Bering Sea along with his $5000 guitar.

We recorded one album at Crabo's house in Astoria, and spent some energy trying to promote it. I came to the eventual, if obvious, realization that Astoria was not a good place to pursue a musical career. Seventy five dollars was a really good wage for a gig and because of the small population there was no way anyone could survive by playing music without having a regular job. When we moved to Portland in 2004 that effectively ended our musical relationship. Crabo had a great sense of humor, and a sardonic way of looking at the world. I miss his stories and his sense of the absurd.

NOT GOOD ENOUGH FOR THE LIBRARY

One day I decided that I really should donate one of my books to the local library in Astoria. I decided that my first book about the music business was something that would be useful in a town where there were a surprising number of aspiring musicians. I took a copy of the book down to the library and talked to the librarian at the desk. She asked me if my book had been reviewed, and if she could see copies of reviews. I felt as though I was on trial. I wondered if she had some notion that my book was pornographic or represented some sort of subversive threat. I explained that the book was published by a subsidiary of Random House and was currently in its third edition. She responded by saying that if I wanted the book to be in the library, I would have to bring reviews with me and talk to a reference librarian.

This event crystallized why Astoria wasn't a tenable place for us to live. It truly offended me. Did I have to pass some sort of loyalty test to donate a book to the library? What sort of town were we living in? Right about that time our house was getting an exterior paint job. The painters seemed to have drug or drinking problems, or a combination of both. Remember that this was a Victorian house, so the expanse of the roof was enormous.

We had received two other bids for the job besides the crew that we chose. One painter regarded himself as an artist, not a craftsman. He had many color pictures of his work, and he had a very specific vision of how the house should look. His vision was so strong that he clearly wasn't listening to a word that Susan said. He entirely ignored the fact that Susan being a painter, might have some useful thoughts about the job. It was impossible to pin this gentleman down on price, "it could cost $15,000, it could cost $25,000, etc. The other person we interviewed was less rigid, but when we asked him for references he would mention client after client, but in each case they might not be a good reference because "we came to loggerheads." Not wanting to come to loggerheads with him, we decided not to go with his bid.

Along with the painting fiasco, we began to be uncomfortable about things like running into someone downtown who would say things like "I see you're mowing the lawn." When you live in a small town everyone seems to know more about your habits than you yourself do.

Meanwhile we were spending more and more time in Portland for R&R. Powell's Bookshop in Portland is probably the best bookstore in the United States. The music section alone is larger than the size of many bookstores. There were also many restaurants and music venues in Portland, and nobody seemed to care about your personal habits. After some contact with several realtors, we found a house in a suburb within the city called Multnomah Village, about fifteen minutes from the downtown.

With some trepidation we put our house in Astoria up for sale. It sold in a single day to a doctor who had recently gotten a job at a nearby hospital. He had some doubts about purchasing a Victorian house, but he had brought several friends with him, who urged him to "go for it." Like the town itself the Astoria real estate market was eccentric and unpredictable. It's the one and only time we have ever sold a house in one day.

REFLECTIONS ON ASTORIA

We still miss the summers in Astoria, where an eighty degree day is considered hot and uncomfortable. We miss the easy access to the Pacific Ocean and I miss our outside porch on the second floor of the house. When the weather wasn't too wet, I'd sit out on the porch and play music. People on the street could hear the music, but they couldn't see me or where it was coming from. In a way that fulfilled my most idealistic notions about music. It isn't important about who is playing music, it's simply something to listen to.

We don't miss the clannishness, the sheets of rain, or the huge hills that make walking less comfortable as the walker ages. Once again, it was time to move on.

THIS LAND IS OUR LAND

About six months before we left Astoria, Scott McKenzie called and asked if I wanted to do a TV show with him in Pittsburgh. The show featured a number of pop-folk artists, including Trini Lopez, Tommy Makem and some other artists. Besides getting paid for the show, the producer had arranged for a recording to be released on Rhino Records.

Scott and I had a few negotiating points to go over. The producers wanted us to join AFTRA, the union that regulates TV musicians and actors. I had been a member of AFTRA when I was in The Journeymen, but since I really didn't expect to sing on network TV again, and wasn't singing on this show, I wanted to be paid through the AFM, the musician's union. Scott refused to join AFTRA again, and he worked out a direct payment with the producers. I was ultimately paid as a musician, which was possible because they had musicians playing bass, keyboard and drums who accompanied many of the musicians.

The contract for the recording arrived from Rhino Records, which paid $750 each to Scott and me. We signed the contract and returned it. A month later another contract arrived with another check. I called Scott, and asked him what he did. Since he was really the featured artist, I didn't want him to get in any kind of trouble. He said something to the effect of "I cashed it, you schmuck." I then cashed my check.

We performed Scott's big hit about San Francisco, and then Scott insisted that they let me do a banjo solo. Of course they didn't use the banjo solo in the actual television show, but we performed before a live audience, and it was fun for me.

I don't have too much to say about the show. Denny and Michelle were there and did quite a bit of the narration. Erik Darling was there with some female singers who re-capitulated the vocal back-ups on Erik's big hit with the Rooftop Singers, Walk Right In. Eric Weissberg was there playing mandolin for Judy Collins, and he also reprised his Dueling Banjos hit, with Tommy Makem's son playing guitar.

THE AFTERMATH

When I got back to Astoria, there was a message on my answering machine asking me to call a place in Cannon Beach about a gig. I was probably feeling a little bit full of myself at the time. After all I had just earned over twenty five hundred dollars for playing all of two tunes. I called the number. It turned out that a fancy bed and breakfast place in Cannon Beach had been re-modeled, and they wanted someone to play at the opening. Knowing that Cannon Beach is one of the best known tourist destinations on the Oregon Coast, I asked the woman what her budget was for the event. She said "oh, you won't get paid, but you'll get lots of exposure, and you might even get on KAST radio". That station, by the way, only plays 70's and 80's rock. The odds of their playing ANYTHING that I have ever done are between 0 and 0. I gently told the woman that I really didn't need any additional exposure at this phase of my career. Back to earth again. Gotta leave this town.

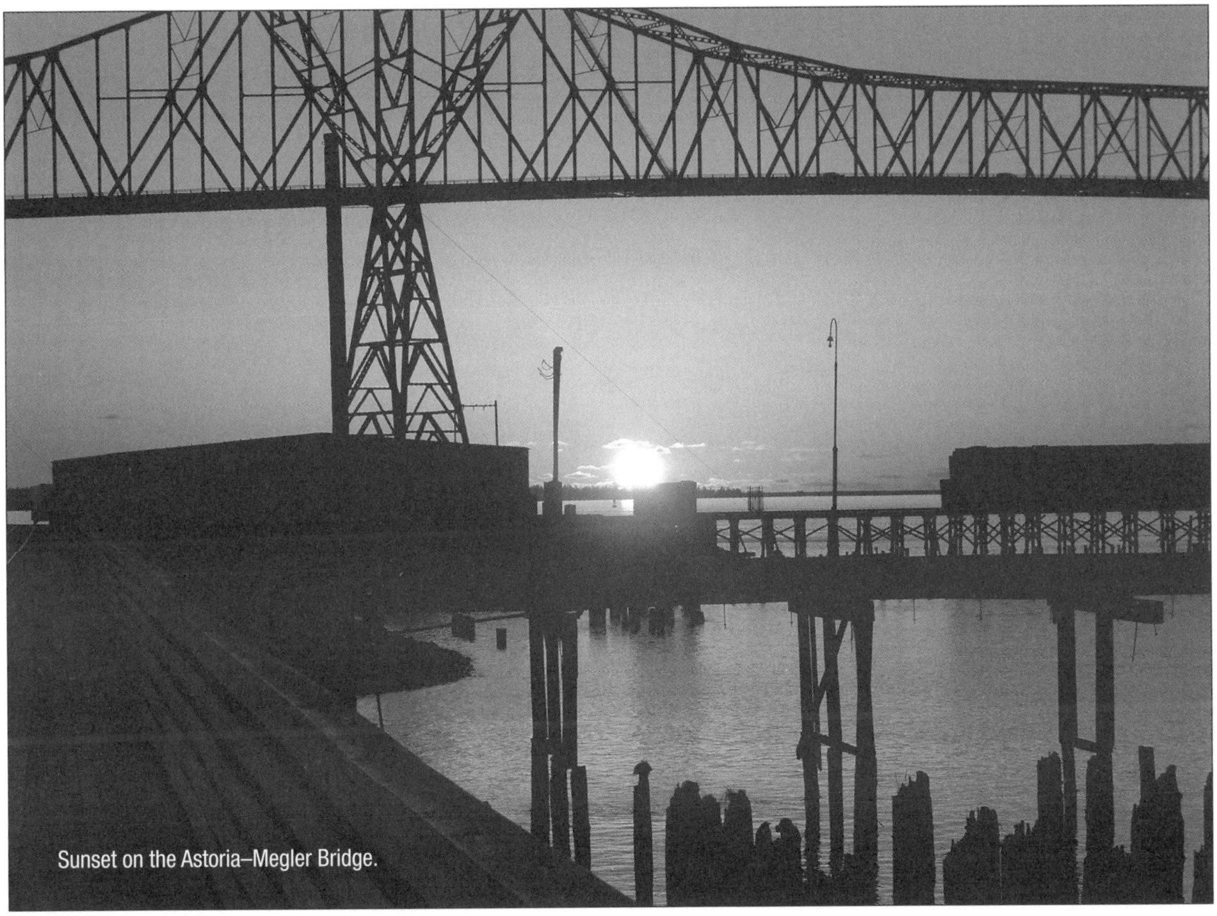

Sunset on the Astoria–Megler Bridge.

Part 3 • Chapter 22

2003-2012
PORTLAND TOWN

It was a relief to be in a town where a variety of art galleries, medical providers, bookstores and restaurants were readily available. I tried to enter the music scene as quickly as possible, connected with the Portland Folk Music Society and became active in the Portland Musician's Union. I joined the Concert Committee of the Folk Society, and a couple of years later became its chair. After all those years of playing music I became a concert promoter! We had been losing money on our concerts, and in general I felt our series had become stale. In general today's American folk scene has increasingly consisted of graying audiences listening to aging performers. I tried to bring in younger performers, and people who had never played in Portland. As a performer myself, I was careful to limit my shows to one a year to avoid the obvious conflict of interest. Since I had been doing shows for the society before I ever got on the concert committee, this seemed reasonable to me. Along the way I made some critical mistakes, especially in my third and final year of booking concerts. Whether I liked it or not, the members of the organization liked their performers to be familiar faces. When I brought in younger performers who specialized in world music, the audiences voted with their wallets and didn't attend. Having had my fill of committee meetings, I elected to disband the committee and do things on my own. In a volunteer run organization this was definitely a mistake. At one concert I had to set up the chairs, introduce the performers, sell tickets and help staff the table where performers' CD's were sold. That is when I started to experience burn out. Incidentally, my successors did better. Restoring the committee format and relying more on old and trusted performers seemed to do the trick. Lesson learned, if not appreciated.

MICHAEL KEARSEY

Through the society I met Michael Kearsey. Michael is a bass and guitar player who has been in a Middle Eastern music band called The Brothers of the Baladi for some years. Besides that commitment he writes music and plays with an old time blues and ragtime band and with several blues artists. The Brothers had a good following in Portland and on the West Coast until 9/11 occurred. Although there has only been, at most, one Arab in the band, any American interest in Middle Eastern Music seemed to be quashed by the terrorist attack on New York. The band has also had poor luck with agents and managers, with numerous promising relationships evaporating for various reasons.

Michael has a great sense of humor, and he and I have spent many hours hashing over our various experiences in the morass known as the music business.

TERRY CURRIER

Terry Currier owns a record store called Music Millennium, which is one of the outstanding outlets for independent music in the United States. He genuinely likes all kinds of music, from hip hop to folk to classical, and whenever possible he sponsors in-store concerts by local and touring artists. I have never heard a bad word about Terry from another musician, which is a remarkable achievement in itself.

When Garth Brooks railed against the sale of used CD's, Terry held a barbecue of Garth's records. He traveled up and down the West Coast, barbecuing as he went, and garnering national publicity. The sale of used LP's and CD's is one of the best profit centers for record stores, which is why Terry started barbecuing. When the store needed a roof, Terry raised over $60,000 with a Kickstarter campaign. I think every musician in Portland that had a dollar to his or her name contributed to the fund. I don't think I have ever met a person active in as many musical causes as Terry is, from the Blues Society to the latest alternative rock, hip hop or folk recording.

THE PORTLAND MUSICIAN'S ASSOCIATION

I was elected to the board of the Portland union. Many of the problems in the local union mirrored what I had experienced in Denver. Portland prides itself on its diverse music scene. As is the case in many cities, the stalwart members of the musician's union are the symphony, who have a collective bargaining agreement that includes compulsory membership in the union, and the older generation of jazz and pop musicians who are often swing band veterans. The younger musicians who play rock, hip hop, folk music, blues and other contemporary pop styles don't tend to join the union unless they record for major record labels. The Portland union hired an organizer who came up with a concept that he termed Fair Trade Music. This was the musical equivalent of fair trade coffee. In other words the notion was that there should be decent minimum wages for all gigs.

Fair Trade Music was intended to help younger musicians understand that they needed to establish minimum wage standards in order to make a semblance of a living. It was not designed for union members as such, but for all working musicians. This in turn was anticipated to eventually bring these people into the union.

The members of Fair Trade included union and non-union members, and they began negotiations with Portland venues to establish minimum wages for all employees. Once such an agreement was reached, the venue would have a sticker in the window to indicate their compliance with the minimum wage scales.

In Portland the campaign stumbled after several years when the organizer who originated the concept was laid off. The initial financial support for his position had come from the national union, but as this amount was reduced over a three year period, the local could not take up the monetary slack. One large group of venues had agreed in principle on the Fair Trade concept, but the sticking point came with larger size bands. The venue owner argued that he didn't tell a group to have ten pieces, for example, and he could not reasonably afford to pay ten people the necessary wage. He felt that it was certainly feasible with groups of three or four musicians.

Subsequently two other locals of the union, one in Seattle, the other a local consisting of traveling folk musicians, were able to implement Fair Trade with some success. Other locals are looking at the possibility of adopting it, but have not committed to doing so.

GETTING THE UNIONS TO UNIONIZE

One of the problems that came up during my three terms on the board was that local unions in other professions often hired non-union musicians. At the same time that they asked us to honor their picket lines or support pro-labor legislation, they didn't seem to understand that music is in fact a working class profession. Fellow board member Noah Peterson and I appeared before a state labor union meeting and were able, with some difficulty to explain to these people that we needed their support as much as they needed ours.

THE SYMPHONY

My guess is that most people, possibly even most people reading this book, think that symphonic musicians are among the happiest warriors in the music trade. Robert Faulkner, who is both a sociologist and a musician exploded this myth in his book The Hollywood Studio Musician. Faulkner found that musicians often hated conductors, who they deemed to be tyrants. Moreover, many musicians had originally dreamed of being soloists, travelling world-wide and making excellent wages. Instead they were performing a rather pedestrian repertoire of pieces that recycle every few years. In other words the musical challenges were limited.

As a board member in Denver and then in Portland I came face to face with these realities. There are a half dozen major orchestras where the minimum annual salary is in the vicinity of $150,000, and another half dozen where the pay scale starts at $80,000-$90,000. Portland and Denver are more in the $50,000 range. When you consider that many of the musicians in these orchestras began their training at the ages of 5-10, depending on what instrument they play, it would be fair to say that their training approaches the level that is expected of doctors or lawyers. In smaller cities, like Colorado Springs or Salem, there is no one who can make a full-time living in the symphony. This is because the minimum salary may be $10,000-$15,000 for a season that lasts ten to twenty weeks.

During my tenure on the Executive Board, we spent many hours on such issues as the behavior of the conductors, intra-orchestra rivalries and grievances, and especially the behaviors and policies of the Board of Directors of the symphony. These individuals were often wealthy people who exercised their clout in terms of orchestra policies, salaries, the number of musicians in the orchestra, and other issues. Not surprisingly, a good deal of time was wasted on gossip that came through certain members of the orchestra and their "insights" into orchestral policies. Whenever any other symphony would cut salaries, reduce the number of musicians in the orchestra, or even go out of business, a tidal wave of panic would hit the local orchestra and become a subject for the board.

NOAH PETERSON AND INTEL

Noah Peterson is a saxophone player who is one of the most promotionally active musicians I have ever met. Originally from Montana, he lived in Portland for about seven years before I hit town, and left in 2012, about the same time that I did. Noah also booked about a hundred gigs a year at Intel, the computer chip company. Intel is the largest employer in Oregon, although it is not an Oregon-based company. The Intel shows were lunch-time gigs at two locations in Hillsboro, a suburb of Portland.

While I lived in Portland Noah developed a solo saxophone show that involved looping, so that he could perform multiple parts with the aid of pre-recorded sound loops. He also became the initiator of loop festivals in Portland, Seattle and Denver. Noah sets up solo tours where he picks up an anchor gig, say in Florida. He will then relentlessly phone or email his contacts and end up with thirty gigs in thirty five days. Noah moved to San Antonio in 2012, and when he's home he plays rub board in a zydeco band, has a jazz rock group, and a smooth jazz group. He also produces many videos and posts them on YouTube, and he has a record label. Noah is almost a paradigm of how a musician makes a living in the 21st century. He does it by pursuing multiple musical careers. When the work slacks off in one area, he is able to compensate with one of his many other projects.

I met Noah at a membership meeting of the union, and we served together on the Executive Board. Noah is strongly pro-union, but his politics are Republican-Libertarian, whereas mine lean more towards anarchism. Somehow our ideas seemed to coincide, and we were often a minority of two in board discussions about what causes to support or what endeavors to undertake.

I played fifteen Intel gigs in a period of about two years. The gigs paid reasonably well, $150 for two hours and a sumptuous lunch. About half of the employees took their laptops to the cafeteria, and were doing some sort of work while the musicians played. They were polite, but somewhat disinterested. It was almost a moral victory to sell the occasional CD, or even to have a conversation with the audience members.

I enjoyed the Intel gigs, because it was like a paid practice session. I even wrote one or two tunes while doing the gigs. I also used this time to play new pieces, then in the short break between the first and the second set I would revise the piece and play it again. Since the second set audience was a new group of diners, it didn't matter. Security at Intel was extremely tight. When you got to the correct building, you surrendered your driver's license and signed in. You could not go to the cafeteria without an escort from the company, so you had to wait ten or fifteen minutes for someone to do that.

In 2012 Intel suddenly suspended their live music

programs. At about the same time they hired Dr. Dre to write a series of jingles for in-house use at various Intel branches. I don't doubt that they paid him more than their collective budgets for live music in Portland for a year. Noah soldiered on, and continues his many musical activities in San Antonio and all over the country.

DICK AND SUSAN IN CONDO LAND

After a brief stay at a house on the outskirts of Multnomah Village, we bought a three bedroom condominium in a 1960's condo complex. We were unaware of exactly how condos function. There were contentious board meetings, and arguments about things like whether a tree should be removed because one resident was obsessed with the notion that the tree was diseased. The fact that arborists didn't agree with her assessment never seemed to stop her from attempting to get her own way. Most of the neighbors were relatively reasonable and pleasant, but our upstairs neighbor was mentally ill and she would provoke us in a number of ways. She stomped on the floor, stood on her balcony taking imaginary cell phone calls, and repeatedly stalked Susan when she left the house. She was a renter, and her landlord who lived in Seattle, refused to take any action against her. It wasn't a good situation, but Portland had experienced a strong real estate boom from around 2003-2007, and moving was unthinkable.

PART-TIME COLLEGE TEACHING

I wrote letters to the music departments of almost every college in Oregon, soliciting summer teaching gigs. I taught for several summers at the University of Oregon in Eugene. The students were intelligent and on a higher academic level than the students that I had taught at UCD. My boss' name was Jack Boss, and we got along well. For whatever reasons, Eugene doesn't attract a large group of summer school students, and enrollment problems caused the bureaucrat above Jack to cancel some classes at the last minute. I then decided that I had reached the end of the road at UO. Playing the lottery to teach a class that didn't pay all that well didn't seem like a productive way to spend my time. My strangest experience as an academic sharecropper in Eugene occurred when I made a proposal for a class about music and politics like the class I had taught in Denver. I had to come up with a final proposal overnight, and one of the more stuffy professors removed me from consideration because of a couple of typos. That very class later was listed in the UO catalog , taught by someone else a couple of years later. The course description was almost an exact mirror of what I had submitted.

CAPITAL HILL COFFEE HOUSE: A CLUB THAT REQUIRED A CONTRACT FOR A JOB WITH NO PAY

A few blocks from our condo was a restaurant that featured music in the second story of its building. I went to check it out, and it seemed as though it would be a good venue for me to play instrumental music. I talked to the manager and she told me that I could submit some music for review. I asked her what the gig paid, and she said that it didn't, but that I should read the contract. Curiosity got the better of me, and I asked for a copy. It stipulated that the artist would exercise his or her best efforts to get friends and fans to go to the club. The hours were specified, the artist was "allowed" to sell CD's and could drink two free soft drinks a night, and could buy food at a 50% discount. I didn't pursue the gig, but I marveled at a club that would actually make a musician sign a contract to play for no compensation. It also hadn't occurred to the owners that most artists' friends already have their CD's. Tempting as it was, I had to turn down this wonderful opportunity.

PORTLAND COMMUNITY COLLEGE & ALLEN JONES

I decided that I would try to do some part-time teaching in Portland itself. Several calls to Portland State University, which is considered a peer institution of UCD, went unanswered. I then called Allen Jones, who was the chair of the music department of the

Cascade Campus of Portland Community College. It turned out that he had read some of my books, and after a brief interview he hired me in 2007. Allen was also a guitar player, and we spent quite a bit of time exchanging stories about guitar players and gigs at lunches in neighborhood restaurants. At the time, he had a really supportive dean in Kate Dins. Each time I came up with a course idea, her attitude was that we should try it. If it didn't make enrollment, we wouldn't do it again. The directness of this approach astonished me, coming from the committee and paperwork citadel of UCD.

I gradually added classes in songwriting and music business to the menu of electives at PCC. The students were a more varied bunch that the ones I taught at UCD. There was a good percentage of black and Mexican-American students, a higher percentage of students were working, and there was all of one departmental meeting a quarter. (the college was on the quarter system.) The pay was pitiful, about $2000 for a three credit class for part-timers, which grew to something reasonable if you taught there for fifteen or twenty years.

I liked my colleagues at the school, who were more down to earth than the UCD profs that I was used to dealing with. Allen and I became good friends and everything was going swimmingly until a new dean entered the picture. I spent a considerable amount of time explaining to him that there was no college with a music business degree in the entire Northwest, but he was set on creating a two year audio program with an AA degree. He was undeterred when we showed him the number of schools that already offered some version of an audio degree. Over time he and Allen clashed over a number of issues, and a few years later Allen retired, and the future of the commercial music certificate program is now in doubt. Since Allen had spent thirty years nurturing this program, this is a sad development.

PORTLAND: THE GOOD, THE BAD AND THE WEIRD

Sometimes it seems to me that every city I have ever lived in, with the exception of New Brunswick, New Jersey has an absolute conviction that it is the coolest, trendiest and hippest place in the United States. During our years in Portland, a once sleepy Republican city of medium size was undergoing an immersion in cool.

My favorite things in Portland were Powells Books, Music Millennium and Artichoke Music. The downtown Powells covers an entire city block. Every day on my email I get a list of the used music books that they have acquired. The number ranges from 30 or so to over 100 books. Every day!

Music Millennium carries many recordings by local musicians, the store has live music several days a week, and Terry Currier, the owner, is often in attendance at music events around town.

Artichoke Music is an acoustic music shop whose very existence was in question when its long-time owners simply burned out. Richard Colombo, with the help of his partner Jim Morris and a group of dedicated volunteers created a whole new level of energy at Artichoke. They instituted three evenings a week of music at the store's café, and expanded the store's teaching staff. They created a special feeling of community for acoustic music musicians and fans.

THE COOL FACTOR

People in other cities often ask if I watch the IFC network TV show Portlandia. I can't watch it, because although many people find it amusing, it is too close to a simple video reproduction of life in Portland. Here's an example of local life from something that happened at PCC. The Cascade campus of PCC is in what used to be a black neighborhood, that is gradually becoming gentrified. The mayor of Portland prior to 2012 was Sam Adams. He was a veteran politico, and had been an administrative assistant to a previous mayor of the town. Portland thought of Sam as being very hip, because he was openly gay, and would sometimes show up in the audience at jazz clubs. Sam spoke a lot about community and the arts, and one morning at a meeting in north Portland, his assistant asked the various storekeepers how things were going.

One store owner complained about the presence of needles on her doorstep as she opened her business each day. The mayor's rep. smiled, and said something to the effect of "great to hear from you Dorothy, what about you, Albert?" Each business owner complained about the neighborhood, invariably followed by the politico's enthusiasm. It was as though she was living in a world made up of her own fantasies, rather than listening to what people were saying.

THE BALLAD OF KIRK REEVES

In order to go from the east side of Portland to the west side, or vice versa, you have to cross over the Willamette River. A man named Kirk Reeves used to play his trumpet and juggle on the west side of the entrance ramp to the Hawthorne St. Bridge. Kirk dressed in a white tuxedo, and wore a hat with Mickey Mouse ears. Kids loved him and many pedestrians walking across the bridge would stop and chat with him. To be absolutely honest, Kirk was not a great trumpet player, but he was a wonderful person. He always had a smile on his face for everyone, especially for kids. When I taught at PCC, I had to cross over from the west side to the east side of town. I often passed Kirk as he stood on a kind of raised area between the two traffic lanes that provided entrance to the bridge. At one point a few people tried to get him removed from his spot, because they claimed that he restricted the visibility of cars entering the bridge. A tremendous outcry of pro-Kirk settlement ended that problem.

In 2012 Kirk went to Los Angeles and auditioned for the tv shows America's Got Talent and Shark Tank. He was not accepted, and he returned to Portland in a severely depressed mood. He also had some physical problems, and was having a difficult time making a living. He ended up committing suicide, leaving a void that affected many, many people who had seen him almost on a daily basis on the bridge.

THE MURAL

Portland built a new light rail bridge between Portland and the suburb of Milwaukie. The public was asked to choose a name for the bridge, and the largest number of respondents suggested that they name it after Kirk Reeves. In its finite wisdom, the committee in charge of naming the bridge decided that Kirk was not a significant enough historical figure to merit such recognition. They went with the name Tillicum Crossing.

The good side of Portland emerged when artist Gwenn Seemel got a grant from the Regional Arts Council to do a mural of Kurt on a building in Portland. This mural is now in place. On my occasional trips to Portland when I across the Hawthorne Bridge I look out at where Kirk used to play. Usually there are homeless people begging in the spot where he liked to play Somewhere Over The Rainbow.

TOM MAY AND WINTERFOLK

One of my musician friends in Portland is Tom May. Tom has had a long career as a singer-songwriter and radio host, and we have exchanged many stories and gigs over the last ten years. Every winter he heads up a list of musicians who perform a benefit at a 600 seat venue called The Aladdin Theater. The benefit raises funds for the Sisters of The Road, a café that services low-income and destitute people. The show sells out or comes close to doing so each year. For many years Utah Phillips headlined the show, but now that he has passed on, different headliners close the show each year. Local performers love playing the benefit, because it is a great audience, especially for those of us who would never draw six hundred people at one of our shows.

Tom is working on his own memoir, and I will not try to tell any of his many colorful stories about Winterfolk, his long-running radio show River City Folk, or his recording and performing career. Tom is one of a number of musicians who supported Artichoke during its worst time of need.

THE ACCIDENT THAT DROVE US OUT OF PORTLAND

In 2010 Susan was walking our two blue heeler dogs, Sam and Dave. She crossed at a school pedestrian walk that was clearly marked. A woman driver approached, slowed down, and appeared to be stopped, as is legally required. In fact she was distracted, looking for a parking space at the school, and plowed into my wife. The dogs were not hurt, but Susan's right leg was broken in four places. I was teaching a night class at PCC and the police called public security to tell me the news.

Two years of a lawsuit and intensive physical therapy followed. The driver called me several times, as did her lawyer, who said to me, "I hope you haven't hired a lawyer!" I'm certain he did indeed hope that this was the case. My son is a lawyer, and through his contacts we found a lawyer named Gordon Carey, who sued on our behalf. A couple of weeks after the accident the driver took a $200,000 loan on the equity from her house. I suspect that she was hoping that no one would notice this. The resolution of the case came some two years later. Our insurance company elected to pay us, rather than going after the driver's insurance company. The driver was an older woman who apparently was taking care of her husband, who had Alzheimer's. We concluded that our company preferred to pay us off than be seen in the courtroom as a persecutor of a "little old lady."

About this time we had become a bit tired of Portland. During the previous two years the rain lasted from September through May, our apartment seemed to be always dark, and the condo meetings started to make me feel as though I was back at UCD. The local art market seemed static and uninspiring.

When we looked for a house in Portland, we couldn't find anything that we liked that was in our price range, or was a single level house. Since we were told that ultimately Susan might be a good candidate for a knee replacement, this seemed essential. We would have had to move to the suburbs to find such a house, and neither of us wanted to do that. That same summer Susan did a one person art show at a gallery in Denver. She sold a reasonable amount of work. My daughter Janelle was visiting from Australia, where she has lived for six years. She found a great house in our price range on the internet.

With the new dean at PCC, I could see that my teaching career there was coming to an end. I was mostly writing books and making records, and I realized that I could do that from anywhere. Both Susan and I had several good friends in Portland, but we also had friends in Denver, and my son and his family lived there

Photo: George Filgate

Chico Schwall - songwriter, teacher and multi-instrumentalist, fluent in many musical styles. He was myy co-coordinator at the Far West annual gathering in Eugene, 2012.

Below: Terry Currier - friend to all Portland musicians. Terry owns the Music Millennium record store.

Photo: Duray Thirdgill

Above: Noah Peterson - master of modern musical self-promotion. He has a one-man sax-looping show and has developed looping festivals across the country.

Below:
Allen Jones - my boss at Portland Community College.

Brothers of the Baladi - a Portland-based band that plays Middle-Eastern music. Because of 9/11 and recent terrorist attacks, the band has experienced difficulties getting work. Michael Kearsey and I have done a variety of musical, writing and teaching projects together. Band members: J. Michael Kearsey, Michael Beach, Charles Pike, Clark Salisbury

Part 3 • Chapter 23

RECORDING MUSIC

Musicians have varied attitudes towards recording. Some artists are not comfortable playing unless an audience is present. I am a member of a second set of musicians who approach the recording studio the way a child does a chemistry set. All of this wonderful equipment at your command can reproduce your vocal or instrumental sounds, or modify these sounds in all sorts of ways. There is something intangible about the way a room feels that also plays a role in what transpires.

From an early point in my musical career my friend Dan Fox and I had talked about attempting a piece that integrated my banjo playing with woodwind instruments. By the late 1980's I started to work on a piece called New Traditions. It ended up as a five part suite with a song as the last movement of the piece.

I don't remember how I met Bob Rebholz, but he was well known in Denver as a saxophone and flute player. I decided that I would use him on soprano and tenor sax and flute. Tim O'Brien was living in Denver in 1987, and I hired him on fiddle, mandolin, guitar and vocals. I played banjo and guitar, Adolph Mares played electric bass, and Tom Doenges, then living in Colorado Springs, played slide guitar. Tim and his sister Mollie sang the song in Part Five. The engineer for the session was Steve Avedis, who I had gotten to know through other session work.

The recording sessions for this album were the fulfillment of a long-time dream. Bob and Tim in particular really made the piece work. During my year in Los Angeles I made some attempts to get a record deal for the album, but I was not successful in doing so. After I came back to Denver in 1989 I became a bit depressed about the possibility of getting a deal, but when I attended a conference on the American folk revival in 1991, I bought a few copies of the demo. I gave a copy to Allen Shaw, who had a company called Folk Era. That record company did mostly re-issues or new releases of typical folk-pop groups like the Kingston Trio or the Chad Mitchell Trio. Allen listened to the recording on his way to the airport. In the car with him was a folklorist and bluegrass musician named Neil Rosenberg, who apparently urged Allen to put the record out. (for the record, so to speak, I have never met Neil Rosenberg.) The rest of the album consisted on a neo-Tunisian piece that I had written after our trip to Tunisia, another long suite called After Kentucky, and a guitar piece.

The last step before an album is manufactured is called mastering. It is often done in a separate recording studio by a different engineer. In this process the sound can still be modified, but since everything is now on two tracks rather than multiple tracks, these adjustments are necessarily somewhat limited. Allen used a mastering engineer in New England, and he sent the album out to him. Either because this engineer didn't like the album or he actually thought that he was improving it, he completely changed the sound of the album. On ninety five per cent of it I had played without the use of picks, which is kind of a trademark of my particular approach to the banjo. The album came back with the banjo sounding brittle and echo-y. I told the engineer I wanted him to re-master it just as it sounded on the original tape.

This album evolved into a series of albums that I am working on to this day. I recorded several albums in duo and trio formats, but my last two albums, Four Directions and Near and Far are the ones that have come closest to my recording the tunes in the way that I wanted them to sound. Both of these albums were recorded in Portland, the first with a fine engineer named Dean Baskerville, and the second with Jordan Leff. Four Directions is a double album recorded in 2008 consisting of new instrumental music and songs written over the last forty years, and performed by various singers. Chico Schwall and I overdubbed quite a few instrumental parts on the instrumental album, simulating a small combo. Near and Far was recorded in 2013 at Jordan's studio, The Secret Society. This studio is the most comfortable room that I have ever recorded in. Part of this quality is the ambience of the room itself, and some of it is due to Jordan's diligence and efficiency. On this album I realized another ambition, which was to use oboe and banjo together.

MITCH IIMORI

When I decided to use an oboe on my album, I checked out various oboe players in Portland. The ones that I encountered either were classical players who couldn't improvise or had rhythmic problems. Someone told me about a fellow named Mitch Iimori. When I spoke to him I asked him if he had an oboe d'amour. That instrument is sort of an alto oboe and has a sound most prominent in the pop music world as the answering element on Sonny and Cher's record of I Got You Babe. When Mitch told me that he had TWO oboe d'amours I realized that I had chosen the right oboe player. I used him on oboe, oboe d'amour and English horn on the album. I subsequently discovered that he also played clarinet, bass clarinet, bassoon, tenor and soprano saxophone, flute and alto flute, and most of the same instruments that I play.

Mitch was born in Japan, and he first heard and fell in love with American folk music when his father brought home some Pete Seeger records. His father worked for Sony, and Pete Seeger had recorded some albums for Columbia, which was bought by Sony. Mitch had an older brother who was a conductor who exhorted him to study classical music. Mitch then went to the Eastman School, one of America's most distinguished music schools, and got a degree in oboe. This together with his natural talent and insatiable curiosity accounts for his ability to play so many different instruments. What is truly remarkable about Mitch is that he not only plays all of these instruments that I have listed, but he gets an excellent sound on each one of them.

RECORDING YOUR OWN ALBUMS

I have played on many recordings by other artists. Playing on your own albums is a bit different. One of the most difficult things to learn is to allow yourself to experiment, and then to have enough objectivity to know when the experiments work or when they are ill-advised or badly executed. When I play multiple parts on my own records, I have discovered that I come up with the new parts very quickly and rarely have to do them more than twice. I don't entirely understand why this is so, but it has been particularly evident on my last two albums. It also seems to make no difference whether I have written the new part, or if it resides entirely in my head

There are still more recordings to come, as I will explain in the last portion of this book. Much of my recorded music can be heard on my website, www.dickweissman.com

Jordan Leff - engineer on my last two albums and several other projects that I have been involved with.

Multi-Instrumentalist, Mitch Iimori. He played boo d'amour, oboe, English horn and clarinet on my last two albums.

Part 3 • Chapter 24

BOOKS AND INSTRUCTION BOOKS

Earlier I mentioned my first forays into the music instructional and book publishing worlds. The book that you are now reading is one of twenty two books that I have written or co-authored. I have also written or co-authored over forty instructional books on various musical subjects. This came about in a variety of ways

Hal Leonard, by far the largest music print publisher in the United States, also has a book division. The company is mostly based in Milwaukee, but the book division operates out of Montclair, New Jersey. The CEO of the book division is John Cerullo, and he had worked at Big 3 Music. Big 3 published my first banjo method. From 1990-2010 Hal Leonard Books has published four of my books about the music business, songwriting and music and politics.

In 2003 I met Richard Carlin. Richard is himself an author, an excellent concertina player, but he is best known as an editor. From 2003 to 2010 the various publishers that Richard has worked for have published three of my books, and three others that were collaborations.

My 2010 book Understanding The Music Business was the first book that I have written that was specifically intended as a college textbook. I wrote this book in an attempt to write an understandable and thorough book about the music business.

Another example of how book deals evolve came to me in 2004. I felt that there was room for a book on the American folk music revival. Since I was both a participant and observer in the revival, I felt qualified to write such a book. I was contacted by Evander Lomke, who had wandered onto my website. Evander had been an assistant editor at Crown when I wrote my first book about the music business. The book, called Which Side Are You On? An Insiders History of the Folk Music Revival, was published by Continuum Press in 2005, and was a finalist for the Oregon Book Award in non-fiction writing in 2006.

SOME UP-DATED THOUGHTS ABOUT THE FOLK MUSIC REVIVAL & THE FOLK ALLIANCE

At various times I have attended the North American Folk Alliance annual meetings, and when I moved to Oregon I became active in their regional branch, which is known as Far West. Almost all the regional meetings follow the national model. This means that participants stay at a rather up-scale conference hotel, pay a registration fee to attend the events, and if they wish can purchase exhibition space at an exhibit hall to help promote their career. There are also annual awards, which in the case of Far West are known as Best of the West. Each conference has official showcases, which performers audition for through tapes or videos, and the so-called guerrilla showcases, which are held later at night in hotel rooms. The problem with guerilla showcases is that a dozen or more of them may be going on simultaneously, and so the audience for such a showcase can vary from three people to forty or fifty attendees, playing in cramped hotel rooms.

Since I have been closely involved in studying, writing and teaching about the music business, over the years I have had increasing misgivings about these events. The regional conference fees range from around $150-$200, based upon when the participant registers. The conference hotels for Far West usually cost in the range of $125 a night and up. The event lasts 3-4 days, so there is a minimum of three nights lodging involved. Unless the participants live in the conference city, they must also drive or fly to the conference, and there is little point in attending unless you have promo packages to give away which include CD's, MP3's, videos, photos and bios. These promotional expenses have been somewhat diminished through the use of electronic press kits and web sites, but to make an impression on live human beings who attend the conference there is still some necessity for creating physical copies of the promotional materials. Some performers rent hotel rooms which serve as a combination of sleeping quarters and rooms where they can showcase their music. These rooms are a bit more expensive than simply renting the hotel room as a place to sleep.

I think it would be fair to say that attending these conferences is going to cost in the neighborhood of $1500 for anyone attending who doesn't live in the conference city. Some people double up or triple up to reduce the cost of hotel rooms, and there are some scholarships awarded that eliminate the registration fee. However, the inevitable question comes to mind: is it worthwhile to participate in one or more of these events?

EUGENE AND FAR WEST 2011

Plagued by our inability to come up with the answer to the above question, Chico Schwall and I undertook the responsibility of co-chairing the conference for 2011. We did two things to reduce the cost of the conference. Instead of using a conference hotel for our musical events, we rented a wonderful concert and music teaching facility called The Shedd, where Chico teaches. We only held two events at the Conference Hotel, the Best of Awards and a final meeting on the last morning of the conference. Because the conference was held in downtown Eugene, we were able to provide attendees with a list of nearby motels, which ranged in price from $40-$60 a night. Those who needed a luxury hotel could stay at the Hilton, for about $110. We also lowered the cost of attending the conference by about $50. We didn't only deal with the issue of cost. We held panels on folklore, writing instrumental music, and an actual panel on getting gigs in specific towns and in Europe. Through the cooperation of Local 1000 of the American Federation of Musicians, we were able to arrange an inspiring keynote speech by John McCutcheon the long-time president and co-founder of Local 1000.

One result of our efforts that we had not anticipated was that the organization made more money than it had ever made at a conference. I recall that the amount was $13,000. In general people liked the conference. A few people made the justifiable complaint that we hadn't provided transportation between the Hilton and the Shedd, so that some older or disabled people suffered some hardships in getting from place to place.

An odd artifact of the conference was that one particular show had less than optimum sound. Chico was bitterly attacked for this problem, which was more of a scheduling problem with the hosts than anything else. The other concerts probably had the best sound that Far West had ever experienced, because the sound technicians were familiar with the rooms that they were working in, and the rooms were designed for concerts. Most hotels do not have rooms that are specifically intended for music, and this means bringing in sound technicians from outside the conference, adding to the general expense of operating the conference.

The next year Far West went back to the conference hotel format, which continues to this day. Chico and I went back to being musicians, not promoters.

SCOTT McKENZIE

Scott and I were not especially close in The Journeymen. He was four years younger than I was, and to be honest, not especially mature for his age. Starting with the ill-fated John Phillips recordings in the mid--90's we became good friends. Scott didn't like to talk on the phone, and at times he would become depressed. He also began to suffer from Guillain-Barre Syndrome, and he started to curtail his performing activities. That essentially resulted in dissolving the Mamas and Papas Revival Band. Except for a few brief foreign tours, and a session where he recorded a single song, Scott really left music behind.

He lived in the Silver Lake section of Los Angeles in a rented house without a car. He became a virtual recluse, who lived his life on the internet and on his web site. Scott attended my 70th birthday party in Santa Barbara in 2005 and we exchanged emails. I only called him when he didn't answer emails, because I sensed that his depression was kicking in. I visited him once and stayed at his home, but a few other times when I went to Los Angeles, he didn't want to receive visitors. In the spring of 2012 he became quite ill. Towards the end I considered visiting him in the hospital, but I was told that in his final days Scott only wanted to sleep.

Scott made his transition to another world in August, 2012. Just prior to his death he wrote a poem based on a dream that he had. In the dream he rode an Appaloosa pony high above the "stench" of the world, on a voyage that he did not anticipate returning from. In October some of his closest friends organized a musical memorial at the Whisky A Go Go. Harry Tuft and I attended the gathering, and we performed one Journeymen song together, I did an instrumental, and I did a song about The Journeymen that I had written a few years before. Changing the names of the three of us to Jimmy, Eddie and Jerry. The verse about Scott went like this:

"Jimmy and Eddie traveled, together,
They sang together so well,
Jimmy spent all of his time, making money,
Didn't notice Eddie going through hell.
Now he's gone to another place,
Chasing a dream of his own,
Every morning he waters the garden,
He doesn't like to talk on the phone".

Very few of Scott's famous "friends" attended the memorial. Michelle Phillips did, and Barry McGuire also played some music. He performed the song Creeque Alley, John and Michelle's paean to the folk rock years. Oddly the song mentions almost everyone in that genre, except for Scott. It does however, mention Barry himself several times. I thought to myself, this really is Hollywood. I imagine Scott would have appreciated the irony.

THE FOLK REVIVAL TODAY

When I became involved in the folk music revival in the middle and late 50's, many of the musicians who were in the revival were interested in a wide variety of music. Dave Van Ronk for example, was initially known as a blues singer. Before that, Dave had tried to sing jazz. As he put it, "I wanted to play jazz in the worst way, and I did." As his career evolved he performed songs by Joni Mitchell and Brecht and Weill. I could cite numerous other examples, like that of Frank Hamilton. Frank is interested in world music and jazz, as well as all kinds of roots music.

One of the problematic aspects of the current direction of the folk revival, is the emphasis on singer-songwriters. They clearly dominate both the national and regional Folk Alliance conferences. I think it would be fair to say that a considerable number of the singer-songwriters are actually striving for the level of success and financial reward that is the end game of pop music. You can also observe the other musical factions at the folk gatherings: the Irish and blues enthusiasts, the bluegrass and old-time music folks, etc.

The odd thing about all of this is that it is occurring at the same time that more and more musicians are emerging who are capable of playing in a variety of styles that are informed by traditional music but delve into aspects of jazz, classical and international music styles. I am thinking about Bela Fleck, Chris Thiele, Tony Trischka, and some younger musicians like mandolinist Matt Fliner and banjo player Jayme Stone.

I have one final observation about awards, whether they are state awards, Grammy awards or Folk Alliance Best of trophies. I don't think that music is a bowling tournament. How can you possibly maintain that someone is the best guitarist in the world. Are we talking about a flamenco master like Paco de Lucia, a classical guitarist like Julian Bream, a rock guitarist like Jimi Hendrix, a folk-country guitarist like Doc Watson, bluesman Robert Johnson, or any one of dozens of wonderful musicians. In the words of Rodney King: "can't we all just get along?" The only meaningful award that I can visualize is one in a category like Musicians Deserving Further Recognition.

INSTRUCTIONAL MATERIALS

My later instructional books have been published by Alfred Music and Mel Bay. In 2008 I wrote the book Banjo A to Z: Everything you need to play 5-string banjo in every style. Although the sub-title is a bit over-hyped, it discusses the various styles of banjo playing that I have used over the years on various CD's. It is published by Alfred Music. In 2009 I finally realized the fruit of all my thinking about non-jazz improvisation in a series of books that I co-authored with Dan Fox. They are books for banjo, flute, guitar, mandolin and piano, and they are published by Mel Bay.

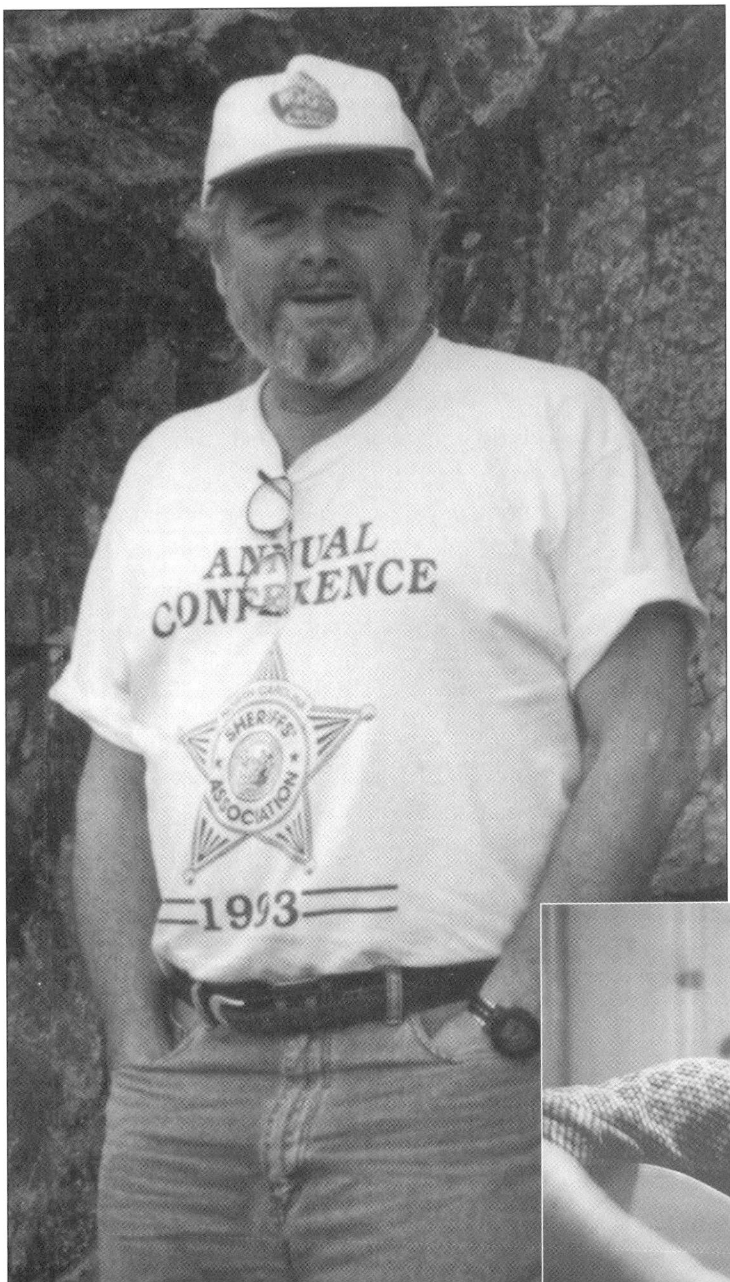

Scott McKenzie in the 1990s. Standing on the Dock of the Bay, and playing in the studio.

Part 3 • Chapter 25

2013-? BACK IN DENVER AND BEYOND

When we moved back to Denver in 2013 I decided to scale down my college teaching even further and to concentrate on writing and recording music and writing books about music. The only college teaching that I have done since then is short workshops or brief classes through the University of Denver's University College.

In 2015 I recorded another CD with Jordan Leff in Portland, featuring Mitch Iimori on oboe, English horn, clarinet, bass clarinet, dulcimer and soprano saxophone. I will release this album on my own label, Longbridge Recordings in conjunction with the release of this book. The title of the album is Night Sky.

I received a small grant from the Puffin Foundation in 2014 to write, record and produce an album of songs of social commentary. So far I have recorded two of the four or five songs that I have completed for this project. The project also involves singer Harry Tuft, who came up with the concept, which he calls The Bottom Rung. This refers to the large group of people at the bottom rung of the ladder of success. Our goal is to get this project out in 2016.

As far as books go, there is the one you are currently reading, and a revision of my music business textbook. I have been working through a company called North Star Media that places music in film and television. Finally, I have been elected to the musicians union board in Denver. Unlike most locals in the federation we are gaining members, and hope to hire an organizer soon. When musicians or students ask me about the union, I throw the question back at them. Although the union often has pursued outdated initiatives, what other option do musicians have? Who else represents them in negotiations with record companies, club owners, or symphony orchestras? For me the best path for a young musician to take is to become involved with the union and to help it modernize, rather than just be a bystander.

HOPES, REGRETS, DREAMS & REALITIES

I am eighty years old at this time. By and large I feel that I have been a "fortunate son." I have been able to make a reasonable living pursuing various jobs involving music. I am more or less at peace with the choices I have made over the years.

My children are out in the world pursuing their objectives in ways that works for them. My daughter Janelle is the deputy director at an international women's rights organization in Australia, and my son Paul works with a company that puts together financing to build and rehabilitate affordable housing projects. Susan is able to do the work that matters to her with drawing and painting. At times she would like to have more outlets for her work, but I suppose you could say the same thing about me.

I am happy that I no longer teach music business at college. It seems that these college programs have expanded at the same time as job opportunities have diminished. The internet and social media have created opportunities, but they also have taken many jobs away. If I were starting a program now, I would cap the number of students at some number like fifty students, and I would strongly suggest to these students that they explore multiple careers.

This is not economically feasible at the great majority of programs, but it would reflect the realities of the business. I would encourage students to explore multi-media and sports marketing, besides the courses that most colleges currently offer. In looking back on my life, pursuing multiple careers is exactly what I did. In my case it wasn't the result of careful planning, but as various opportunities came up I explored them. It's quite possible I would have been a better banjo player if I hadn't wanted to spend an almost equal time playing guitar. Similarly I probably would have been a better songwriter, record producer or writer if I had restricted myself to a single activity. Truthfully it wouldn't have fit my personality, and I probably would have left music out of boredom. If I were doing it all today I'd probably do pretty much the same thing, but out of necessity rather than choice. Very few musicians are going to be able to stay with a single career in the 21st century.

I cannot really say how long I intend to write music or books. Inevitably there will come a time when I will not be able to play up to my own standards. I hope that I am realistic enough to not perform in public when this time comes. I have seen too many musicians perform until their later performances became an embarrassment to themselves and their greatest supporters.

If I have a problem with the modern world, beside the usual gripes about omnipotent cell phones and shallow news coverage, it is the general tendency for detailed explorations of the obvious. If you watch television or listen to the radio or explore the mighty internet, you know what I mean. What I want to do is to try to maintain the integrity of my work, and allow my work load to diminish as the inevitable becomes the ordinary. Until then, I want to spend time with my family and friends and use my skills in whatever ways I can. I want to do at least one more album with a larger ensemble, and I am still thinking up additional book projects. In the summer of 2015, through my friendship with banjo player, author, storyteller and traditional music scholar Stephen Wade, I taught at a summer program where we explored traditional music and music based upon it. The program is at the Rocky Ridge Music Center near Estes Park, Colorado. I hope to continue doing that work as a kind of capstone of my teaching career.

Recently I had a conversation with Harry Tuft about our musical tastes. Our tastes are truly opposite. He likes a fairly narrow band of music, but within that grouping many performers. I like many musical styles, but within each of those genres I really relate to only a handful of musicians. In a world of frequent standing ovations, what constitutes a good performance? I recently read a book about creativity which was generally simplistically positive. Then I got to the part where Branford Marsalis, the saxophone player, maintained that anyone who claims to have had constant peak experiences playing music is simply deluding himself. He recalled maybe three such moments in his career. It was very gratifying to see a musician this celebrated being so honest about what constituted significant moments in his own musical performances.

In a world of over-hype it is important to be open to these moments. In spring, 2014 I saw a performance by five musicians, playing newly commissioned pieces. I loved the concept, but the first half of the show really didn't reach me. In the second half the quintet played a piece called Evolution by mandolin player Matt Flinner. It was a wonderful piece of music. Each of the players seemed to play their parts with more conviction and integrity than they had shown during the earlier part of the concert. It was as though he had written the piece with those specific musicians in mind. I rarely have this sort of listening experience. As long as it happens, however irregularly, I am happy to commit myself to listening to and playing music.

THE FRENCH GUITAR

In October of 2014 Susan and I met my French-speaking daughter Janelle in Paris. Prior to going there I had idly searched the internet for old guitars. I discovered some interesting music stores and to my surprise I noticed that a French luthier was making guitars that he sold under the name Larson Brothers. The Larson Brothers were two luthiers in Chicago who made guitars from around 1900-1940. They never used their own names for the guitars, but they were sold under the names Euphonon, Maurer, Prairie State, Stahl and JB Stetson. Guitarists prized these instruments, which were noted for their versatility.

While exploring the city we chanced upon a store called Woodbrass. This is actually a group of music stores, with one store specializing in guitars. They had two of the "Larson Brothers" instruments. One was a Stetson, which was made either in Mexico or China, but the other was a Prairie State, made in

France. I played the guitar in the store for about an hour. It was as though I were in a trance. One of the things that determines whether I will actually buy an instrument is whether it seems to have a unique voice. I almost felt as though the guitar was guiding me, patiently asking me to play it with bare fingers, with a flat pick, in different styles and different registers of the instrument. I ended up buying it, but because we already had considerable luggage I had it shipped home.

A month later the guitar cleared customs in Miami, and arrived on my doorstep. Sort of. It was a day and a half later than Federal Express had promised to deliver it, and I had given up on getting it that day by 5PM. It was snowing and very cold that night, and Susan thought that she'd step outside and see how much snow was falling. There was the guitar, in a shipping box marked Fragile in four places, lying in the snow. Despite the weather and the markings Fed Ex had left it outside in the snow. When I took the guitar into the house, the hard case was saturated, but fortunately the guitar itself was not wet.

Playing this guitar has been a real learning experience for me. I often feel that it is leading me more than I am directing it. I wrote a piece called Night Sky, which is on my website, and it will give you some idea of what the Prairie State sounds like.

WHAT IF?

In another life I might have taken a shot at professional tennis, and if I were re-incarnated as a musician again I probably would play woodwinds and not fretted instruments. In the long run these sounds and textures have the most appeal to me. I have never toured in Europe, and as the clock winds down, it seems unlikely that this will ever happen. But I have music to write, and some 300 CD's that I'm behind in listening to. There are also books to write and books to read, places to travel to, and people to share ideas with. That's good enough for me.

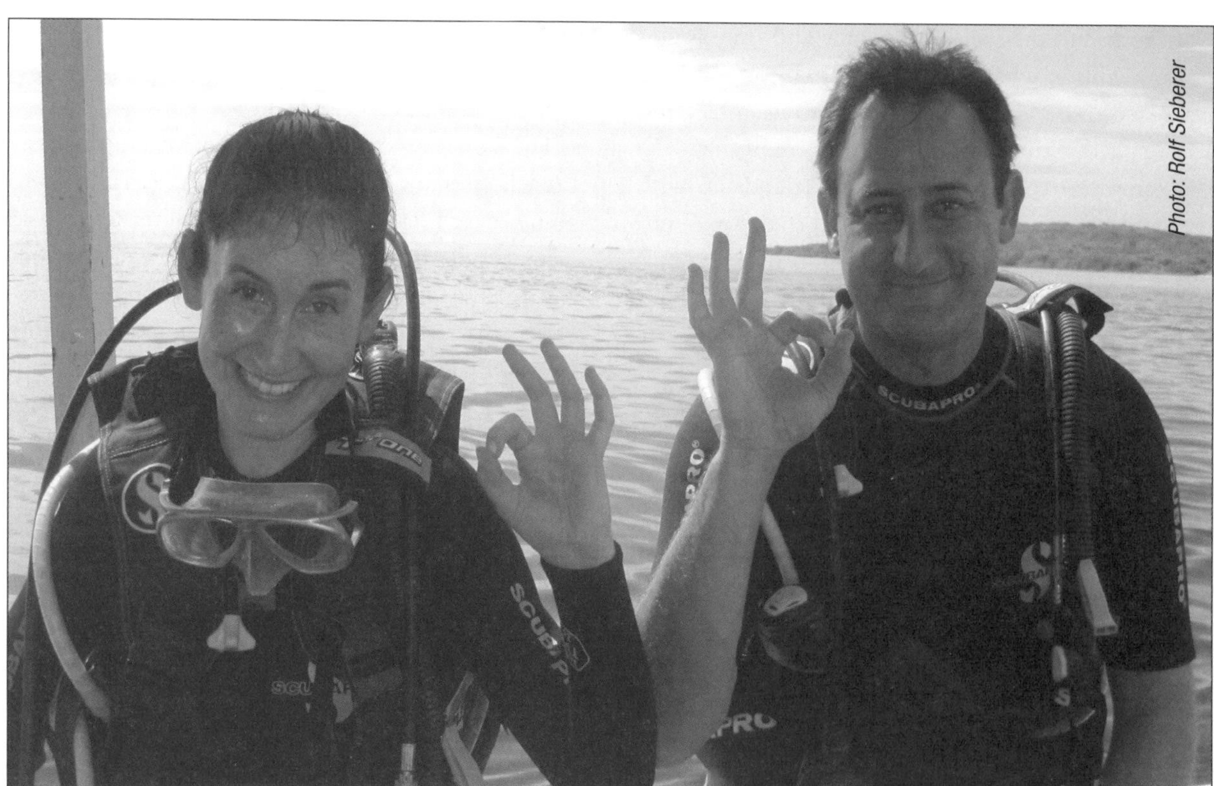

Janelle and Paul- Weissman (my kids) - scuba diving in Australia.

Photo courtesy Ome Banjos

Above: Peggy Seeger, widow of folksinger-playwright-songwriter Ewan MacColl and half sister of Pete Seeger. This photo comes from around 2010, and was taken outside the Denver Folklore Center.

Left: Tanya and Chuck Ogsbury holding the 55th Anniversary Ome Banjo at the NAMM show in Los Angeles. My banjo of choice is still the Ome Muse (made by Chuck in 1962!)

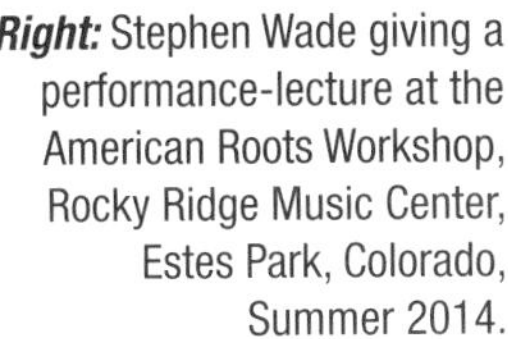

Right: Stephen Wade giving a performance-lecture at the American Roots Workshop, Rocky Ridge Music Center, Estes Park, Colorado, Summer 2014.

Photo courtesy Rocky Ridge Music Center

Appendix

Below are a few short takes on mostly musical subjects that don't necessarily fit into the story line of this book.

SONGWRITING

Most important artists of any kind go through a maturation process in their skill set and the thinking process behind their art. In music it would be unthinkable to imagine that Mozart, Bartok, or John Coltrane did their best compositions before they were thirty years old, and suffered a serious artistic decline after that. When we examine contemporary American songwriters, we see that like mathematicians, they seem to burn out very quickly. Bob Dylan himself has acknowledged that he is now incapable of writing anything as adventurous or significant as the work he produced in his youth. I would also argue that the same could be said about Joni Mitchell, James Taylor, and the bulk of revered pop songwriters. In Joni Mitchell's case, her deepest songs, like The Circle Game, or Both Sides Now were written in her early twenties.

Of course there are exceptions to the rule. Curtis Mayfield's black exploitation movie songs in the film Superfly are quite different from his earlier gospel-tinged hits of the 60's. John Phillips continued to write songs well after the successes of The Mamas and Papas. In his case, the songs, regrettably, are largely uncirculated because he had lost the vehicle to perform his songs.

Is there something inherently limiting about the three or four minute pop song, or is that the trappings of success and money turn the writer in the direction of duplicating his or her prior work? I don't have an answer to this question.

MUSICIANS AND ENTERTAINERS

We recently spent a few days in the town of Salida, Colorado. The town had just experienced a mini-Woodstock music festival, with two lead acts and a dozen others making up the supporting bill. One of the townsfolk told me that one of the well-known lead acts did a great show. She added that they didn't sing or play very well.

This highlighted for me the difference between musicians and entertainers. Entertainers are charismatic, attractive people who often are excellent dancers. This doesn't preclude them from being musicians, but isn't specifically relevant to that purpose. There are obviously people who are skilled in both areas, but then there are people who are great musicians but poor entertainers, while others are great entertainers but poor musicians.

Many music critics focus more on audience reactions to music rather than the music itself. Possibly this is simply a realistic assessment of the way most people relate to music. When I was teaching at UCD, I asked my students how many of them listened to music without any sort of additional distraction. Almost none answered that they did. They used music while reading textbooks, doing dishes, having conversations, or pursuing other activities. These students were all music majors, by the way.

It is essential to be entertaining on some level to gain an audience, but in my opinion the entertainment element has overwhelmed most people's ability to concentrate on listening to music.

WRITING MUSIC AND SONGS

I know many people who write music and/or songs. Although I have read many musical memoirs, almost none of the authors talk about their compositional process. Since I assume most readers of this book at the very least are interested in music, I thought I'd devote a few paragraphs to describing how I work.

When I write songs, I generally start with a concept of what to write about. I then pick up an instrument and try to integrate my concept with a melody. I usually sketch out a very rough lyric, and come up with a complete melody fairly quickly. I then go back and re-work the lyric. I think that most people are more skilled at writing either lyrics or melodies, and I clearly fall into the latter group. It can take days, weeks, or even months until I am satisfied with a lyric, but I rarely make many changes in the original melody.

When I write instrumental music, I usually pick up a banjo, guitar, or occasionally I go to the piano. More recently I have been playing an octave mandolin called an octafone. Sometimes I have a clear idea of where I am going from the very beginning. At other times I go to various banjo or guitar tunings in an attempt to challenge myself to find new directions. Sometimes the tune is in my head before I even play. Sometimes I try out various techniques on the instruments that I play to find the groove or attitude that I want to work with. Sometimes the music comes out of a groove or rhythm, occasionally it comes out of a chord progression. Sometimes it's a matter of playing in different registers of the instrument, or even changing where I place my right hand. Each of my instruments has a different sound, so the very choice of whether I play a nylon string guitar, a steel string or a twelve string are going to bring out different creative impulses. I try to avoid using a consistent method of composing in order to keep from repeating myself. It's also important to me to try to recognize when a new piece of music is not worthwhile. An intriguing musical fragment in an unsuccessful piece can become the starting point for a complete different work.

THE BANJO IS A MUSICAL INSTRUMENT

Contrary to my colleague at UCD who didn't want to hire me because the banjo is not a musical instrument, I believe that there are any number of banjo players who have refuted that pompous notion. Having said that, there are some phenomena in the banjo world that never cease to puzzle me

When I was a young musician, guitarists would say to me, "do you play rhythm or lead?" Now I admit that these are two distinct ways of playing the guitar, but from the beginning I felt that this was a strange and meaningless separation of playing styles. On the banjo the way that this clannishness presents itself, is "do you play clawhammer and old-time music or do you play bluegrass?" Surprisingly I have been asked this question by some prominent banjoists.

My point is that the assumption that there are two, and only two ways to play the banjo is ridiculous. Most of the many summer banjo camps are set up in exactly this way. The problem with thinking of the banjo in this way is that it eliminates blues, classical music, world music and any sort of style that fuses different techniques and musical approaches. Every style has its strengths and its limitations. The primary limitation that I find in bluegrass banjo is that up to now all of the prominent players who play bluegrass use fingerpicks. There are, of course, reasons for this choice. Volume, speed and intensity are among them. I have a fantasy of a bluegrass player emerging who plays a nylon string banjo without fingerpicks. Before you dismiss this odd notion, think about flamenco guitar. Flamenco players certainly play with every bit of intensity and volume that bluegrass banjo players do.

As for clawhammer or old-time banjo, why settle for a single musical sound? Another problem is that clawhammer or as we used to call it frailing, is a generally harsh sound that isn't appropriate for every song or every musical style. Our new banjo motto might be: Think Before You Pick!

THE NEW MUSICIAN

Good musicians have always had boundless curiosity. A new if mostly middle-aged sort of musician seems to have emerged towards the end of the twentieth century. Musicians like Don Byron, Bela Fleck, Matt Flinner, Bill Frisell, the Kronos Quartet, Ron Miles, Jenny Scheinman and Chris Thile represent a breakdown in the concept that a musician should play in only one style. These musicians are interested in and capable of playing music that moves back and forth between classical, jazz and folk music

Although some of these musicians have carved out successful careers and have some notoriety, others are better known to musicians than to the general music listening public. Some of these musicians are also composers, and some are not.

I look forward to the emergence of more musicians and composers who will create new music beyond what they themselves can imagine.

Bibliography / Discography

Below is a partial list of some of the books that I have written or co-authored. All are currently in print, except for the Folk Music Sourcebook.

BOOKS

THE FOLK MUSIC SOURCEBOOK
Original edition published by Alfred Knopf in 1976,
Revised edition published by Da Capo in 1989.
Co-author, Larry Sandberg.
Winner of the 1977 Deems Taylor
ASCAP Music Critics Award.

WHICH SIDE ARE YOU ON?
An Inside History of the Folk Music Revival in America.
Continuum Press, 2005.
Finalist for the Oregon Book Award
in non-fiction writing, 2006

SONGWRITING;
THE WORDS, THE MUSIC & THE MONEY
2nd Edition, Hal Leonard Books, 2010.
Includes CD and DVD.

TALKIN' BOUT A REVOLUTION;
Music and Social Change in America.
Hal Leonard 2010.

UNDERSTANDING THE MUSIC BUSINESS
Published by Prentice-Hall, 2010,
reprinted by Taylor & Francis, 2015.
Revised edition, Taylor and Francis,
to be published in 2017

RECORDINGS

NEW TRADITIONS
Folk Era Records
FE1400CD 1991

REFLECTIONS
Folk Era Records
FE1444CD 1998

FOUR DIRECTIONS
Long Bridge Recordings 2008

NEAR AND FAR
Heron Bay Records HB071 2013

THE JOURNEYMEN
(with Scott McKenzie and John Phillips)
Collectibles

Note: I have played on dozens of recording sessions and produced many albums as well.

My favorite projects are:
Judy Roderick
WOMAN BLUES
Vanguard CD6366 CD
Re-issue 1993

And the regrettably out of print
FRUMMOX FROM HERE TO THERE
Probe LP4511S

Look for my new instrumental CD
Night Sky on Longbridge Recordings in 2016

Also keep an eye out for
The Bottom Rung Project
A CD of songs of social commentary
with Harry Tuft and others.

To hear some of my music go to my website,
www.dickweissman.com

You can write to me at ***r2s@comcast.net***

More Great Books from Centerstream...

COWBOY GUITARS

by Steve Evans and Ron Middlebrook
foreword by Roy Rogers, Jr.

Back in the good old days, all of America was infatuated with the singing cowboys of movies and radio. This huge interest led to the production of "cowboy guitars." This fun, fact-filled book is an outstanding roundup of these wonderful instruments.

00000281 Softcover (232 pages)..$35.00
00000303 Hardcover (234 pages)..$55.00

REGAL MUSICAL INSTRUMENTS:1895-1955

by Bob Carlin

Regal Musical Instruments 1895-1955 is the only book to trace the history of the Chicago musical manufacturer. With its roots in Indianapolis, the Regal familiar to most collectors and players was spun off of music giant Lyon& Healy in 1908. Regal Music Instruments 1895-1955 draws upon period trade magazines, distributor catalogues, as well as the never before published memories of Regal factory employees to paint a complete picture of the company's history. 330 pages with full color throughout.

00001484..$45.00

SPANN'S GUIDE TO GIBSON
1902-1941

by Joe Spann

This detailed look at the inner workings of the famous musical instrument manufacturer of Kalamazoo, Michigan before World War II. For the first time, Gibson fans can learn about the employees who built the instruments, exactly where the raw materials came from, the identity of parts vendors, and how the production was carried out. The book explains Gibson's per-World War II factory order number (FON) and serial number systems, and corrects long-standing chronological errors. Previously unknown information about every aspect of the operation is covered in-depth. Noted historian Joe Spann gathered firsthand info from per-war employees, and had access to major Gibson collections around the world. Long time Gibson experts, as well as casual collectors, will find this volume an indispensable addition to their reference shelf.

00001525 302 pages..$39.99

THE GIBSON L5

by Adrian Ingram

Introduced in 1922, the Gibson L5 is the precursor of the modern archtop guitar. This book takes a look at its history and most famous players, from its creation, through the Norlin years, to its standing today as the world's most popular jazz guitar. Includes a 16-page full color photo section.

00000216 112 pages..$29.95

THE GIBSON 175
Its History and Its Players

by Adrian Ingram

Debuting in 1949 and in continuous production ever since, the ES-175 is one of the most versatile and famous guitars in music history. The first Gibson electric to feature a Florentine cutaway, the ES-175 was also one of the first Electric Spanish guitars to be fitted with P.A.F. humbuckers and is prized for its playability, craftsmanship, and full rich tone. Written by noted author/guitarist Adrian Ingram, contents include: the complete history of the 175, The Players, a beautiful ES-175 Color Gallery, Chronology, Shipping Totals, and more. This book is a must for every guitar player and enthusiast or collector.

00001134 ....$24.95

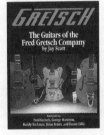

THE GIBSON 335
Its History and Its Players

by Adrian Ingram

Gibson's first "semi-acoustic" the ES-335, which was neither totally solid nor fully acoustic, is the guitar of choice used by many famous guitarists such as Andy Summers, Elvin Bishop, Lee Ritenour, Jay Graydon, Robben Ford, Freddie King, John McLaughin, Jimmy Page, Chuck Berry, Tony Mottola, Johnny Rivers, Jack Wilkins, Bono, Grant Green, Eric Clapton, Stevie Ray Vaughan, Alvin Lee, B.B. King, Emily Remler, Otis Rush, Pete Townshend, John Lee Hooker, and Larry Carlton. This book includes the complete history of the 335, the players, a beautiful color section, chronology, shipping totals and more. A must-have for every 335 player and guitar enthusiast or collector!

00000353 120 pages..$29.95

GRETSCH – THE GUITARS OF THE FRED GRETSCH COMPANY

by Jay Scott

This comprehensive manual uncovers the history of Gretsch guitars through 32 pages of color photos, hundreds of black & white photos, and forewords by Fred Gretsch, George Harrison, Randy Bachman, Brian Setzer, and Duane Eddy. It covers each model in depth, including patent numbers and drawings for collectors.

00000142 286 pages..$35.00

THE HISTORY & ARTISTRY OF NATIONAL RESONATOR INSTRUMENTS

by Bob Brozman

This book is a history book, source book and owner's manual for players and fans that covers the facts and figures necessary for serious collectors. In addition to many black and white historical photos, there is a 32-page color section, and appendixes with serial numbers for all instruments, a company chronology, and a Hawaiian Artist Discography.

00000154 296 pages..$35.00

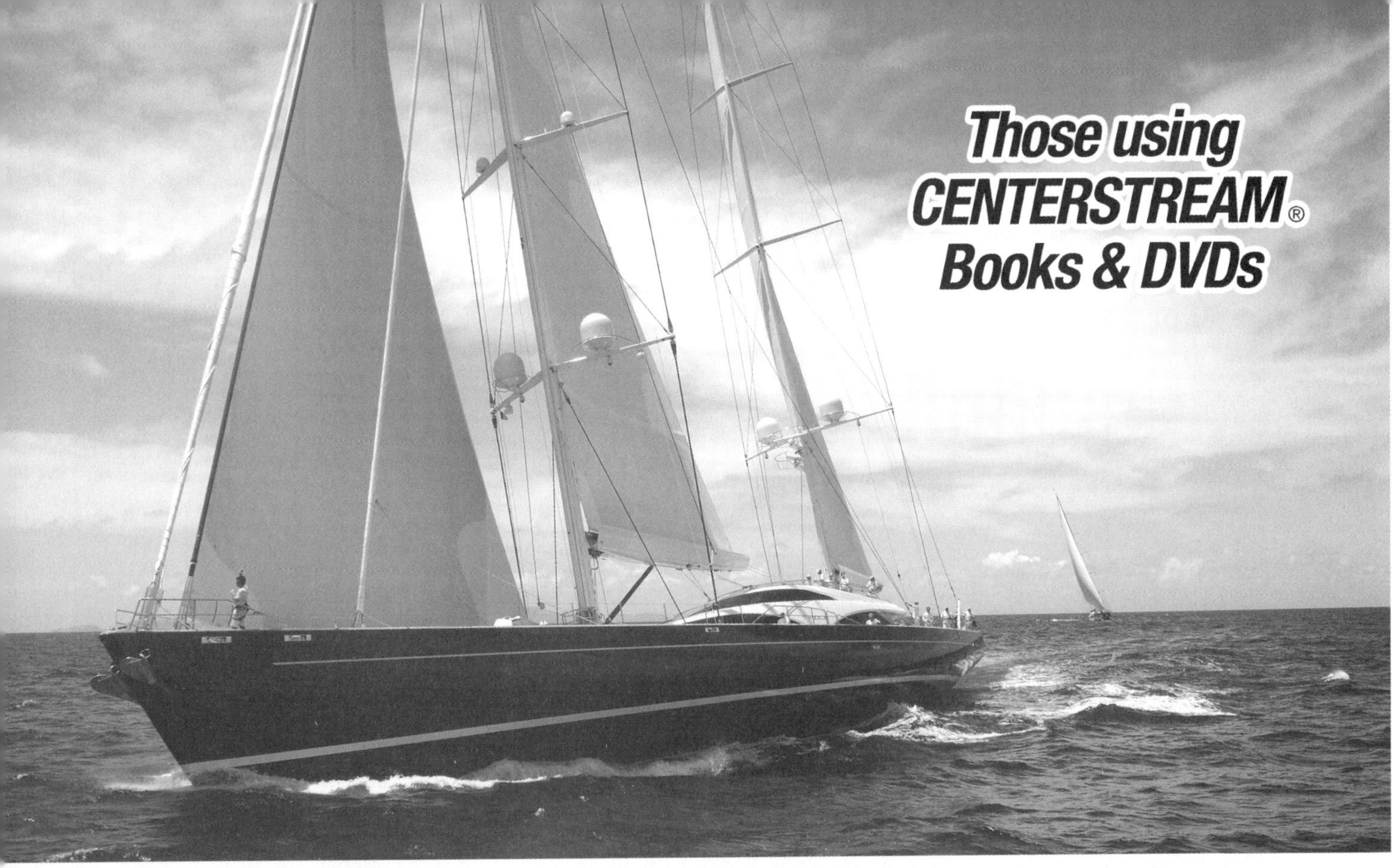
Those using
CENTERSTREAM®
Books & DVDs

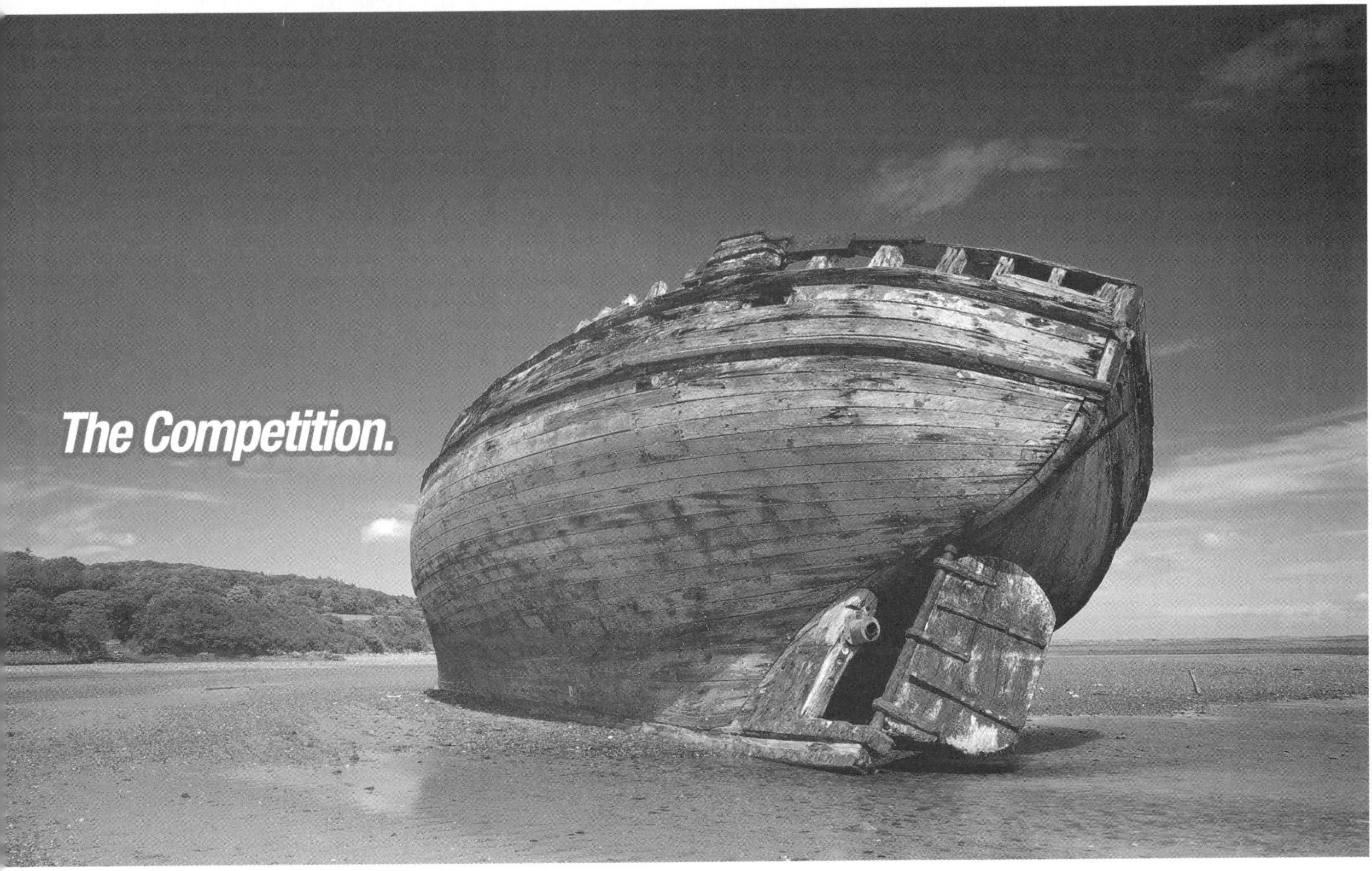
The Competition.